What We Save Now . . .

An Audubon Primer of Defense

THE
AUDUBON
LIBRARY

What We Save Now . . .

An Audubon Primer of Defense

Edited by Les Line

Illustrated with photographs and drawings

PUBLISHED IN COOPERATION
WITH THE NATIONAL AUDUBON SOCIETY
BY HOUGHTON MIFFLIN COMPANY, BOSTON : 1973

THE AUDUBON LIBRARY

Alaska: The Embattled Frontier
by George Laycock

What We Save Now . . .
An Audubon Primer of Defense
edited by Les Line

First printing ʌ

ISBN: 0-395-16613-6
Library of Congress Catalog Card Number: 74-132785
Printed in the United States of America

Title page photograph of a great blue heron by Molly Adams

*To the men and women
who defend wild America
with typewriter and camera*

What we save now is all we will ever save.

—Allen H. Morgan
Executive Vice-President,
Massachusetts Audubon Society

Contents

Illustrations

The Making of
a Preservationist

MEMORIES.

Of a wild little river. Of a village green.

First, the village green.

The town was Sparta, a pleasant community of two thousand in the apple and peach country of western Michigan. By New England criteria, its park wasn't much. No long, sloping greensward. No ancient elms and oaks. No colonial courthouse or tall-spired church. No granite monuments to Revolutionary War events or heroes. Just a patch of grass enclosed by a spiraea hedge on a Main Street corner. At one end was the requisite bandstand, and next to it a hand-lettered roll of honor for two World Wars.

My earliest memory from a Midwestern childhood is of sitting on the grass on a summer Saturday evening and listening to Sousa marches being played by a band of high school musicians and alumni. I was proud that the snare drum was the responsibility of my Uncle Fred, and I would contribute the rhythm from the same place at the back of the band shell ten years later.

We marched to the park every Decoration Day to honor our veterans. We gathered there to rejoice when the village fire siren and church bells signaled V-E Day and then, four months later, V-J Day. We built autumn bonfires there to cheer our football teams on to championship seasons. And every summer the town folk and farm folk met there after their Saturday night shopping to exchange news and hear some inspiring, if not inspiringly played, music.

Then the village council sold the village green.

Sold it to the town bank so it could build a modern brick-and-glass edifice, complete with drive-in window, on that coveted Main Street corner.

As part of the deal, the village fathers got the old bank for the municipal offices, and some swampy lowland at the outskirts of town for a new park. They built another bandstand there, but few people ever came to the summer concerts again. It was too far to walk, and the mosquitoes were too many and too fierce for sitting on the sparse grass that managed to grow in the dried clay.

On Decoration Day, now, the band and the Scouts and the veterans march to the side of the bank, where a bronze plaque lists in small type the dead of four wars. Taps is played and a wreath left on the sidewalk.

And the last time I was home, the Junior Chamber of Commerce held its annual chicken barbecue, one of Sparta's big summer social events.

Held it in the parking lot of the bank.

As for the river of my boyhood (a creek or a river is an integral part of growing up in the country), it wasn't particularly distinguished either. On the map its name was spelled Rogue, but everyone pronounced it Rouge, which is how it appeared on the early records. It was neither red nor a rascal, however. Just a modest river of normal color that twisted for thirty-two miles through nice second-growth forestland and tangled bottomlands. Even where it sliced through a farm or pasture, its banks were densely wooded.

The Rogue was never so wide that a boy couldn't cast a Dardevle into an eddy beyond some tree roots on the opposite bank, where a grandfather pike might be lurking. My river abounded in northern pike up to eighteen pounds in size, plus native and introduced trout and swarms of spawning suckers when the current warmed up in the spring. To reach the best fishing spots, a boy had to slosh across meadows decorated with wild blue flag and then fight his path through stinging nettles and intertwined willows. Moreover, in those pre-repellent days, one wore mosquito-proof clothing on the hottest midsummer days.

I almost caught my first fish in the Rogue, but it shook the hook free (and made off with my minnow bait) before my father could position the landing net. I cried. The Rogue would yield my fair share of fish before I left home, however, along with river ducks and, from its woodlands, fat fox squirrels and cottontail rabbits and ruffed grouse and morel mushrooms. And the experience of wildness over a whole boyhood, long before it was possible for the man to visit faraway mountains and canyons and forests and islands and great swamplands where the wilderness was real.

Not that the Rogue was pristine. We always fished north of the outfall from the Sparta sewage treatment plant, for it was obvious to the eye that the sewage wasn't being treated in any way whatsoever. One might bump into a cow more often than a white-tailed deer, and there usually was a road within earshot. Still, it was a shock and an outrage that summer when the walking draglines moved in and began systematically to destroy the northern and wildest one-third of the river.

The project was simply make-work for the county drain commissioners, but it was done with all the zeal and cruel efficiency of the channelization schemes of the Soil Conservation Service and the U.S. Army Corps of Engineers. The circuitous Rogue was routed straight as a gutter, its banks stripped of all vegetation, its bottom gouged of anything that might conceal or nourish a fish.

The cause for such ruination was never explained. Presumably flood control was the excuse. The Rogue would escape its banks during the spring freshets, and a few cows might be stranded for a day or two on high ground. But the nearby farms were mostly hardscrabble and, indeed, much of the channelization took place in the middle of a state forest preserve.

The last time I was home, the local newspapers announced a grand plan by county officials to dam the Rogue River and flood the wild parts that were still left. They want to create a big, long lake for water-skiiers and motorboaters. This in a glacier-sculpted county that is already chockablock with natural lakes of all shapes and sizes.

I suppose it was inevitable.

I recite these stories not because they are unique (although how many village greens have been sold to banks?) but because I have often been asked what led me to a career in conservation. The answer, I believe, lies in those two incidents from my boyhood.

When the village council quietly gave away the town park, no voices were raised in protest. To a fourteen-year-old, it seemed a wrong thing to do. It seemed terribly wrong, not long thereafter, when a wild little river was ravaged for reasons that were dubious at best. But I could only watch in frustration as the bandstand was ripped down, and as the steam shovels ground onward. There was a feeling of utter helplessness. And the hope that, one day, I could do more than anguish at such iniquities.

If words, skillfully written words on the pages of a national magazine, can accomplish what a boy could not (and I know that they can), then I consider my quest a success, my job the very best in the world. The words are not my own, for the most part, but those of the finest writers in conservation. With them, and their magazine, rests a great responsibility. These men and women must be the environmental conscience of America. They must defend our natural heritage by informing, educating, stimulating, exhorting, by creating awareness and appreciation, by exposing ecological errors and environmental outrages.

Some one hundred thousand of those words have been gathered here in a collection of recent articles (all carefully updated) from the pages of *Audubon*, the magazine of the National Audubon Society. They do not constitute a tract, for far too many books of that kind have been published in these days of heightened environmental concern. Rather, they are a quiet plea. And good literature. One would expect nothing less from the respected authors whose contributions are included herein. There are warnings, to be sure, but not of the popular doomsday school. There are success stories, too, and thoughtful essays, and even humor.

I grew up in a day when conservation meant the propagation of creatures of fin, fur, and feather for the hunter's bag and the fisherman's creel, and not the saving of village greens and country rivers. Indeed, up to a very few years ago those of us who tried to stop the despoilers (whether they were great bureaucracies and industries or merely local drain commissioners and bankers) were simply ignored, as a boy in Michigan tried to ignore the Rogue River mosquitoes.

Mosquitoes, however, demand man's respect. Now a new breed of conservationist has developed a bite that the despoilers should respect. Instead, they have chosen to swat. They spend their public relations dollars trying to create an "environmental backlash." When they could easily mend their governmental and corporate ways, they have fought back by calling names and throwing stones. Wilderness advocates have been labeled "woodsy witchdoctors of a revived nature cult" by a spokesman for the timber industry. These "modern Druids," he explains, "would sacrifice jobs and fulfillment of human needs . . . in order to achieve their own selfish goals." Developers have hurled multimillion-dollar law suits at citizens who testified against housing projects at public hearings.

The most popular epithet of the despoilers is "preservationist." It is used liberally to label those who insist on sane national policies and priorities and restraints on such matters as oil exploitation, highway construction, pesticide spraying, mining, logging, land development, power-plant siting, the building of airports, the damming and straightening of rivers, the pollution of air and water, the commercialization of wildlife, the poisoning of predatory animals. It has even been used by old-line conservation clubs to disparage their nonhunting colleagues who would curtail open seasons and bag limits to aid dwindling game species, or end unsportsmanlike shooting practices.

Indeed, "preservationist" has replaced "little old lady birdwatcher" as the favorite expletive of the despoilers, since the latter term hardly applies to today's broad-based environmental movement.

The despoilers, I suggest, should consult their dictionary. There they would find "preservationist" defined as "one that advocates the preservation of a species from extinction," a cause that hardly seems so despicable.

Man, they tend to forget, is also a species. The saving of brown pelicans and prairie dogs and butterflies, the protection of native rivers and great swamps and untrammeled wilderness, the opposition to the ravishing of the land and the poisoning of the ecosystem — all have as their ultimate goal the preservation of a meaningful life for the human species.

The men and women whose words you will read, and their editor, are proud to be called preservationists.

Les Line,
Editor, *Audubon*

I. The Assault on Diversity

A young golden eagle, shot dead on a sheep ranch

JOSEPH WOOD KRUTCH

In Dubious, Desperate Battle

NEVER IN THE HISTORY of the world has there been so much
concern over man's violation of the natural environment and
the disappearance of what was once an abundant wildlife. This
is an encouraging fact, but it carries a discouraging implication.
We are more concerned today because never before have the
destructive processes operated at such a rapidly accelerating rate.
Despite new legislation and the establishment of new parks and
wilderness areas, the tide is still running against everything except
the growth of the human population, and the consequent elimination of everything that is not man-made and man-dominated.
Even Africa, which seemed not long ago a great reservoir of
the wild and the beautiful, is now threatened by its own "developing nations" — despite international concern and the establishment of protected areas.

Pessimists sometimes insist that if the population explosion
continues there will be no room for anything except human beings
and then, presently, no room even for them. Mankind, as
geophysicist Harrison Brown pointed out, "is behaving as if it
were engaged in a contest to test nature's willingness to support
humanity, and would, if it had its way, not rest content until
the Earth is covered completely to a considerable depth with
a writhing mass of human beings, much as a dead cow is covered
with a pulsating mass of maggots."

If this prospect were absolutely inevitable, then conservation would be no more than a rearguard or delaying action. But if it is just possible that the human race will discover in time how to avoid both mass destruction on the one hand and mass starvation or mass suffocation on the other, then it is surely worthwhile to preserve as much as we can of all the beauties, animate and inanimate, of our Earth. Destroyed buildings can be rebuilt; destroyed works of art may possibly be replaced by new creations; but every animal and every flower which becomes extinct is lost forever in the most absolute of all deaths.

If the concern which many feel is to be effective, the public at large must know what is happening and must feel very strongly that it ought not to happen. More than a hundred years ago, Thoreau wrote in his *Journal:*

> When I consider that the nobler animals have been exterminated here — the cougar, panther, lynx, wolverine, wolf, bear, moose, deer, the beaver, the turkey, etc., etc., — I cannot but feel as if I lived in a tamed, and, as it were, emasculated country ... I take infinite pains to know all the phenomena of the spring, for instance, thinking that I have here the entire poem, and then, to my chagrin, I hear that it is but an imperfect copy that I possess and have read, that my ancestors have torn out many of the first leaves and grandest passages, and mutilated it in many places. I should not like to think that some demigod have come before me and picked out some of the best of the stars. I wish to know an entire heaven and an entire earth.

Nothing less than a conviction as passionate as Thoreau's can resist the process which, unless determinedly arrested, will end in the elimination of every animal except man (and presently man himself) from the terrestrial globe. It is not only that they are being crowded out. Even when space is left them, the environment becomes modified in so many ways that they cannot survive. Poisons passing from organism to organism along one of those food chains which are a fundamental part of the living macrocosm reach at last the end of the line in birds and mammals — and may ultimately reach man himself. No more than a decade ago conservation meant almost exclusively the protection of the land and its creatures from the too successful human race. Today, overcrowding, pollution, chemical poisons, and fallout make conservation of the human species itself a pressing problem.

In our own country the destruction of the natural environment and its population has reached a state somewhere between that of Europe on the one hand and Africa on the other. In Africa man is just beginning to threaten the existence of its wildlife, including what Thoreau calls the nobler animals. England and the European continent have been so impoverished by deliberate destruction, and more importantly, by the simple preempting of available space, that naturalists can hope for no more than the preservation of a pitiful remnant. We in America, on the other hand, have just recently reached the point where saving rather than clearing the forests typifies what ought to be our ambition, although many continue to talk as though we were still pioneers in an empty land and boast of inexhaustible resources when, in fact, resources as indispensable as space, pure air, and pure water are approaching exhaustion.

Comparatively speaking, so much open country and surviving wildlife are left us in national parks and wilderness areas, as well as in certain still sparsely populated regions, that a visiting naturalist like James Fisher is moved to exclaim: "Never have I seen such wonders or met landlords so worthy of their land. They have had, and still have, the power to ravage it; but instead have made it a garden." As he realized, no European country ever dreamed of a national park system until it was too late.

James Fisher's tribute was uttered some fifteen years ago, but it sounds more ominous now than it did then. For a time it had seemed that the movement to conserve, which Theodore Roosevelt did so much to channel, had permanently arrested the attempts to violate many spectacularly rich and beautiful areas. But recently the attacks upon them have been intensified. Advocates of dams in the last unflooded canyons will not give up, and they pour ridicule and vituperation upon those who oppose them. Loggers and prospectors watch for any possible opportunity to force their way into wilderness preserves. Road-builders are demanding the right to cut superhighways through areas once sacred to peace, quiet, and air free from gasoline fumes. Those who wish to preserve and those who wish to ravage are joined in dubious and desperate battle.

Thoreau's lament over a maimed and imperfect nature reminds us that though the maiming has recently proceeded at a frightening pace, it has been going on for a long time — almost since the white man arrived on our continent. It reminds us also that many of the smaller as well as many of the nobler animals which still survive have disappeared from large areas where they were once plentiful. To use another of Thoreau's matchless sentences: "The squirrel has leaped to another tree; the hawk has circled further off, and has settled now upon a new eyrie; but the woodman is planning to lay his ax at the root of that also."

Neither laws aimed at some sort of conservation nor others intended to encourage killing are new. In 1630 the Massachusetts Bay Company provided a penny bounty for each wolf killed, which was no doubt justified at a time when men had only a precarious foothold on the continent they were presently to conquer all too thoroughly. But we are only now beginning to get rid of the senseless poisoning of coyotes by the government and the bounty payments on pumas in some of the Western states.

Sixty years after the first payment of a bounty on wolves came the first measure directed at conservation, when Massachusetts established a closed season for deer and followed it in 1710 with a law prohibiting the use of camouflaged canoes, or boats equipped with sails, in the pursuit of waterfowl.

Both were admirable measures, and have been followed by many others. But they are usually too little and too late. Hunters continue to slaughter the nearly extinct desert sheep in the fastness to which it has retreated. In Mexico's Baja California, where most game laws are either nonexistent or unenforced, they have all but exterminated this once plentiful animal by lying in wait for it at the widely scattered waterholes where it is possible to kill in a single evening all the desert bighorns which have come from over a large area to this one watering place.

Who cares? Many do, but not everyone does. It is said that when Audubon sought the subscription to *The Birds of America* from a wealthy citizen he was answered by the declaration "I would not pay that much for all the live birds in the United States, much less for pictures of them." Indeed, it is not uncommon to observe a sort of backlash provoked by increased public concern with conservation. Human needs, it is said, come first though the question "What needs of what people?" is seldom asked. The whole assumption that some contact with the natural world is conducive to physical and emotional health is often rejected. Once proposals to conserve were met with nothing worse than indifference. Now they are sometimes met with rationalized arguments ranging all the way from a simple enthusiasm for superhighways to the theory that the aim of civilization is not the preservation of the natural but its ultimate elimination — including the destruction of everything which does not serve the primary needs of an exploding population. As a dean at Massachusetts Institute of Technology recently put it, "in hedonic potential, megalopolis is no more and no less a natural environment for man than Athens or a peasant village."

Much of what the United States will be like a few generations hence may well depend upon the extent to which this thesis prevails. Perhaps it would be worthwhile to suggest some of the lines along which a refutation might be made.

Certainly the conflicting attitudes are as old as civilization. Christianity often followed the lead of its Hebrew sources in assuming that animals had been created for no purpose except that of being useful to man, and modern Catholicism sometimes accepts that premise so completely that an American bishop could recently brush aside the protest of some of his fellow religionists against what they regarded as cruel experiments, and repeat in the simplest and most unqualified form the premise that whatever might in any way profit mankind was legitimate no matter what abuse of animals it might entail. But even in the Middle Ages, St. Francis was not unique, and in the legends of the saints there are many tales concerning their tenderness toward the lesser creatures. When the Age of Science began, heavier stress began to be laid upon the argument, which was not really new, namely, that only by his works was the glory of God manifest. As John Ray, the seventeenth-century English biologist, put it: "Let us then consider the works of God and observe the operation of His hands . . . None in the subluminary world is capable of doing this except man, and we have yet been deficient therein." While still at Harvard, Thoreau unconsciously echoed and characteristically exaggerated this pronouncement when he wrote: "This curious world which we inhabit is more wonderful than it is convenient; more beautiful than it is useful; it is more to be admired than to be used."

Today most people would be inclined to reply to a defense of megalopolis by citing recent experimental evidence which seems to demonstrate that crowding not only reduces "hedonic potential" but also produces many disorders unknown where adequate elbowroom is available. Others (and I would include myself among them) are inclined to insist that there is such a thing as human nature and that it needs the contact with the natural world of which it is a part. Perhaps the late William Morton Wheeler, an impeccable technical scientist, put the whole thing most succinctly when he wrote about our fellow creatures: "That, apart from the members of our own species, they are our only companions in an infinite and unsympathetic waste of electrons, planets, nebulae and stars, is a perennial joy and consolation."

A female green turtle lumbers back to her realm after depositing her eggs on a Costa Rica beach

ARCHIE CARR

Great Reptiles, Great Enigmas

ONLY A LITTLE WHILE AGO the oceans seemed unassailable —
too big and stable to be hurt by man, too teeming with life
to let him ever go hungry. But now we know better. Suddenly,
even the myriad creatures of the sea are suffering from human
intemperance. The offal of cities circles the world in the global
currents; beaches are strewn with the cast-off artifacts of men
two thousand miles away.

It is not just the quiet inhabitants of reefs and clam beds that
are declining. The marching shoals of shrimps are dwindling,
the peregrine sardines and tunas cycle fewer every season. Even
as we came to know our dependence on the sea, our disruptions
there were spreading.

For nearly two decades most of my research time has been
spent working with sea turtles, a group of animals that now are
caught in the crossfire of ecologic decline and overexploitation.
I was drawn to sea turtles partly because in those days there
were gross blank places in their known natural history, and partly
because I saw a hawksbill come ashore out of phosphorescent
surf one night and dig in the sand while a thin moon climbed.

Today the plight of sea turtles is widely known, and efforts
to learn more about them and slow their decline are in progress
almost wherever they occur. But the concern was dangerously

slow in coming. In the *Red Data Book* of the International Union for Conservation of Nature, three species of sea turtle are listed as endangered, and by the criteria the IUCN employs that is a reasonable judgment. But if, as the measure of peril, trends are used rather than fixed population levels, there is no cause for complacency over the survival outlook of any kind of marine turtle.

It is really not known how many kinds of sea turtles there are. An ornithologist would find the taxonomy of the group in an inconceivably rudimentary state. So the people whose ideal it is to save every single recognizable and genetically different form of every sea turtle genus are not even able to define the objects of their concern. As a first step in coping with the multiplying threats, somebody ought to tackle the job of showing how many genetically distinct forms there are among the various wholly separate breeding colonies.

At the moment, the recognizable kinds of sea turtles seem to me to be eight in number. There are surely many more, and some of them have been named, but I can't see that they have really been defined. There are five sea turtle genera: *Caretta,* the loggerheads; *Lepidochelys,* the ridleys; *Eretmochelys,* the hawksbills; *Chelonia,* the green turtles; and *Dermochelys,* the leatherbacks. Only in *Chelonia* and *Lepidochelys* are there clearly differentiated, named species. The various green turtle colonies of the eastern Pacific are easily told from the Atlantic green turtle, *Chelonia mydas,* although regions of confusion exist; and the flatback, *Chelonia depressa,* of northwestern Australia is a strikingly different animal that superficially looks more like a ridley than a green turtle.

If I had to judge the relative survival outlook of each of the eight kinds of sea turtles, I would list them in this order of decreasing security:

(1) *Dermochelys coriacea.* The leatherback is a spectacularly unique animal. Although nowhere abundant, it is less plagued by exploitation than the other genera. The eggs are taken in most nesting localities, but little use is made of the meat. The skin is not used, the creature has no real shell, and though used in a few places as a cure-all, the oil smells too odd for Polly Bergen to put into cosmetics. Though by no means in reassuring shape — Costa Rica is losing its Matina rookery to egg poachers, and the famous Trengganu rookery in Malaya is clearly over-exploited — the pelagic foraging habits of leatherbacks keep them relatively free of the nets of trawlers, and the new colonies that have been discovered, including an enormous one that has been studied by Peter Pritchard for the last four seasons in French Guiana, put *Dermochelys* a bit ahead of the others as a survival bet. Even so, by my book it is an endangered species.

(2) *Chelonia depressa.* I rank the flatback in this position only because Dr. Robert Bustard of Australia attests so emphatically to its safety. The species has the second most restricted breeding range among sea turtles, and this seems pretty alarming; but Dr. Bustard says that stewardship for wild species runs high in Australia, and that the flatback is under strict protection and sure to remain so.

(3) *Caretta caretta.* If *Caretta* is really a single worldwide species, it may actually be better off than the preceding. The strong protection of the colonies nesting on the Zululand coast of southeastern Africa and at Heron Island on the Great Barrier Reef, combined with the remaining American rookeries, might hold the line for a time. But despite the more or less effective legislation in the United States and the conservation efforts of a number of individuals and organizations, the encroaching development, the wheeled vehicles on beaches and lights on coastal highways, the raccoon predation, and the human egg

poaching that still goes on are all hindering reproduction. At
the same time, drownings of turtles in the nets of shrimp and
menhaden fishermen are steadily increasing.

Besides, it seems unlikely that there is really only one kind
of loggerhead. The Pacific form was separated long ago under
the name *Caretta caretta gigas,* and though the original grounds
for the separation were not firm, there very probably are two
or more kinds of loggerheads in the world. If so, then the Atlantic
form is in bad shape. It has almost disappeared from most of
its range in Cuba and on the Caribbean mainland coasts. Colonies
on the coasts of Turkey and Senegal are exploited with unmonitored intensity. A few carefully protected places on the coasts
of Florida, plus a few islands in Georgia, South Carolina, and
North Carolina, may be the last stronghold of the Atlantic
loggerhead, and the long-term trend is not heartening.

(4) *Chelonia agassizi,* the black turtle of the Pacific. If the
survival of the black turtle depended on its Mexican and Central
American populations, it would be in bad trouble. It is less sought
after for meat than the Atlantic green turtle, but it gets involved
in the vast slaughter the hide hunters and egg poachers wreak
on the Pacific ridley. The black turtle of the eastern Pacific
lacks the numbers to withstand that abuse, and may well become
an incidental casualty along the American mainland shores. To
my eye, however, the black turtle stock occurs elsewhere — in
the Galápagos Islands, among the mid-Pacific Islands, and in parts
of the Indian Ocean. With its range extending through so much
territory, the complete loss of the Mexican and Central American
colonies might not obliterate *Chelonia agassizi;* but here again,
the name, as I am using it, surely covers a number of hitherto
unnamed races. The sooner these are properly defined, the sooner
concern over their plight will be generated.

(5) *Lepidochelys olivacea,* the Pacific ridley. Until lately this

little turtle seemed on the way to extirpation from the eastern Pacific. The inane and catastrophic vogue for turtle leather has focused insupportable slaughter on both the migrating ridley flotillas and the onshore *arribadas,* as the Mexicans call the enormous nesting aggregations. While Mexico has organized programs of research and control, exploitation has far over-reached the restraints, and for a while it seemed likely that the species would be wiped out of Mexico. And so it still may be. The Pacific ridley is probably the world's most abundant sea turtle, but it is also the most massively persecuted. No species better illustrates the inadequacy of population numbers as a sole measure of security. The ridley take in Mexico was more than a million in 1968 — and those were just the legal, recorded landings. The famous *arribada* at Piedra de Tlacoyunque in the state of Guerrero declined from 30,000 in 1968 to a few hundred in 1969.

My reason for rating the species no lower in the list is some recent evidence that the leather trade may be dwindling. It is high time. Sea turtle leather is really not very good; its current vogue results from pure public relations. And with Dr. F. Wayne King of the New York Zoological Society revealing the irrespon-sible shortsightedness of the international traffic, with the Mexi-can population already reduced to a level that is scaring the industry and engendering renewed official protective efforts, and with new *flotas* and *arribadas* recently reported along the Central American coast, the situation now seems more fluid than desper-ate. So I am inclined to keep the antepenultimate place in my list for the Atlantic green turtle, which I think is in somewhat worse shape than the Pacific ridley. I ought to say that Dr. Peter Pritchard, an extraordinarily able turtle man who got a Ph.D. doing research on ridleys, disagrees with this judgment. It goes to show how risky such comparisons can be.

(6) *Chelonia mydas,* the Atlantic green turtle. When I grouped all known "black turtle" colonies, there were left the *Chelonia* populations nesting in the Caribbean, in the Guianas, and at Ascension Island; plus — for lack of any demonstrated grounds for separating them — some Pacific colonies that are obviously not *C. agassizi* and so, simply because of our ignorance, have to be grouped with the Atlantic green turtle as *C. mydas.* The resulting unwieldy, surely unnatural "species" includes a lot of turtles — enough to allay the concern of anyone not aware of the losses and depletion that the genus has undergone during the past two centuries, and of the rising rate of exploitation.

It is these trends, again, and not absolute population numbers, that seem the only sensible basis for assessing the survival outlook of the green turtle. In the case of the western Caribbean green turtle, the course of events is especially dismal. Because long-term tagging has roughed out the migratory cycle of the Tortuguero colony in Costa Rica, it can be shown to be increasingly under attack everywhere. Even in Florida, medieval legislation, staunchly supported in recent political controversy, permits the commercial exploitation of an almost vanished green turtle colony. Some of the Pacific rookeries are located where there are religious taboos against eating meat. In some of these, however, the egg harvests are heavy; and, moreover, when the turtles leave the breeding ground they go out into wholly unknown resident range, where exploitation may be completely unmonitored.

The greatest need is for inviolate sanctuaries where the capture of turtles is prohibited on or anywhere near the beach, and where no eggs are taken. In the case of every existing green turtle sanctuary, migration takes the turtles away to resident range that, if known, is unprotected. For example, the nesting turtles of Ascension Island and at the sanctuaries in Surinam are fully protected, and in both locations poaching is almost nonexistent. But when they leave both places the turtles travel a thousand miles or more to feeding grounds along the coast of Brazil. There the pressure of exploitation is growing almost as fast as it is in the Caribbean.

So despite the sizable remaining populations of *Chelonia mydas*, as I define it here, and despite the rapid spread of anxiety over its decline and the efforts to arrange the international programs required to stop it, the position of the green turtle is clearly degenerating.

Last in the list are the Mexican ridley, *Lepidochelys kempi*, and the hawksbill, *Eretmochelys imbricata*. I have thought a lot about the claim each has to being the most endangered sea turtle, and find it hard to judge between them. Taken together, they graphically show the difficulty inherent in such judgment, because for diametrically different reasons they both have insecure grips on the future. The hawksbill is in danger because it nests too diffusely to be protected, the ridley because it breeds in such concentrated gangs.

The Mexican ridley forms the most heavily aggregated reproductive gatherings of any reptile — any vertebrate animal, probably. Except for occasional isolated single nestings elsewhere along the southern coast of the Gulf of Mexico, its breeding and nesting are restricted to a few mass emergences, in which as many as forty thousand turtles used to come out in a single day on a short stretch of the coast of Tamaulipas near the town of Rancho Nuevo. No other *arribadas* of *L. kempi* are known anywhere, and the occasional lone nestings south and north of the Rancho Nuevo area are probably too isolated to be of any consequence to the ultimate survival of the animal. As to exploitation, the big threat is the hide hunters, who have repeatedly tried to get permits from the Mexican government to raid the colony. An efficient turtling team could reduce the species to half its numbers in one year. By the end of a second season, intensive hunting combined with the chronic background drain imposed by trawl-net drownings and egg poachers would probably insure the subsequent extinction of *Lepidochelys kempi*. The predicament of the Gulf ridley is thus a classic case, in which a small population with minuscule reproductive range is undergoing constant poaching and accidental inroads, and faces the constant threat of sudden disastrous commercial raiding.

The hawksbill is in a very different position. If the main weakness of the ridley is its restricted breeding range, the hawksbill's trouble is overdeployment of its reproductive effort. Hawksbills are spread throughout the world's tropical waters. They forage mainly around reefs, and they nest on almost any stretch of sand shore, no matter how short it may be. No other sea turtle is so solitary in its nesting. In a few places small groups may come out together, but mainly reproduction is carried out by females that go ashore alone, sometimes where other species nest, sometimes on little scraps of beach that any other sea turtle, except possibly a Pacific ridley or Galápagos black turtle, would spurn. The exploitation of the hawksbill has increased drastically during the past two decades. Besides a steady growth of the tortoiseshell market in Europe and Japan, the skins and calipee are bought in some places, and the turtle itself is eaten. As a result, Caribbean hawksbills now bring the hunter as much as $15 apiece, which is usually more than he could earn in a week by any other work available. So, with hawksbill eggs more favored by local people than any other, with scuba divers snatching young hawksbills out of their reef retreats for the hell of it, and with marine curio shops selling young ones stuffed and polished for hanging on your wall, there is cause for the gravest concern over the hawksbill. And its attenuated nesting range makes it impossible to provide adequate breeding sanctuaries. So there is really little choice between hawksbill and Mexican ridley as the most threatened kind of sea turtle. If the tortoiseshell trade could be killed, the hawksbill would probably survive. The fate of the ridley depends on the ability of the species to withstand the casual inroads of the trawlers, on abolishment of the legal commercial turtling still permitted in Florida — which is a main migratory station of the ridley — and, above all, on the good will and good luck of the Mexican government in protecting the Rancho Nuevo breeding ground.

When I first went to Costa Rica with a National Science Foundation grant to study the ecology of sea turtles, my main aim was to work out the routes and stations of the migratory travels of *Chelonia*. I soon found it difficult to stay clear of the complex relationships between turtles and people. It was obvious that the Tortuguero nesting ground, where I had set out to develop a long-term tagging project, was on the way to oblivion. There was organized exploitation along the entire nesting beach. The turtles were turned for the market as soon as they came up out of reach of the surf. Up at the Nicaraguan resident ground, the bag limit was simply the capacity of the turtle schooners to carry turtles away.

It seemed then that the mayhem on the nesting beach was the main threat, and that once that was stopped the colony might withstand the drain to the turtle boats. In fact, it occurred to me that in *Chelonia* the world had a marine herbivore that, with a little study and wise management, could be made a resource of great importance. People were getting nervous over their own growing numbers, and talk of turning to the sea for food was spreading. The green turtle appeared to have special promise in this respect, being not only good to eat but virtually the only edible vertebrate able to harvest the vast crops of submarine vegetation that spread in shallow, warm, protected water. I preached this so hard that lately I have been reproached for having helped snowball the exploitation that now threatens to destroy the resource.

What I had in mind, however, was not green turtle on every table but rather turtle on the tables of the seaside people who had fished out their reefs and couldn't afford the equipment for deepwater fishing. This was Joshua Powers's aim when he organized the Brotherhood of the Green Turtle in 1957, and that of the Caribbean Conservation Corporation that grew out of the Brotherhood. None of us visualized the demand that would come when countries that once were poor grew prosperous, and when seafood restaurants began to feel insecure if turtle was missing on their menus. Just the other day, looking back through some of the first things I wrote about sea turtles, I found this passage in *Handbook of Turtles:*

"Although the green turtle is in no immediate danger of extinction, it will support no resurgence of the industry. It seems almost certain that with modern methods of refrigeration and food preservation to enlighten the inland public concerning the gastronomic properties of this succulent reptile, the pathetic remnant of the once-teeming hordes will be pursued with harpoon and stop net, and the centers of activity will invade even more remote waters until the animal is backed against the wall."

Now the resurgence I spoke of has come to pass, and I am as sure now as I was in 1952 that it is going to be insupportable. It was brought on by three changes in the world: the spread of a more imaginative attitude toward eating in the United States some twenty years ago; the prosperity of Western Europe; and an increased demand for turtle by-products. The first factor came into play after the Second World War, when a lot of GIs came home more open-minded about victualing than they once had been. Seafood restaurants broke out all up and down the steak-and-potato belt. They made big industry out of the shrimp business, and green turtle became the touchstone of the exciting menu. This latter vogue — and it is really more vogue than gastronomy, because restaurant turtle steak is mostly dismal — has practically wiped out the feeble remnant of the Florida green turtle population. Coming on top of the original luxury soup trade, it is a major new threat to the green turtle in the western Caribbean.

As to the effect of European opulence, the demand that it has generated is a brand new and surprising factor. The biggest market for turtle outside the United States is now West Germany. According to Alfred Knopf, a reliable source of such lore, the best turtle soup in the world is now West German. John Lusty, proprietor of the famous London turtle soup factory and grandson of its founder, disagrees. Mr. Knopf's opinion is a straw in the wind all the same. Turtle soup used to be ritualistically English, although always the fare of the elite. Such days are gone. Mr. Lusty makes instant turtle soup tablets, and German initiative is ransacking the Earth to supply the chefs of Munich and Frankfurt.

The only hope to save the Atlantic populations of the green turtle is wholehearted international cooperation and an as yet unborn willingness to put the survival of the species before immediate self-interest. The first effort to generate that kind of shared responsibility was made by the Caribbean Conservation Corporation. Through its Operation Green Turtle, a dozen countries and islands were for eight years made partners in a joint restocking effort and were provided whatever information or techniques came out of the Tortuguero project. While no new breeding colonies have as yet been detected, a realization of the plight of *Chelonia* in the Caribbean was planted in places where none had been before. Meantime, the CCC has continued its monitoring of the Tortuguero nesting ground, and has provided facilities for varied research projects there and elsewhere in the Caribbean. Its operations in Costa Rica were a point of condensation for a Tortuguero National Park, one of three projects of the vigorous new national park service of Costa Rica.

More recently, the International Union for Conservation of Nature vastly extended the outlook for international sea turtle stewardship by establishing a special committee of its Survival Service Commission. The members of this Marine Turtle Group were carefully chosen for their involvement with sea turtle biology or conservation in strategic localities around the world. The World Wildlife Fund has financed two meetings of the group at IUCN headquarters in Morges, Switzerland. There was nothing ceremonial or perfunctory about those meetings. Each time, a dozen or more people from practically everywhere spent five days sharing information, hopes, and forebodings, and objectively searching for answers to problems and ways to avert disasters. Some rays of hope came out of the sessions, but the main advance was the shared understanding of the scope and gravity of the problems presented by avidly exploited animals with international migratory ranges.

With the possible exception of the Australian flatback, no kind of sea turtle can be given a sure survival outlook by protecting it within the frontiers of a single country. To date, there is no international program protecting a species throughout its range. There almost was. The world's first approach to a closed system of migratory sea turtle protection almost materialized in 1969. Disturbed by the poor nesting season, we had reported at Tortuguero for 1968, and urged on by expressions of concern from a great many people, a group of high-level delegates from Costa Rica, Nicaragua, and Panama met in a *conferencia tripartita* in

San José. Nicaragua was there because, according to calculations based on our tag returns, at least two-thirds of the Tortuguero nesting colony is derived from the extensive turtle grass pastures off the coast of Nicaragua. Panama is a resident ground or migratory station for perhaps half of the remainder. So those three countries working together could almost certainly insure the survival of *Chelonia* in the western Caribbean.

After three days' deliberations, the delegates agreed to call a three-year moratorium on turtling in all their home waters, while they worked out a permanent plan that would give Costa Rica, custodian of the nesting ground, a fair share of a strictly controlled yearly harvest without raiding the nesting colony. Then they went home to obtain what was expected to be automatic ratification. When Billy Cruz, Costa Rican representative of the CCC, cabled me the news, I happily telephoned colleagues who for years had been hoping that some such thing would happen. I wrote IUCN headquarters, too, suggesting that congratulations were in order, and there was great rejoicing. The day of international sea turtle conservation had dawned.

Only it hadn't. What Nicaragua did was sweep the San José agreement under the rug and build two big, modern turtle processing plants, kick out the Cayman turtle schooners, and seduce the Miskito Indians — the Turtle Indians, probably the most specialized turtle culture in the world — into killing feverishly for the factories. Now the Miskitos are taking home a little cash instead of meat, and with it buying an inadequate diet to replace the good one provided for ages by the turtle colony with which their society had evolved. Dr. Bernard Nietschmann of the University of Michigan has a forthcoming article on this debacle in the *Journal of Human Ecology*. It is a hair-raising story, not only because of what is happening to the Indians and the turtles, but because the development killed the rising resolve of the Costa Rican officials to curb the turtling at Tortuguero.

For Costa Rica also has two turtle-processing plants. They are supplied by boats that cruise along the nesting shore from June through August and harpoon the mating pairs or the females going ashore or returning through the surf. Taking turtles on the beach has been illegal for twelve years. But the harpoon boats come in so close you might as well turn the hunters loose on shore.

Two special aspects of this situation make it stick badly in my craw. One is the absence of any extenuating ignorance by the parties involved as to what they are doing. *Chelonia* is the best known of the sea turtles, and the life cycle of the Tortuguero nesting colony is better known than that of any other population. Both countries know that Costa Rica has charge of the only green turtle breeding ground remaining in the western Caribbean, and that the Nicaraguan pastures are populated by turtles that hatch on the Costa Rican shore and nowhere else. This simple ecologic picture has been repeatedly made plain. And still they continue to subject the declining resource to growing exploitation. The other bitter pill is that both countries are depriving the poor coastal people of turtles they desperately need, while at the same time espousing an export industry that is bound to obliterate the resource.

So the world's first international agreement for sea turtle conservation has disintegrated, and about all we can do is wait and see whether new losses, sure to come, will scare the decision-makers into making a new effort at cooperative control. Meantime, turtles still come to Tortuguero to nest each season, and we still see tags that we have put on them as long as eight or ten years before. As time passes, these contacts accumulate, and various kinds of new information are emerging from the records of such repeated encounters with individual nesters.

The usual motive for tagging a migratory animal at its breeding ground is to find out where the colony comes from — whether the animals are derived from a single year-round habitat, or from several distant places. That was the first aim of the tagging program at Tortuguero when I set it up in 1955. To turtlers and fishermen, green turtles were already known to be long-distance migrants, but this had never been demonstrated to the satisfaction of zoologists, and was, in fact, generally doubted. Why, I was never able to figure out. It seemed to me that, over and above the risk involved in ignoring lay opinion on such matters, the mere distribution of the nesting sites vis-à-vis the nearest feeding pastures indicated periodic long-range travel. In any case, only a few months after our first season at Tortuguero an international tag return came in. It was from up in the Miskito Cays, where the Cayman turtle boats were operating, and it reinforced what the captains had told me: that the Nicaraguan turtles nested in Costa Rica.

As years passed, repeated long-distance recoveries soon filled in the pattern of migration. They showed that while Nicaragua was the main source of the colony, other sizable parts of it came from Panama, the Guajira Peninsula of Colombia, and the Yucatán Peninsula of Mexico. Returns from more far-flung localities — Trinidad, Florida, and Martinique, for example — have slowly trickled in. Later on, the relative volumes of returns from different places began to give some indication of the relative sizes of the resident colonies there.

A significant aspect of the long-distance recoveries is that none has been made on any other nesting beach. However, we have recently learned that turtles from two different rookeries may mix on the feeding ground. This was shown when the northern-most Brazilian recoveries of turtles tagged at the Ascension Island nesting ground began overlapping the southernmost recovery localities for turtles tagged in Surinam by Dr. J. P. Schulz and his associates, and by Dr. Peter Pritchard.

The growing pattern of long-distance recoveries strongly suggested that the migrants are accomplished open-sea navigators, and the tagging program at the midocean nesting ground at Ascension Island was organized to test that possibility. The consistent recovery of Ascension females on the coast of Brazil confirmed the existence of an island-finding ability, and of some kind of advanced navigation mechanism.

Those are the things to be learned from long-distance tag recoveries. Over and above their intrinsic interest as natural history, the results led into two separate collateral avenues: research to explain open-sea orientation, and planning for the international conservation efforts obviously necessary to save the green turtle. But further insight into the life cycle comes from repeated contacts with the turtles at the nesting beach. These contacts are of two kinds: short-term recoveries, made after the twelve- to fourteen-day renesting intervals of a female during her stay at the nesting beach; and remigration returns, the successive migratory visits that an individual turtle makes at intervals of two or more years. One thing we hoped to discover from these was the growth rate of the female turtles after they reach maturity. Being reptiles, they supposedly had no definitive upper size limit, but simply kept on growing after reaching maturity, as rattlesnakes or largemouth bass presumably do. The females that come to Tortuguero range widely in shell length — from around 28 inches up to the 46 inches of the big wind-turtles, as the local people call them. It seemed reasonable to attribute this wide range in body length to age, but as time passed we could detect no growth in the turtles we measured. Whatever increase there was could not be reliably measured with the big wooden calipers we used. Finally, however, when the data had accumulated for a dozen years, we took the whole lot over to the statistics department and got back a tenth of an inch per year as the average increase in overall body length.

The figure was surprising, and its bearing on our studies of the colony became apparent when, after the bad nesting season at Tortuguero in 1968, nesting was very heavy in 1969, and we began trying to account for the sudden increase. Naturally, we looked for evidence of the arrival of an unusually big group of new nesters. But how do you identify a first-time nester? With only the negative evidence of her failure to bear a tag, there was always the chance that the turtle was merely one that had been missed by the tagging crew during an earlier nesting season. This problem of spotting the true neophytes among the untagged arrivals was aggravated by the excruciatingly slow growth rate, which suggested that the wide range in shell length meant simply that the females matured at different sizes — just as humans do. So we couldn't just tally all big, untagged turtles as old ones that we had missed earlier, and all small ones as new recruits to the breeding population. Some of the big ones were big because they were old; while some were already big, because of genetic or ecologic factors, when they made their first trip to the nesting beach.

Nevertheless, there was bound to be *some* relation between size and age, and finding it seemed important to our understanding of what was going on in the turtle population. My wife closeted herself with the tagging logs, and after long toil came up with a size group that was almost self-evidently neophyte. It was the 36-inch or shorter shell-length class. Any turtle encountered with an overall shell length of no more than 36 inches could be tallied as a new addition to the nesting colony without introducing any important error. This may seem a small advance, but it wasn't. It was a way of determining whether part of the nesting peak in 1969 was produced by the maturing of new recruits. And that turned out to be the case. There was a marked increase in the number of 36-inch nesters that year.

But those newly matured females were not wholly responsible for the peak. Another factor was an internal, lifting-yourself-by-your-shoestrings kind of change, which, like the growth rate, came to light only because we had stayed in the tagging business so long a time. We had known for years that the females of the western Caribbean population nest on dual cycles — that some of them come back to the beach after a two-year absence, and some after a lapse of three years. The three-year cycle is the more frequent, in ratio of about two to one. We have never recorded a return to Tortuguero after a single year's absence. You find such nonannual breeding rhythms in some kinds of birds — condors, albatrosses, penguins, the sooty tern — but they have in no case been accounted for. It seems possible that they simply represent the amount of time the female requires to prepare for the physiologic tour de force of traveling hundreds of miles to a breeding ground and then, in the case of *Chelonia*, remaining along an almost foodless shore until as many as five, or possibly even six or seven, nesting emergences have been carried out at two-week intervals.

Perhaps this feat requires more than one year's physiologic preparation. And perhaps the two-year and three-year dichotomy just reflects variable feeding conditions in the home range of the individual turtles. That the Surinam green turtles often nest annually does nothing to clarify the puzzle. Little is known about fluctuations in the productivity of turtle grass pastures; but currents wax, wane, and shift about in the western Caribbean, and the hurricane belt moves back and forth. Such changes probably affect the condition of the pasturage or interfere with the daily grazing regimen, and thus influence the reproductive cycle. In any case, it seemed most likely that some kind of ecologic changes at the resident ground caused the shifting between the two cycles. But whatever the cause of the duality in nesting cycles, the bearing on the productivity of the population was clear: the more prevalent the two-year cycle, the more young the colony would produce.

It took ten years to learn that an individual female may shift back and forth from the longer to the shorter cycle, or vice versa. We had to await the accumulation of two-time returns of tagged females to the nesting beach, and we have now recorded 50 of these, as well as five three-time returns. These include cycle shifts in both directions. Changes to the shorter cycle have been far more frequent than the other way around, however. There was a rash of shortened cycles in 1969, and this should probably be considered, along with the coming of newly matured females, as a factor in the increased nesting of that year.

Besides those two well-documented, interchangeable nesting cycles, we have slowly grown to suspect that occasional female turtles may wait four years between nestings. This is hard to prove because the four-year intervals that we have recorded might merely reflect defective patrolling of the beach — cases in which a turtle nesting on a two-year cycle was missed on her first return, and then seen again on a second migration four years after she was originally tagged. It will take statistical analysis to prove the reality of the four-year cycle, and for that the efficiency of the sampling done by the tagging crews has to be known. It will probably turn out that a four-year reproductive cycle is infrequent but normal in the Tortuguero population.

If so, one is tempted to reason further that western Caribbean green turtles must take whatever amount of time is necessary to prepare for their arduous breeding venture — that none can get ready in a single year, that some need two years to prepare, some three years, and others still longer times. This possibility can only be tested by statistics that we accumulate through continued tagging.

A very different way the renesting and remigration tag returns have paid off is in our studies of the goal sense and site fixity shown by the females when they return to nest. It is a challenge to explain not only how a thousand-mile open-sea course is navigated, but also how the journey can so often wind up with the migrant hauling out within a few yards of where she nested two or three years before. Practically, it is important to restoration efforts to know what goal sense it is that attracts a female ashore at the point she chooses as a nesting site.

Back in 1952 and 1953, I did a lot of scouting of Caribbean beaches, looking for sea turtle nesting grounds. Local people kept telling me that if you marked where a turtle came ashore on a given night, you only had to go back there two weeks later and you would find her again at exactly the same spot. The same thing is said by resident turtle people all around the world. While it is not altogether true, it is true enough to make you wonder how such insight ever comes to the people who tell you about it. All I can suggest is that the discovery of site tenacity is not made by turtle hunters, but by egg hunters, who don't kill the turtle but only sit waiting beside her till she has laid her eggs, and so have the chance to memorize her scars, deformities, or peculiar patterns of barnacles. Otherwise, the only way to learn about nest-site homing would be by the purposeful tagging of turtles, discovering first that they come ashore more than once in a given season — which, obviously, would not be self-evident — and then noticing that second nests are often dug close to the first ones.

The amazing reliability of that folklore has kept me open-minded when talking to backcountry people about turtles, even when their yarns had a wild sound to them. We have been tagging at Tortuguero for seventeen seasons now, and have gradually refined our system of marking the beach so that the positions of nests can be accurately recorded. What the records now show is that the females neither scatter at random along the rookery shore, nor come back to precisely the same spots each time, but instead recognize short *sections* of shore, and come back there time after time to nest. Although the occasional female nests five or six miles from a former landing place, the average separation of the points at which a turtle nests on two successive visits to the Tortuguero beach is about 1000 yards. But the more arresting figure is the *modal* distance — the *usual* separation between two landings. This has proved to be 200 yards, just under an eighth of a mile. The figure is almost the same for the separation of the nests of a given season, of which we have thousands of records, and for the 500-odd intermigration returns after two or three years or more.

There have been so many of these 200-yard intervals, spread through so many nestings and so many years, that they alone seem all the proof you need that a sea turtle recognizes and returns to, not some familiar topographic feature, but a home section of shore that is most often 200 yards long, and is marked off for her by utterly unknown signs. What kind of delimitation could she possibly be using to locate such a strip of beach, with no durable topographic skyline behind it; where there are only dunes and coco plum ledges that grow or disappear through the years; where the surface of the sand is constantly scoured by torrential rains and occasionally is stripped away completely and relaid by storms; and where strong longshore currents vary sporadically in direction and speed, and in the volume of freshwater they carry from the coastal rivers.

It seems impossible to put your finger on any mark that would last through a single two-year cycle, much less through the decade and more that some of our records cover. The local people, wise as they sometimes are, are no help in this case. They tell you vaguely it is Turtle Mountain — a 500-foot volcanic relic that rises alone just back of the northernmost end of the nesting beach — that directs the turtles in to their landing places. But over and above the fact that sea turtles see poorly above water, it seems unlikely that a seaside hill at one end of the nesting beach could be the beacon for such performances as the return of a female that we recorded ashore eight times in six years on one half-mile span of the twenty-mile nesting shore, and in a position from which the mountain was completely out of sight from the eye level of a turtle.

So for quite a while smell has seemed a logical possibility as the landing sense. When a female turtle comes ashore she repeatedly pokes her chin and muzzle into the sand and holds it there a moment, sometimes moving along while her nose plows through the sand. All the shelled turtles — that is, all sea turtles except the shell-less leatherback — do this, some more industriously than others, but all often enough to demand an explanation. So for want of an explanation of site tenacity, we put two and two together and started calling sand *nuzzling* sand *smelling*.

But now that we have a lot more data on the fineness of the homing returns, I don't know what to think. Unless some smell-able essence of the home strip oozes up from the groundwater and keeps reimpregnating the sand with a characteristic odor, there seems no way in which smell could guide the female.

Whatever the guide-signs, they must be imprinted in the young at the time they hatch out, or while they travel down the beach to the sea and swim through the surf to begin a developmental migration that lasts six years or so. Although it is conceivable that the little turtles inherit their instructions for finding their hatching place when they return to nest, the capacity to be imprinted with the guide-signs seems a much less complex adaptation. The best assumption is that baby turtles leave their natal place with some indelible olfactory impressions that help them recognize the site six years later.

An observation that might lend strength to that idea is the dearth of nesting on sections of the Tortuguero shore where people live. You might be inclined to say that the people just scare the turtles away from the beach in front of their *ranchos*, but this is doubtful. There is no coastal highway at Tortuguero, no stream of car lights behind the dunes — only a few people in thatched dwellings, where the dim lamps are turned out early in the evening. What seems more probable is that through former decades the killing of nesting turtles and taking of eggs simply deleted from the colony the individuals that, as hatchlings, were imprinted with the tendency to nest in front of the little settlement.

Conversely, when big storms chop up a section of the shore where a turtle has faithfully returned to nest for years, she often will keep coming back there year after year, even though coco plums have been uprooted, old palms have fallen, and she has to climb a four-foot, wave-cut bluff to get to good nesting sand. Obviously, this neither proves that hatchling imprinting occurs, nor gives any clue as to what signs are imprinted.

In our theorizing about the phenomenon of green turtle navigation in the open ocean, imprinting has again been appealed to. At one time it was my tendency to relax and say that turtles probably find midocean islands by celestial navigation — the same way birds migrate, according to some ornithologists. But the more I thought about this, the harder it was to visualize the monumental evolutionary process it would take to build the

necessary almanac instinct, the sense of the relation of changing
signs in the sky to points on the surface of the Earth. Then
Dr. David Ehrenfeld and Dr. Arthur Koch found that green turtles
could hardly see anything with their heads out of water, and
this further weakened the celestial navigation theory by ruling
out stellar orientation.

As a matter of fact, there is no good explanation of the open
ocean navigation of any animal, either aerial or aquatic. But
in the case of the South Atlantic green turtle, which cruises across
1200 miles of featureless ocean and makes pinpoint landings on
Ascension Island, the steady current that flows from the island
to the Brazilian resident grounds makes smell a reasonable
component of the guidance process. The theory is that an
Ascension smell fans out downstream in the South Equatorial
Current, stays smellably strong until it reaches Brazil, and serves
to keep the migrants to Ascension in the latitude of the island
as they travel eastward. The necessary easterly heading, the
theory suggests, is maintained by a compass sense, which now
has been found to be widely prevalent among both vertebrate
and invertebrate animals. The main virtue of this theory is that
all it would require of evolution would be a built-in capacity
to be imprinted by, and to perceive and judge relative concentrations of, a special smell — and not the fantastically complicated
map sense that celestial position-finding would require.

The most frustrating aspect of my work with sea turtles has
been our efforts at electronic open-sea tracking. The olfaction
theory could easily be tested if the migratory paths of the turtles,
or sections of them, could be accurately tracked. If smell is
actually the key to latitude in the Ascension journey, female
turtles taken from the island before completing their nesting,
and released a hundred miles or so across the current from
Ascension, should prove unable to establish proper return head-

ings. Others, carried downstream, should make successful approaches to the island, perhaps on zigzag courses indicating appraisal of the home smell in the current coming from the island. Our efforts to get these track plots by long-range, surface-to-surface radio contact have yielded only meager results.

It would be comforting to find the smell part of the open-ocean navigation theory also involved in landfall recognition and nest site tenacity. But what kind or combination of odors could guide a migrant in, at the end of her trek across hundreds of miles of open water, to one 200-yard stretch of beach? We really have made very little progress in accounting for either the long-range navigation of turtles, or their ability to recognize their hatching place.

The things I have been speaking of all bear on the practical problem of saving sea turtles from overexploitation and loss of habitat. It has never been clearly known, for instance, what in the eyes of a turtle constitutes a good nesting beach. Why do green turtles more often than not travel hundreds of miles from their year-round pasture ground to nest on a piece of beach that looks, to a man, like hundreds of miles of closer shore? The answer may partly be that the beaches that now are empty were long ago exhausted by overexploitation. Certainly, mass nesting once was much more widespread in the Caribbean than it is today, when big assemblages gather only at Tortuguero and Aves Island, a tiny islet in the middle of the eastern Caribbean. But there are cases in which no such explanation seems to apply.

The question of nest habitat choice is important to any effort to establish new breeding colonies. In Operation Green Turtle, the Caribbean Conservation Corporation, using transportation provided by the U.S. Navy, moved thousands of eggs and hatchlings from the Tortuguero rookery to eighteen likely-looking beaches around the Caribbean. No new breeding colonies have as yet grown up, and nobody knows why. Perhaps the inoculations were just too weak — too few hatchlings were put out in each locality. Or possibly the surviving hatchlings went back to Costa Rica when they reached breeding age. But there is also the nagging thought that the places where the releases were made were unacceptable as nesting ground. An effort was made to select sites where nesting had once occurred; but perhaps changed conditions had made them unfavorable for nesting.

It has been suggested that there is a relation between nesting and the size and shape of sand grains, but exceptions in this respect make generalization profitless. Certainly a beach with too much clay or mud in the sand, or one composed of overlarge shell fragments, is never chosen; but practically anything else in the way of texture seems acceptable, providing drainage is good. So in trying to account for the clumped nesting of the green turtle, something other than the obvious physical features of the shore has to be proposed. After reviewing the case for olfactory piloting in a recent paper, I suggested that perhaps, in the opinion of a green turtle, a good nesting beach is any well-drained ocean shore swept by a current that (1) carries dissolved chemicals that the migrating adults can smell or taste a long way off and (2) transports the hatchlings to wherever they spend the first months of their lives. For these practical implications, as well as to gratify biologic curiosity, it seems urgent to test the idea that smell is used as a guide-sign.

In the long run, marine turtles, like the seas themselves, will be saved only by wholehearted international cooperation at the governmental level. That is an almost legendary substance. While waiting for it to materialize, the critical tactical needs seem to me to be three in number: more sanctuaries, more research, and a concerted effort by all impractical, visionary, starry-eyed, and antiprogressive organizations, all little old ladies in tennis shoes, and all persons able to see beyond the ends of their noses, to control the international commerce in sea turtle products.

For some time, organizations concerned with the survival of species of animals that are being commercially exploited have been faced with the obligation of deciding whether to mount international campaigns to discourage the use of products derived from the animals, or to encourage artificial culture projects. Actually the two courses are not mutually exclusive, but the aspirant farmers say they are, and they bemoan any move to depopularize products derived from animals that they say they will one day save from extinction by farming.

If things are left as they are, the commerical sea turtle industry seems certain to go on cynically mining to exhaustion its sources of supply. In the process, some of the species involved will probably be dragged down to nonviable population levels. In the case of the green turtle, prospective farmers say that if conservationists will only hold back in their trade-killing campaign, a commerce based on artificial culture can be developed, and this will quickly make poaching and commercial turtle hunting unprofitable.

The same is said by the people who plan to farm crocodilians. Superficially it sounds good, but there is fuzzy thinking in it. I have yet to see or hear of a work plan for any reptile ranch that shows in realistic detail how it expects to achieve a volume of production so great that it will do anything other than *increase* both demand and prices. If the enterprise is a commercial one, it will obviously do everything possible to create new markets. Just as obviously, it will not be able to satisfy these, and so will exacerbate, rather than relieve, the predicament of the natural populations.

And meanwhile, because nobody has yet worked out the

problem of breeding sea turtles at production levels in enclosures, turtle farms will remain dependent on natural sanctuaries for the eggs from which they get the little turtles they propose to grow to slaughter size, and to flood the market with. Individual female green turtles have mated and laid in captivity, but nobody has ever approached the successful production of eggs in volume.

It obviously will be many years before turtle farms will do anything other than weaken the position of wild species. If turtle farming — as an alternative to depopularization — is to be espoused by people interested in the survival of natural species, the only effort to be encouraged should be a nonprofit, government-sponsored campaign in which many small, widespread, purely experimental projects simultaneously attack the problems of nutrition, disease control, and captive breeding; and which, from the beginning, freely share all information bearing on procedure and results. That sort of cooperative, nonprofit, pilot program might possibly lay groundwork for a pantropical turtle farm industry that would be able to spring into existence and from the beginning fill any new demand that it created. If this appears a reasonable possibility, then conservationists might logically give the campaign support.

For the time being, however, the only realistic course is a worldwide effort to discourage international traffic in sea turtle products of every kind. The demand can be built back quickly in that distant time when the farms are prepared to meet it.

FAITH McNULTY

The Silent Shore

FOR THE PAST FIVE YEARS reports from the California coast have
been increasingly ominous. In one instance after another there
are signals that birds, and perhaps even fish and mammals, that
inhabit these waters are in serious trouble. It is possible — though
as yet unproven — that these are the early symptoms of a coming
catastrophe. But even if things become no worse than they are
at present, there is enough to mourn.

For the past several years, brown pelicans and cormorants have
failed to reproduce. On the offshore islands, where thousands
of these birds annually gather in noisy, busy, breeding communities, biologists have found almost no young; only abandoned nests
and scattered eggshells.

On the Farallon Islands, 30 miles west of San Francisco, where
thousands of murres and ashy petrels nest, eggshells are measura-
bly thinner than normal, giving warning that, like the pelicans
and cormorants, these birds, too, may reach the point where
reproduction is impossible.

The peregrine falcon is already a ghost. It has virtually
disappeared from California. Where there were once more than
200 known nesting sites, a search in 1970 found only two breeding
pairs. Four young peregrines were fledged; no more.

Bald eagles and ospreys have likewise vanished from the

Southern California coast. The great blue herons and common egrets that nest in a canyon near Point Reyes have abnormally thin eggshells and are showing some symptoms of reproductive failure.

All along the coast the sea lion nurseries held less than the usual complement of young. A biologist reported that on one of the major sea lion islands, San Miguel in the Channel Islands off Santa Barbara County, he had found 348 dead pups and only 20 pups alive during the spring. Many of these seemed weak and unlikely to survive. There has been an extraordinary rise in the rate of premature birth, or abortion, in sea lions. A biologist who counted 135 such aborted young on San Nicolas Island off Ventura County during the spring of 1969 found 442 in 1970, an increase of more than 200 percent in one year.

Hundreds of miles south, on the rocky islands off Baja California, birds and mammals are having the same reproductive difficulties; there are fewer young than normal of either kind. Besides the fact that they are in difficulty, there are other significant factors common to all these different species. First, they are fish-eaters. Second, the fish they eat inhabit waters that are among the most pesticide-laden in the world.

In fact, it is through analysis of the bodies of these seabirds and mammals that we get an inkling of the extent to which the coastal waters for thousands of miles carry such contaminants as pesticides, mercury, and polychlorinated biphenyl (PCB). PCB is a DDT-like compound used in industry whose persistence and danger to the environment have only recently been identified. That certain persistent pesticides cause reproductive failure in birds has now been firmly established. There has been less research on sea lions and seals to prove, or disprove, a connection between these pesticides and increased mortality or abortion. But very recent evidence strongly suggests such a link.

We have definite data on the reproductive problems of a long list of birds. The peregrines, eagles, ospreys, pelicans, cormorants, murres, herons, egrets, and petrels all nest in places where they can be observed and a nesting debacle can be documented. We know of the raptors' decline because, although they are for the most part solitary nesters, their nests are conspicuous, are used repeatedly, and many have been on record for years. The seabirds on the list of birds that we know are in danger nest in communal rookeries, largely on islands off the coast, and a massive nesting failure is apparent to anyone who goes to look. In addition to these residents there are 20 or 30 other species that feed in coastal waters at some time or other. Their status is not known, simply because they move on and nest elsewhere, often in remote northern regions where an adequate census is very difficult.

However, on the basis of what is happening to more resident species, it is reasonable to surmise that any birds that linger and feed in the contaminated waters off California will be affected by the high level of persistent pesticides.

It seems incredible that such an enormous body of water as the coastal areas of Alta and Baja California can become polluted. It seems equally strange that a poison applied on land, perhaps hundreds of miles from the ocean, can ultimately wind up concentrated in the tissues of fish, seabirds, and seals, but the mechanism of pesticide concentration has been thoroughly explained, and the pathway from cropland to ocean water has been traced.

Water and air are the two most mobile components of the environment, and chlorinated hydrocarbons such as DDT travel freely along with them. One of the important characteristics of these compounds is that they are very insoluble in water and can be suspended in it. Attached to particles of sediment, they can be picked up by droplets of water and move with them wherever that water flows. Waters constantly meet and intermingle. The ultimate destination is the sea. As Rachel Carson wrote, "It is not possible to add pesticides to water anywhere without threatening the purity of water everywhere."

On the other hand, when water containing DDT evaporates, the DDT goes into the air along with the water. Thus it can rise into the air from a treated field along with the morning dew — or a particle of dust — and be carried around the world by the wind in a few weeks. Chlorinated hydrocarbons originating in Europe or Africa have been detected in Barbados. Scientists believe that the amount of pesticides carried to the tropical Atlantic Ocean by the trade winds is comparable to that carried to the sea by the major river systems. Air and water give pesticides wings.

Once a chlorinated hydrocarbon has entered a body of water the process of "magnification" begins. It happens because of another important characteristic of the chlorinated hydrocarbons — their solubility in fat. All living things, no matter how small, contain fatty compounds called lipids. When a marine organism, be it a tiny one-celled plankton, a mollusk, a worm, or a fish, takes chlorinated hydrocarbons into its system (in food, in water, or through absorption), the stuff dissolves in the organism's fat, and there it remains. Thus, particle by particle, chlorinated hydrocarbons are strained out of the water and added to the systems of living things.

It is, of course, the fate of everything ultimately to be eaten. Each organism eats many organisms from levels of life beneath it. In the sea, particularly, the predator of one species is often the prey of another. As each creature feeds on pesticide-laden food, the food is digested and expelled, but much of the pesticide is stored in the fat. With each meal more is added.

The concentration of DDT in organisms depends on the rate of intake and can rise by amazing multiples. A fish that eats some contaminated food, and some uncontaminated, may only double the concentration in the food supply. But a seabird that eats nothing but contaminated fish may carry ten times the amount, or more. Creatures at the top of the food chain may carry residues at a concentration more than a million times greater than their environment. Thus water containing an amount of pesticide so small it can barely be analyzed may nevertheless contaminate very heavily the creatures that live in it. In order to determine the contamination of an ecosystem it is necessary to analyze the creatures living in it, not the water and air that are the media of transport.

Concentration also depends on still another characteristic of the chlorinated hydrocarbons — their persistence, or ability to resist change as they pass from one organism to the next. Most natural substances decompose as they are metabolized in the body of organisms that eat them, but the chlorinated hydrocarbons do not. DDT can be metabolized into a closely related compound called DDE, which unfortunately is also toxic and persistent. DDE is very slowly degraded. As one scientist remarked, "We have found no bacteria that would eat it on a platter." The principal way it can be lost is if it sinks so deep into the ooze at the bottom of the ocean that it is below the reach of even bottom-dwelling organisms. Once let loose, most chlorinated hydrocarbons remain in the environment for a long time; just how long is still a matter of debate.

The reason that chlorinated hydrocarbons are spread around in the first place is that they are poisons. They are nerve poisons that in heavy concentrations cause tremors, convulsions, and death. There is no immunity; only a difference in the amount needed to bring about this effect. In general, if an organism has nerves, the chlorinated hydrocarbons can kill it. At sublethal concentrations, however, they cause subtle and complicated changes in body mechanisms — changes that have taken biologists by surprise. In the case of birds they bring about changes in the sex hormones. One result, thinning of eggshells, has been discovered only within the past five years, but it is now well understood and documented. The discovery came about because pesticides have destroyed, nearly completely, the peregrine falcon. Peregrines exist now only in the remote, outer limits of their former range where pesticides have not yet reached a critical concentration.

The fact that peregrines were disappearing was first noted in Britain. Peregrine falcons prey on other birds, and British pigeon fanciers complained of increased predation on their birds by the falcons. As a consequence, a British ecologist, Derek A. Ratcliffe, undertook a census of peregrines in the early 1960s. He discovered, to his dismay, that most of them had disappeared. Furthermore, those that remained were not succeeding in raising a normal number of young. There were many instances of nests in which the eggs broke. Obviously some sort of catastrophe was overtaking the birds.

Ratcliffe analyzed the remains of peregrine eggs and found high residues of the chlorinated hydrocarbons and particularly DDE. At about the same time American ornithologists became aware that the same thing was happening to peregrines here. Roland C. Clement of the National Audubon Society, Dr. Joseph J. Hickey of the University of Wisconsin, and Roger Tory Peterson discussed the situation in 1963, and in 1965 a conference of American and European raptor experts, including Ratcliffe, was called. The conferees discovered that peregrines had melted away from all the agricultural areas of Europe and the United States. They suspected that somehow pesticides were to blame, but the mechanism was mysterious.

It was not until 1967 that the most conclusive evidence incriminating pesticides was provided. It came from Derek Ratcliffe. He had been struck by the peculiar look of peregrine eggs. The shells were so fragile they dented at a touch. It occurred to him to measure the thickness of these shells and compare them with peregrine eggs laid before the introduction of modern pesticides. Fortunately, museum egg collections provided sufficient material for comparison. The difference was clearly apparent; the shells of eggs laid before 1946, when the new pesticides were introduced, were 20 percent heavier than those laid after.

Ratcliffe wrote to Dr. Hickey, who was able to duplicate the results of Ratcliffe's comparison perfectly. This was followed by experiments in which DDT was fed to caged sparrow hawks and mallard ducks at the U.S. Fish and Wildlife Service research center at Patuxent, Maryland. These showed that even a very tiny dose of DDE, the breakdown product of DDT, caused thin eggshells in mallards.

The case against DDT was conclusive, but the way in which the damage was caused had remained mysterious. A Cornell chemist, Dr. David Peakall, has now shown that DDE induces over-production of an enzyme that destroys estrogen, the hormone governing many aspects of the reproductive process, such as the time of breeding and the storage of calcium. In addition, DDE may interfere with enzymes that enable calcium and carbonate to be transported to the eggshell.

DDT and other pesticides have, of course, been washing into all our rivers and coastal waters for more than 20 years, but in California the story has a special twist. Not only have pesticides been used there in greater volume and variety than in any comparable area on Earth, but in addition a particular circumstance — a weird industrial "accident," a giant blunder, a monumental example of unconcern for the consequences of pollution — has made the California coast a special and critical case. To the already colossal burden of agricultural chemicals applied to the land, a manufacturer of DDT gratuitously added the straw that broke the camel's back.

The story begins in 1947, in the innocent days when it was believed that every substance the chemists bestowed upon us was an unmitigated blessing. That year the Montrose Chemical Corporation built a plant for the manufacture of DDT on a site in Torrance, California, on the outskirts of Los Angeles. Its plumbing system, as was the common custom of the times, hooked up to the county's sewer line. Thereafter, until 1970, the waste products of the plant, laden with DDT, were drained into the sewer and spewed into the Pacific Ocean a few miles away. When, more than ten years ago, overwhelming evidence showed that DDT could have serious effects on the environment, the officers of Montrose were unimpressed. They joined chemical industry propagandists in disputing any charges against persistent pesticides. And they continued to pour DDT down the drain.

Just how much DDT Montrose put into the water as a by-product of its manufacturing is not definitely known, since Montrose's officers have refused to discuss it, but Dr. Robert Risebrough, a young biochemist at the University of California at Berkeley, investigated the situation and made some estimates. He discovered that the plant's capacity is 7,500,000 pounds a month. In 1967 it was operating at 80 percent of capacity and making 6,000,000 pounds a month. In any manufacturing process a certain amount of the product is bound to be "lost," spilled, left adhering to containers and machinery, the clothes of workers, and so on. Most of this would be washed down the drain. But more important, the waste liquids of the manufacturing process itself contain significant amounts of DDT. These, too, went into the county's sewer line. A reasonable estimate for such losses is one-half of one percent. If Montrose lost that much DDT it would amount to 1000 pounds of DDT a day washing into the sewer.

Calculations as to what this could have meant over 24 years until 1970 are staggering. In that time, operating at full capacity, the plant could have produced 2,160,000,000 pounds of DDT. A half of one percent of that is 10,800,000 pounds. Even if that production estimate is whittled down to three-quarters, it is still a colossal amount of DDT. Dr. Risebrough believes that it accounts for most of the DDT that now all too evidently pollutes the entire coast of California and threatens so much of its bird and animal life.

In retrospect it seems incredible that through all the years of discussion of the effects of DDT no one, until very recently, gave thought to the level of pollution in the Pacific or to the Montrose plant in particular. If the officers of Montrose thought about it, they kept it very much to themselves. But it is reasonable to wonder how Samuel Rotosen, the president of Montrose Chemical Corporation, who attended DDT hearings in Wisconsin in late 1968 and early 1969 and listened to hours of testimony about the harmful effects of DDT, could return to his home in Los Angeles, read in his local newspapers about what was happening because of DDT in the waters of California, and still allow the Torrance plant to continue draining DDT into the county's sewers.

In 1965 Dr. Risebrough, who has a Harvard Ph.D. in molecular biology, joined the Institute of Marine Resources at the University of California, which was embarking on a study of pesticide pollution in coastal waters.

Everyone assumed that the heaviest accumulations of pesticides would be found in the San Francisco Bay area, where the river systems that drain California's great agricultural lands pour into the sea. Dr. Risebrough found that there was indeed a heavy load of DDT in marine organisms in the bay and all along the coast, but when he sampled fish caught near Los Angeles, the results were astonishing. They carried 20 times as much DDT in their tissues as did fish caught elsewhere. Risebrough found this mysterious, intriguing, and alarming. As he went on with his sampling, it occurred to him to look at some of the birds that feed on fish along the shore. Again DDT levels turned out to be high in the tissues of these birds. The highest was in a pelican taken near Monterey. This turned Dr. Risebrough's thoughts to pelicans.

In October 1967 a group of lawyers and scientists came together to form the Environmental Defense Fund, Inc., known as EDF, for the purpose of seeking remedies in the courts for abuse of our land, water, sea, and air. Dr. Risebrough became one of their scientific advisers. In 1970 EDF sued the Olin Corporation, a DDT manufacturer in Huntsville, Alabama, which had been pouring DDT-laden waste water into streams feeding the Wheeler National Wildlife Refuge. Rather than remodel its plant to prevent this pollution, Olin quit the manufacture of DDT. This left the Montrose Chemical Corporation as the sole U.S. producer. Naturally it occurred to EDF that if Olin had produced a great deal of DDT-laden waste, Montrose might also.

An officer of Montrose denied that it was responsible for any pollution, but EDF nevertheless asked Dr. Risebrough to look into the matter. Certainly the location of the plant coincided remarkably with the high levels of DDT in marine organisms. At the same time the fate of the pelicans had given dismaying evidence that DDT was having far-reaching effects along the coast.

The pelican debacle had been discovered by Risebrough on March 19–20, 1969. He had been wondering about the West

Coast brown pelican for some time before that. He was aware that a huge disaster had already wiped out the entire population of brown pelicans on the Gulf Coasts of Texas and Louisiana. It had happened suddenly in the late 1950s. Before anyone had realized that the 60,000 pelicans that nested there were in trouble, they had disappeared, leaving scientists who attempted to explain their disappearance with little to analyze except empty air. Nevertheless, some biologists were convinced that pesticides were to blame. There was, they felt, circumstantial evidence linking the pelican disaster to the death of millions of fish killed by pesticides in the Mississippi River.

Despite this catastrophe to the Gulf Coast pelicans, there was, as late as 1967, little information on the status of the brown pelican of the California coast, one of the most common birds seen in the area. On the Pacific Coast pelicans nest on rocky offshore islands. The northernmost nesting site is the Channel Islands, but there are others off the coast of Baja California and in the Gulf of California. Pelicans are communal nesters, building their nests nearly within pecking distance of each other in colonies that may number several thousand birds. No one had checked up on pelican colonies for some years until 1968, when the Smithsonian Institution's Pacific Ocean Biological Survey program sent out two biologists, Ralph W. Schreiber and Robert L. DeLong. Their study, like so many other things today, was a by-product of military activity. It was initiated not by concern for the pelican but by the fact that the Department of Defense was searching for an island on which to test deadly biological weapons. It wanted an island free of birds that might carry germs to the mainland. The biologists, innocent of the intent of their mission, were sent off to survey birdlife along the coast.

They visited Mexico's Los Coronados Islands, off San Diego, where a large nesting colony of pelicans had been seen ten years

On California's Anacapa Island, an empty brown pelican nest and a crushed eggshell — the legacy of DDT

earlier, and found only a few nonbreeding birds. They moved on to the Channel Islands, where nesting pelicans had flourished in the past. They found them breeding only on Anacapa, the most easterly of the chain of islands off Santa Barbara. Anacapa is a narrow spine of rock whose breathtakingly steep cliffs are extremely difficult to climb. Schreiber and DeLong saw perhaps 200 birds, apparently nesting, but were unable to reach the colony to examine the nests. A month later they visited Anacapa again, but this time concluded that the birds were no longer nesting. They noted a low proportion of young birds. Their observations were somewhat equivocal, but suggested a decline in the number of brown pelicans breeding on the California coast. Their report pointed out the link between reproductive failure and certain pesticides, so recently discovered, and warned that if the California brown pelican was having difficulty these chemicals might be implicated.

The following year, 1969, Robert Risebrough was determined to collect pelican eggs for analysis. In March, together with biologists from the San Diego Natural History Museum and the Point Reyes Bird Observatory, he went to the Channel Islands. Again there were no nests anywhere but on Anacapa, where a colony was located on a ridge of the highest peak. There seemed to be about 200 birds there. The men climbed up to the site and were startled and dismayed to find a scene of almost total devastation. Where there should have been eggs or nestlings they found empty nests, broken eggs, and no young at all. They examined 298 nests. Only 12 held eggs, and most of these were single eggs. Broken eggshells were scattered about. The men collected bits of broken eggs for analysis and left within 20 minutes in order to keep disturbance of the birds at a minimum. The eggshells were later measured and compared with eggs collected at the same spot before 1943. The recent eggshells

were 50 percent thinner.   It was no wonder they had broken.
Dr. Risebrough returned a week later and found that even
the few eggs he had seen previously had disappeared. The adults,
startled from the nests, showed little inclination to return. Clearly
the colony was being abandoned. Risebrough's findings alerted
the California Department of Fish and Game and the Bureau
of Sport Fisheries and Wildlife, and they, too, paid several visits
to the islands. Late in June Risebrough made a final visit and
at a second nest site found a single, downy chick. From combined
observations it was possible to estimate that 1272 nests had been
built and possibly had produced a total of four chicks. The nests
of cormorants in the vicinity of the pelicans were also empty.

In January 1969, a few months before the discovery of the
nesting failure, the famous Santa Barbara oil spill had bathed
the shores of Anacapa in crude oil. When news of the pelicans'
plight was made public, apologists for DDT wondered aloud
if the oil might not be to blame for their nesting failure. This
possibility was ruled out with the discovery that the problem
extended much farther than the oil.

In April, Joseph R. Jehl, Jr., of the San Diego Natural History
Museum and L. C. Binford of the California Academy of Sciences
visited the pelican islands in Mexican waters. On Los Coronados,
14 miles south of San Diego, where thousands of pelicans once
nested, they found 300 pairs trying to nest, but as at Anacapa,
their nests held only crushed fragments. By May the colony was
deserted. At San Martin Island, 156 miles farther south, a large
colony of pelicans was having somewhat better success. Many
nests contained full clutches, but there was also evidence of
broken eggs. On analysis the eggshells turned out to be thicker
than at Los Coronados, and the DDE content was somewhat
lower. On the San Benito Islands, 80 miles at sea, the searchers
were at first reassured to find relatively little egg breakage, but

on a return trip in June they found only about a hundred young birds when there should have been several times that many. Evidently the birds that had nested there had spent time feeding in contaminated waters.

If anyone had hoped that the 1969 nesting catastrophe was peculiar to that year, the hope was dispelled in 1970. The California Department of Fish and Game hired an associate of Risebrough's, Franklin Gress, to make a study of nesting pelicans. From mid-February he watched as the colony of pelicans on Anacapa went through its nesting routine in tragic futility. The birds courted, paired, and nested normally, but within a short time broken eggs littered the colony and the attempt was abandoned. A new colony was formed with the same sad ending. On July 29 Gress paid a final visit. He found one tiny survivor; a baby pelican about two weeks old. It was the only bird to hatch on Anacapa that year.

As in the year before, double-crested cormorants fared no better. Gress counted 50 pairs nesting side by side with the pelicans. Only one nest produced young birds.

In the spring of 1971 Gress again watched the Anacapa colony. This time he refrained from landing on the island in order to avoid any element of disturbance, but watched the nests with binoculars from a boat. By the end of the season he had spotted seven nestlings among 600 nests.

With the discovery of the disaster to the pelicans on the Pacific Coast it became important to know what was happening to the pelicans that nest on islands within the Gulf of California. DDT pollution there is mostly related to Mexican agriculture and to the waters of the Colorado River and so far is not as heavy as that in American waters. In 1969 biologist James O. Keith, with the financial support of the National Audubon Society, visited four of the larger pelican colonies in the Gulf. He found thousands of birds nesting and producing young, but there was also evidence of trouble. Many eggshells were near normal in thickness, but empty nests and collapsed, dehydrated eggs were also in evidence. The number of eggs per nest was less than normal.

A return visit to the Gulf of California in 1970 confirmed the impression that while the problem is not currently as serious as that on the California coast, danger exists even there. Keith noticed that there was a massive mortality among young birds as they neared fledging and that the population seemed to be unhealthily weighted toward older birds. In 1971 the Bureau of Sport Fisheries and Wildlife assigned a biologist, Daniel W. Anderson, to study the brown pelican in the Gulf of California. Although Anderson found many carcasses of young birds that had died before fledging, nesting success was much better in 1971 than it had been in 1970. But still, collapsed thin-shelled eggs were evident.

The fact that nests with abnormal eggs are side by side with nests containing normal eggs leads to the thought that some birds in the colony migrate north when nesting is over and pick up DDT in the more heavily polluted waters off California. To test this theory, Anderson is tagging young, hoping to keep track of their later wanderings. His findings will give a clue to the ultimate future of California pelican colonies. If there are enough nonmigrants in the Gulf population, there may be a reservoir of less contaminated birds that could, someday, if DDT levels ever sink below the danger point, repopulate the northern coast. Of course their survival rests on the premise that DDT in the Gulf doesn't rise, and there is no guarantee of that.

Recent studies suggest that pelican eggs can survive a certain degree of thinning. Thinning occurs in direct proportion to the amount of DDE in the bird, and the breaking point seems to come when the eggs are 20 percent thinner than normal. On this basis we are able to assess the danger to the pelican populations that remain in the East. Pelicans on the west coast of Florida are in the best situation. So far their eggs are only 10 percent thinner. On the East Coast there are pelicans from Key West to the Carolinas. In general the eggs become thinner as one proceeds farther north. At the worst spots they are 16 to 18 percent thinner — on the edge of the critical point.

Pelicans are long-lived birds, surviving 30 years or more, and so, for some years to come, there will be pelicans at Anacapa, courting, breeding, and building their foredoomed nests. With no young the colony will, of course, dwindle every year through natural attrition. If recruits from farther south linger at Anacapa, it is likely that they too will be unable to raise young. But the public will still see migrant pelicans — though not nearly so many as they saw in former years — loafing and fishing along the coast, ornamenting buoys, or sailing majestically over the waves. Many people may not notice the decrease in their numbers until they are gone.

During the period that the misfortunes of the pelicans were coming to light there were signs of trouble at other checkpoints — the Farallon Islands, west of San Francisco, and the Audubon Canyon Ranch on Bolinas Lagoon, near Point Reyes, where herons and egrets can be observed on their nests.

The Farallons, now under state and federal jurisdiction, have the largest seabird colonies in the United States. Western gulls, three species of cormorants, the ashy petrel and Leach's petrel, the pigeon guillemot, Cassin's auklet, and the common murre all nest there. They have been beset by man for more than a hundred years. In the 1850s birds were so numerous that there was a lucrative trade in their eggs. Old records show that from May to July, 20 men worked all day gathering eggs for the market in San Francisco. Over the years millions and millions were taken. The robbery ended in 1909 with the establishment of a wildlife refuge. Then spilled oil began washing up from time to time. Now DDT is an even greater danger.

There are 30,000 murres breeding on the Farallon Islands. In 1968 and 1970 Risebrough analyzed a number of eggs and compared them with museum specimens. He found a 13 percent decrease in shell thickness. At this degree of thinning there is no abrupt nesting failure, but rather a slight decrease in the percentage of successful nests. As every gambler knows, you can't win with the percentages against you. It is the same story for the ashy petrel. Petrels are pelagic birds and feed entirely in the open ocean, yet their eggs are showing a 9 percent decrease in thickness. Dr. Risebrough points out that these birds serve us as living sampling devices, giving us information on the pollution of the ocean waters that we could obtain no other way.

Audubon Canyon Ranch, on the shores of Bolinas Bay, north of San Francisco, is a unique nesting spot for great blue herons and common egrets. The canyon is walled by steep sides, and from the rim it is possible to look down into the treetops. Second-growth redwoods some 80 feet high rise from the floor of the canyon, and their upper branches provide secure platforms for the nests of about 100 pairs of egrets and 50 pairs of herons. In other colonies it is impossible to see what is going on in the nests, but here, with a balcony seat on the canyon rim, an observer can keep track of the activities of the entire wading bird colony.

In 1967 members of the local Marin Audubon Society began watching the nests. One of the members, Mrs. Helen Pratt, became especially intrigued and kept complete records of nesting success. She also noticed that now and then peculiar-looking eggshells could be found on the canyon floor beneath the nests. She collected them and gave them to Dr. Risebrough for analysis. Predictably, the shells were thin, and the pesticide residues were high. Since then Mrs. Pratt has worked faithfully to provide data for a study of the nesting success of the colony that will be particularly valuable in providing comparative data from year to year.

Both herons and egrets are shoreline feeders. While they are nesting the Audubon Canyon Ranch birds feed in Bolinas Lagoon, which has a rather low pollution level, but evidently their winter wanderings take them to pesticide-laden waters. In 1970 egret eggshells were 15.2 percent thinner, and heron eggs were 10.4 percent thinner, compared to pre-1947 thicknesses. The birds' nesting success is declining accordingly. Eggshells found on the ground below the nests have been soft-shelled, like the collapsed eggs of the pelicans and cormorants on Anacapa. In 1970 several adult egrets were found dying in convulsions. Analysis of their tissues showed high levels of DDE and other pesticide residues.

The question of seals, sea lions, and other mammals on the Pacific Coast is a different problem. DDT in the tissues of California sea lions has been investigated by Dr. Burney J. LeBoeuf of the University of California at Santa Cruz. He has found such extraordinary levels as 2678 parts per million in blubber, or an average equivalent of three-quarters of a pound of DDT compound per sea lion. Until recently, however, there was no direct evidence that linked these high levels to the alarming rate of abortion among sea lions. But this spring an apparently incriminating coincidence was discovered. Three West Coast researchers, William Gilmartin, John Simpson, and Robert L. DeLong, examined six female sea lions who had just aborted their young and four females who had borne healthy pups. They found the two groups were similar in age and general physical condition but the aborting females had approximately eight times as much DDE in their blubber as did the nonaborting females. This is a dramatic and ominous finding filled with

implications not only for the various kinds of sea mammals but
for their relatives in the human species.

In October 1970 the Environmental Defense Fund decided
it had sufficient evidence that Montrose was polluting coastal
waters to ask the court for an injunction. In November two
graduate students working with Dr. Risebrough took water samples from the sewer below Montrose and found that at least 300
pounds of DDT was flowing through the sewer line daily. At
the same time EDF discovered that the Los Angeles County
Sanitation District, the municipal body responsible for sewers,
had measured the effluent months previously, found that 600
pounds a day was going through the sewer, and privately asked
Montrose to desist. Montrose claimed it was complying but it
resisted EDF's suit with various legal maneuvers and sought
revenge against Dr. Risebrough through complaints to the university's Board of Regents that he had no business analyzing the
city's waste water. Eventually Montrose decided to revamp its
plumbing so that waste water could be recycled. It now seals
residual DDT in barrels and buries them in a landfill dump.
What will happen when, in time, the containers disintegrate
is a problem for future ages.

No one can predict if brown pelicans will ever again nest
successfully off California. It depends on whether there is a
sufficient decline in pesticide levels and if the decline occurs
while there are still brown pelicans to repopulate the old colonies.
California agriculture is phasing out the use of DDT, and the
gross pollution from the Montrose Chemical Corporation has
ceased, but it may be a long time before the pollution level
in coastal fish sinks significantly. Dr. Risebrough has made a
guess that it will be 20 or 30 years before the coast is once
again a healthy spot for fish-eating birds.

And so Montrose's mammoth experiment in adding tons of

DDT to the ocean has shown us what we can expect wherever pesticide levels rise to a critical concentration.

We know now that if the silence Rachel Carson envisioned comes, it will come first to the shores of lakes and seas. The seabirds and the shorebirds, those that skim the waves for fish or harvest small marine creatures from the wet sands, will be the first to surrender. We know, too, the form in which death will come. It is unlikely that the birds will drop from the sky to litter the beaches. Instead they will fade gently — like shadows at twilight. Along our coasts fewer birds, first of one species and then of another, may appear in their accustomed places each year. And then, suddenly, on long stretches of shore, there might be none of certain species at all. A beach or an estuary that had formerly been dotted with wading birds feeding in the shallows would be deserted. Over a rocky headland, where other seabirds used to ride the wind, the sky would be empty. There would be no flotillas rocking on the offshore swells, no sudden splash where a swift dive had broken the surface. If the level of persistent pesticides in our coastal waters continues to rise, we will indeed have a silent shore.

A late-summer monarch butterfly sips the nectar of goldenrod

JO BREWER

How to Kill a Butterfly

ON A HALF-MILE STRETCH of dirt road adjacent to our island summer home, the favorite nectar plants of our Maine butterflies once were so plentiful and the feeding butterflies so numerous and so fearless that there was no problem in photographing them day after day at a distance of 18 inches. Then, in the mid-1960s, the roadsides were cut, mowed, and sprayed with herbicides, and the massed thistles, goldenrod, asters, primrose, milkweed, and steeplebush have not yet recovered. I do not doubt that this destruction was the primary cause of an almost total lack of butterflies along our road until the summer of 1970. For most of the species — the red admiral, painted lady, great spangled fritillary, aphrodite, atlantis, three kinds of commas, question mark, meadow fritillary, and silver bordered fritillary — could be found elsewhere on the island in undisturbed locations.

Mine is only one observation of a very small area. But joined with scores of similar observations by lepidopterists throughout the world, there emerges a distressing picture of a planet inhabited by markedly reduced numbers of butterflies.

Concern for butterfly survival was expressed as early as 1956 by Dr. J. W. Tilden, writing in the Lepidopterists' Society *News* of the apparent extinction of the peculiarly endemic butterfly of the sand dunes near San Francisco, the xerces blue. "Only

a few years [ago]," he reported, "it had been the most characteristic butterfly of the coastal sand dune area known as the Sunset
District, but a complete settlement of the area left it no habitat
to inhabit . . . In the larval stages xerces fed on a species of lotus
(*Hosackia*). This species was a low-growing, matting type of sand
dune plant which could not tolerate disturbance of the soil."

A few years ago the *New York Times* reported a far more
dramatic event that took place in Sikkim, an Indian protectorate
in the Himalayas. The meadows and marshlands of this little
principality were at the time the habitat of 600 different butterflies, including some of the world's most exotic species. They
were also the habitat of malaria mosquitoes. The area was
massively and successfully sprayed with DDT to eliminate the
mosquitoes. As a result there are now hardly enough individual
butterflies left to interest the collector.

Butterflies as a group, of course, are not considered pests and
are simply innocent casualties in man's war against unwanted
plant growth and destructive insects. Only the white cabbage
butterfly, whose caterpillars feed on such vegetables as cauli-
flower, cabbage, and Brussels sprouts and the alfalfa-nourished
orange sulphur are listed as specific targets for pesticides. As
pollenizers, butterflies are second only to bees. In a great many
cases the caterpillars of butterflies feed upon and probably help
to control so-called pest weeds such as thistles, nettles, sheep
laurel, chickweed, sneezeweed, milkweed, and water hemlock.

The few butterflies that lay their eggs on garden plants or
ornamental shrubs or trees do not destroy them. The cloudless,
orange barred, and large orange sulphurs are prolific, and their
larvae eat the blossoms of cassia, but even they do not do massive
damage to a large tree. One larva of the little spring blue may
eat two or three buds of dogwood. The caterpillar of the
satin-winged pipe vine swallowtail is nourished by half a dozen

leaves only, but most homeowners would hasten to kill this horny, dark-brown creature — nearly three inches long when fully grown — if they saw one crawling on a Dutchman's-pipe vine. This species probably is in greater danger from people than from pesticides — a warning to the butterfly lover to develop a caterpillar tolerance. A nature-loving neighbor of mine was recently seen in her yard frantically attacking a small willow tree with a hand sprayer "because it is simply alive with worms, and they are completely destroying it!" The "worms" were full-grown caterpillars and would have done no more damage, but out of ignorance this well-meaning lady had eliminated a colony of mourning cloak butterflies that two weeks later would have added life, color, and beauty to the entire neighborhood. If she had looked at the "worms" through sympathetic eyes she might even have found the frosty, scarlet-studded caterpillars quite handsome.

Of the butterflies found east of the Mississippi, 99 species have caterpillars that eat weeds, wild grasses, or wildflowers; 38 eat the leaves of shade trees or ornamental trees. Only 25 species feed on fruit trees or food plants. Of these last, seven eat wild berries. Nine others are so small and so sparse that what they consume is negligible, and several eat parts of the plant or tree not consumed by people, usually foliage. This leaves our three native whites, which eat cabbage, and the black swallowtail, which eats parsley, as encroachers on man's food supply.

Economically speaking, therefore, butterflies do neither great harm nor great good. But their aesthetic value cannot be calculated in terms of dollars and cents. And the biochemists who evolve the pesticides, the manufacturers who make them, the businessmen who sell them, and the farmers who use them neither try to kill butterflies nor save them. They simply ignore them.

Most commercial orchards have been so saturated with insecticides — first with persistent chemicals like DDT and dieldrin, now with the less persistent but often more toxic organophosphates — that they have become barren of both butterflies and birds. The giant swallowtail, whose caterpillars feed on citrus leaves, is not considered a pest and is not a target of spraying. But it will eventually disappear from citrus groves that are regularly sprayed, and the groves will be made poorer, not richer, by its loss. The blemish-free fruit we buy may have been paid for in part with the lives of the viceroy, the red spotted purple, and the little striped hairstreak, which can no longer safely lay their eggs in plum, apple, and cherry orchards. Fortunately, some of their larvae also feed on trees that are not routinely sprayed.

Indeed, survival for a butterfly species may depend upon an ability to utilize a varied diet, with the result that certain trees are hosts to a variety to caterpillars. The willow, for example, serves as food for at least eight different species. The gray, green, and hoary commas all eat the leaves of wild blueberry and currant as well as willow, while some of the lesser fritillaries have also been found on strawberry. Again, sprays take their toll, but these species eat other leaves, and so far a precarious balance has been maintained.

Happily, the spraying of shade trees has fallen into disfavor since the effect of DDT on songbirds became apparent. Elms are often selectively sprayed with methoxychlor, and no doubt this kills many larvae of the handsome question mark, but this species can also live on nettles or hackberry.

There is hope, moreover, that butterfly populations will be able to reestablish themselves as pesticides are used with greater caution and understanding. Adult butterflies that live and fly independently of each other in open meadows and are highly mobile may be able to escape a massive spraying that some insects — a hive of bees or the population of flies in a barn — cannot. However, insecticides are generally used to attack insects not as adults but during the larval stages when they are confined to their food plant or food area, and when their destruction will prevent the rise of another generation. In the larval stages butterflies are just as vulnerable as any other insect.

Fortunately, the usual haunts of butterflies — wild meadows, fields, and open woods — are seldom heavily sprayed. As long as these areas remain intact, the various flowers, grasses, trees, and other larval food plants can continue to maintain present populations of butterflies. The clover will nourish the little sulphurs; wild violets, the fritillaries; grasses, the wood nymphs.

But survival does not depend on food plants alone. The total habitat, which means a combination of all the elements favorable to the entire life cycle of any given butterfly, must be maintained. If the female tiger swallowtail is to lay her eggs on the leaves of birch trees, the habitat of the tiger must have not just one birch but many, for she flies about from tree to tree laying her eggs one at a time.

When the early spring tigers emerge from overwintering chrysalids, the males appear first and soon form "drinking clubs" while they await the advent of the females. Large numbers of males — hundreds of them at times if conditions are right — gather by the edges of streams, at mud puddles, or in damp sand, each spending an hour or more sucking up moisture and at the same time excreting small drops of clear fluid at about ten-second intervals. This may be some sort of cleansing action, or it may be the butterflies' way of introducing some kind of beneficial bacteria into the intestine. The most popular "clubs" meet in cow pastures or other areas where animal manure is present. Contaminated water is therefore likely to be part of the tiger's habitat.

The tiger swallowtail spends its time flying in and out of the woods, retracing the same route many times, stopping to visit flowers as it circumnavigates the meadow, disappearing into the woods only to reappear a few minutes later. The woods afford this lovely yellow and black insect a perfect camouflage as it rests on the branch of a tree with the sun streaming through the leaves onto the streaks of its wings. After mating, the female tiger lays her eggs on the birches' new growth — often among the high sunny branches. When August comes, the full-grown caterpillars of the last brood usually crawl or drop to the ground in search of a sheltered spot where they can pupate, to remain hidden and camouflaged until the following spring.

The birches, the woods, the contaminated water, the meadow, flowers, and sufficient debris for hiding places thus combine to form the habitat of the tiger swallowtail. There must also be a balance of the other forms of life within the confines of the habitat, each species keeping others in check so that parasites cannot kill all the swallowtail caterpillars, birch leaf miners cannot use all the caterpillars' food supply, small animals foraging for food cannot consume all the swallowtail chrysalids, and birds cannot snap up all the newly emerged butterflies.

Each kind of butterfly, further, requires its own food, protection, and climate — so there must be many habitats free of herbicides and insecticides. Within the United States, climates range from tropical to subarctic, vegetation from jungle to desert, and environments from alpine to oceanic. Each has its own butterflies. Each butterfly has its own time cycle, its own optimal moment for coming out of hibernation. Countless different circumstances, therefore, may determine the effect of a pesticide, and it is hardly surprising that lepidopterists do not agree as to the effect of the chemicals on butterflies. Dr. John M. Burns, Associate Curator of Lepidoptera at the Museum of Comparative

Zoology at Harvard, sums up the problem: "Pesticides are certainly damaging to butterflies, but there are so many variables that with the information presently available, it is not possible to say to what extent they are responsible for a general decline in butterfly numbers."

New pesticides are being marketed constantly and are applied in varying intensities by various means. Some of the newer, persistent insecticides are claimed to be selective in action, but this selectivity is characterized mainly by a decreased toxicity to warmblooded animals, and the butterfly is not taken into account. Doubtless it will be susceptible. Pesticides are being developed that, when sprayed on the leaves of a plant or dusted on the ground around it, penetrate the plant's whole system and render it deadly to certain insects feeding on it. These systemic insecticides, as they are called, can be used to protect one zinnia, one ornamental shrub, or one whole orchard. But if they can destroy a leaf miner, will they also destroy the tiger swallowtail and other orchard butterflies?

The value of systemic pesticides can be enormous. Most do not kill on contact. They make it possible to limit the area and the number and variety of plants treated. One application a year can effectively immunize many garden flowers against their most annoying and destructive pests. Greatest success to date has been in the control of aphids, leaf miners, thrips, red spiders, and leafhoppers — all sucking insects. Will these systemics be equally fatal to foliage-eating insects? We know at least one lepidopterous insect, the pine-tip moth, that can be fully controlled by this method. If one kind is doomed, why not others?

Do the poisons introduced by systemics extend to the nectar of the flowers and render them poisonous to bees and butterflies? An insect breathes through stomata, openings on its body, and systemic poisons kill by causing the stomata to close, thus depriving the insect of oxygen. Some caterpillars may become immune to these systemics, as has happened with other chemicals, but on the whole the butterfly is likely to lose out.

Biological controls are another way of controlling pests. Insect hormones sprayed on leaves can prevent larvae that ingest them from entering the pupal stage. The caterpillars simply grow to enormous size and eventually die. But many species respond to the same hormone spray. How many? Which ones? Who knows?

Some butterflies are less threatened by pesticides than others. Those that live on grasses, weeds, and wildflowers are relatively fortunate. These plants thrive on undeveloped land, no one protects them, no one sets out to exterminate them. Like the butterflies themselves, they are ignored. They nourish the butterflies, the butterflies pollenize them, and they live together in symbiotic peace. Where there are thistles there can be painted ladies, red admirals, and great spangled fritillaries. As long as there is milkweed there can be queens and monarchs. But how long will there be enough wild meadowland to supply milkweed from south to north so that the monarchs may lay their eggs during their northern migration?

For the solution to the plight of the butterflies is not simply in protecting them from pesticides, but also in protecting them from a much greater threat — loss of habitat. Even in the unlikely event that pesticides harmful to them could be eliminated, butterflies could not maintain their present population levels in the face of the accelerating destruction of their habitats.

Few would argue with Dr. Charles Covell of the University of Louisville who points to increased use of land for buildings and crops as the primary cause of habitat loss. Wide-ranging reports from lepidopterists provide some specifics. From Florida comes the observation that while populations of the dainty sulphur may survive pesticide spraying on avocado farms, they fall victim to the chopping down and burning of their larval food plants such as fetid marigold, common chickweed, and sneezeweed. Drainage of bogs in northeastern Colorado and most of Nebraska for agriculture has reportedly eliminated the grass nymph from most of its former range. The rapid development of resorts in central Colorado is altering the largest bogs inhabited by a rare fritillary and other choice alpine bog species. Reforestation of 3 million acres of meadow and open lands in Maine effectively eliminates 3 million acres of butterfly habitat. And Dr. Burns, whose special interest is in skippers, joins those who feel habitat destruction is the greatest threat to lepidoptera and laments, in particular, the filling in of marshes with the loss of cattails, reeds, and sedges on which a number of skippers depend for larval food.

In a paper delivered to the Lepidopterists' Society in 1970, Lloyd Martin, for many years curator of the Los Angeles County Museum, described the excitement and pleasure of butterflying in the vicinity of Los Angeles 40 years ago. Of Exposition Park, a speck of green land in the center of a 77-square-mile area of buildings and streets, he says: "The park gardeners planted *Buddleia*, or butterfly bush, around the edges of the rose garden. Here one could get *Papilio rutulus* [tiger swallowtail], *Agraulis vanillae* [Gulf fritillary], and all sorts of common butterflies. In fact, one young collector in 1940 took 23 different butterflies in one day. In the park today it is a very rare occasion to see even one specimen of *rutulus.* Even the lawn skipper is not as common as it used to be.

"On numerous occasions I have tried to rear larvae on plants found in the park, but with no success; even after washing the leaves to remove the crust of smog, the larvae would refuse to eat the leaves. There is some chemical action taking place within the plant to offset the smog chemicals, that the larva cannot digest. *Papilio rutulus* pupae were quite common on the sycamore trees in Exposition Park during the 1930s, and I could go out and get 15 or 20 within a half hour or so. Not anymore! I have tried to rear larvae on leaves from the same trees that used to produce good, healthy pupae. Now the larvae die in a few days."

By protecting the habitats of butterflies, people may well be protecting their own. Butterflies need clean air and open spaces, woods and thickets in which to hide, sunlight to warm their bodies and shine on their wings, and undisturbed fields where weeds and grasses and wildflowers grow. Conservation groups have long been champions of man's environment, and in at least one case their efforts resulted in the salvation of a butterfly. In July 1963, David McCorkle, a biologist at Oregon College of Education, noticed a small sphagnum bog near Yakima, Washington, in which the silver bordered fritillary was flying. This is a rare and very localized species on the West Coast. He made known his find to the Nature Conservancy, and in 1966 the fourteen acres forming the habitat of this little butterfly, the last surviving colony in the state, were purchased by the Conservancy. The former owner retained use for cattle grazing, and the wild violets used by the butterfly as larval food were saved from death by draining. Today as many as 75 butterflies at one time can be seen flying there in season.

Such events are heartwarming to the lepidopterist. But to avoid the destruction of many species, help is needed at governmental levels. Legal protection has been afforded butterflies in a few instances in the United States, the best known being in Pacific Grove, California, where it is a crime punishable by a fine of $500 to disturb the thousands of overwintering monarchs clustering in the treetops. Protection within our national parks varies from collection under supervision to complete protection, as at Grand Canyon National Park where one ringlet and one wood nymph cannot be taken. Efforts to control collecting are also being made in other countries, including Mexico, Switzerland, Ecuador, and El Salvador.

But government action at best is hardly adequate to solve the problem. People can increase their own enjoyment of the world around them by including the larval food plants of a few butterflies in their gardens and by seeing caterpillars with an open mind and a sympathetic eye. Merely leaving a patch of thistles or a stand of milkweed alone rather than destroying it may open the door to a whole new adventure for the nature lover as he watches the butterflies hovering and darting among the blossoms. One can recapture a child's sense of wonder and share the excitement of discovery by caging a full-grown caterpillar and watching it change first into a chrysalis and then into a butterfly. A little corner of flowering meadow is the butterflies' share of the world. A community fortunate enough to have such an area should jealously guard it. For, like the butterfly itself, once the meadow has been destroyed there is no opportunity to restore it to life.

A male red-winged blackbird attacks an ear of corn, first shredding the husk from the top, then feasting on the soft kernels

FRANK GRAHAM, JR.

Bye-Bye Blackbirds?

"Sometimes they appeared driving about like an enormous black cloud carried before the wind, varying its shape every moment; sometimes suddenly rising from the fields around me with a noise like thunder; while the glittering of innumerable wings of the brightest vermilion amid the black cloud they formed, produced on these occasions a very striking and splendid effect."

This was Alexander Wilson, the "father of American ornithology," describing a flock of red-winged blackbirds early in the nineteenth century. During the intervening years, unfortunately, not everyone has watched in rapt admiration as the great flocks of redwings approached. Some have met their advance with scarecrows, firecrackers, and shotguns. Today, in a small area of northern Ohio, where an estimated 10 million redwings mill about in the cornfields after the nesting season, a group of farmers and their spokesmen in government press for an all-out attempt to eradicate them. The proposed weapon? A broad-spectrum chemical pesticide; any kind will do.

"We feel these migratory blackbirds are a national and international problem," a Sandusky County farmer, William Warner, told a conference on "Blackbird Depredation in Agriculture" several years ago. "We feel that our government should take

proper steps to enter the roosting area near where I live along
Lake Erie and destroy a large number of these birds immediately
. . . I am pleased at the progress we have made in the last year
and a half, but every year at blackbird time I wish care had
been taken of all of them."

Sentiments like these, spoken by a farmer who has just demonstrated considerable damage to his corn crop by great flocks of
redwings, are likely to produce an enormous effect upon his lis-
teners. The birds are present in undoubted numbers; they have
taken a measurable toll of the ripening corn. And so the farmers
want to attack the problem as they would a pestiferous insect
invasion — with deadly chemicals.

But will a mass slaughter of redwings in northern Ohio solve
the problem? And even if a significant dent can be made in
the redwing population there, is such a broad-fronted assault
justified? Ecological action is on everybody's tongue today. In
the Ohio redwing story we find the elements that could make
this a classic case history in ecological literature.

There is no such thing as a pest per se, of course. In northern
Ohio the redwing is a pest for only about one month a year,
and for rather special reasons. For the remaining eleven months
it is not only an aesthetic ornament to the landscape but a benefit
to the farmer as well.

Plumage and nomenclature combine to make this bird one
of the first ornithological prizes in our childhood vocabulary.
After all, what could be simpler? A black bird with red in its
wings that is called, logically enough, a "red-winged blackbird."
And, for many of us, it remains throughout our lives one of the
glories of the springtime marsh: spreading its tail, ruffling its
feathers, lifting its wings to present those two marvelous scarlet
shoulder patches, then pouring out its liquid trill: *konk-la-reeee!*
No creature capable of making such a display can be all bad.

Nor is it. Redwings, especially during their nesting season, consume enormous quantities of destructive insects, including snout beetles and leafhoppers. Even later in the summer, when they are nibbling at the farmers' corn, the greater part of their diet still consists of weed seeds.

But like the passenger pigeon before it, the redwing's great numbers cause extensive damage at certain locations during certain times of the year. In Ohio this occurs when the redwings gather in flocks of hundreds of thousands just before beginning their migration to the South. Many farmers trace the trouble to what they believe are a couple of recent developments: a tremendous "population explosion" among the birds, and their abandonment of nesting grounds in marshes and swamps in favor of new breeding sites in upland fields. Both assumptions invite some examination.

According to the U.S. Fish and Wildlife Service, the continental United States today supports a population of a half-billion "blackbirds" (a convenient nomenclatural blanket which includes not only redwings but such other species as grackles, cowbirds, and even the unrelated starlings). The Fish and Wildlife Service estimates that redwings comprise about one-third of this total.

Starlings, and probably cowbirds, are increasing their numbers. Each of these species presents special problems, and the Fish and Wildlife Service is coming around to the conclusion that they should not be "lumped." Starlings, for instance, take some grain; but they are apt to be more damaging around fruit crops, on which they feed, and around holly, on which they roost, spoiling it for the holiday market with their droppings.

Like starlings, cowbirds often gather at livestock feedlots in large numbers. This is a growing problem in areas where animals are taken at certain stages of their growth and herded into feedlots for a quick and economical fattening before slaughter. Cowbirds and starlings eat part of the grain intended for the livestock, a loss that the owners usually survive without great hardship. The more serious charge is that these birds may also contaminate feed and water with their droppings, thus putting a damper on the livestock's appetite so that they fail to fatten up on schedule.

But what of the redwing population? There is some doubt that what we are witnessing is a real redwing increase. The Fish and Wildlife Service, after much investigation, has concluded that redwing numbers do not represent "a recent population explosion, but mainly reflect more knowledge of these populations. However, local population changes are apparent. Man's land use and agricultural practices doubtless have influenced blackbird numbers and distribution."

In other words, there is little hard evidence that there are any more redwings in the United States today than there were a century ago. Rather, the fault lies with modern farming practices, which tend to attract and concentrate the birds in local areas where they become outstandingly apparent and troublesome. This is true in the Ohio counties bordering Lake Erie. Redwings nest in the millions in the Canadian province of Ontario, which forms the northern boundary of the lake. Indeed, Dr. Melvin Dyer of the Fish and Wildlife Service reports coming across a statement made by a local observer in 1759 in which doubt was expressed whether agriculture ever would succeed in Windsor, Ontario, because of the blackbirds' numbers.

After nesting, the redwings begin migrating across southwestern Ontario. They take the shortest route south that is consistent with their distaste for crossing large bodies of water, which means they are funneled across the western end of Lake Erie on the way to their traditional winter roosts in the Southeast. Arriving on the Ohio side of the lake, they encounter at once the great Lake Erie duck marshes — now backed up by huge cornfields that misguided farmers obligingly have planted in the redwings' path.

And the trouble begins. In their postnuptial molt the redwings are not yet ready to undertake long flights and so they are quite willing to remain awhile in the vicinity of an ample food supply. The birds congregate in roosts of many thousands in marshes near the cornfields. In the mornings they leave to find food. Once they have located a cornfield, the birds mill about for a time, then drop down onto the inviting crop.

Unfortunately for the farmers, their corn is most vulnerable to the blackbirds precisely at this time. The corn is still in the milk stage, or else the kernels are just beginning to harden. The birds proceed to shred the husk from the top of the ear, exposing the soft kernels, and begin to feed. The extent of the damage varies with the size of the flocks and the distance to the cornfields from roosting areas.

"While the immediate damage is the loss of corn to birds," says John DeGrazio of the Fish and Wildlife Service, "it is sometimes compounded during wet years by moisture entering the opened husk, causing the undamaged grain to mold."

Annual damages to Ohio's corn crop have been set by farmers and agricultural specialists as high as $15 million. Although this figure is now believed by Fish and Wildlife Service personnel to be exaggerated, the cost may amount to $5 million, much of it concentrated in Ottawa, Lucas, Erie, and Sandusky counties along the southern shore of Lake Erie. Some farmers have wisely abandoned corn and turned to such alternate crops as soybeans.

Agricultural authorities also estimate that the blackbird population in the United States and Canada increased by 300 percent during the early 1960s. This increase is often attributed to the redwings' "new" habit, supposedly acquired since the widespread draining of marshes began, of nesting in alfalfa fields. High in moisture and food content, while deficient in the redwings' natural enemies, alfalfa fields offer ideal nesting sites.

But is this truly a new development? The literature on blackbirds suggests that it is not. Arthur C. Bent, in his monumental *Life Histories,* noted long ago that "Although the birds prefer the vicinity of water, their nests are often found on dry uplands, sometimes at a considerable distance from any water, in fields of tall grass, clover and daisies, where they must be built close to or even on the ground. Nests in bushes and trees also have been reported by several observers."

And Arthur A. Allen, early in this century, found evidence that in its nesting habits the redwing is not wholly attuned to the complexity of the cattail marsh. "The first nests built are located in the dead stubs of the cattails that have been burned over during the previous fall," Allen wrote. "At first they are not sheltered by any vegetation of any kind, for the new growth is barely above the water . . . As the season advances and the vegetation grows, green stalks are included in the support. At first these are not sufficiently strong to serve alone as a support, and consequently the nests are always attached on one side to the dead stub . . .

"This is true of most of the nests constructed in early May, and it generally results in disaster. So firmly are the nests fastened by the strands of milkweed fiber, that the side attached to the green blades is carried upward by their growth, while the other, attached to the dead stubs, remains fixed. As a result, the one side is lifted at the rate of almost an inch a day until the nest is inverted. The birds continue to incubate until the last egg is rolled out."

More recent investigations show that redwings may nest first in a marsh, and later in an upland habitat — in the same season! By resorting to alfalfa fields, then, the redwing is merely beginning to adapt itself as best it can to a changing environment.

It has shown similar adaptability in converting other aspects of man's activities to its own benefit — turning to the loose grain found around the fast-spreading animal feedlots and the rice grown in what once were its roosting areas in southern marshes and swamps. All of these man-inspired developments help to concentrate the birds in pest numbers.

During the 1960s cries began to be heard in Ohio for the government to launch an eradication campaign against the redwings. Leading the chorus were such farmers as William Warner. Warner had chosen to assemble a number of farms in Sandusky County and plant them to corn despite the fact that he was flying in the face of environmental fact: the farms lay on the route of one of the most concentrated redwing migrations in the country.

"Early in my farming career I decided that I like cattle and corn," Warner said. "Working from there, whenever a farm came up for sale that seemed to fit my purpose, I would buy it. Eventually I ended up with about four big farms and four big sets of buildings which I thought would be suitable for feeding cattle. But with this blackbird situation making it almost impossible to raise corn, how are you going to fill those four big barns with corn and pay the high rate of taxes that keeps going up all the time?"

Ohio farmers formed an organization called "Bye-Bye Blackbirds" and began agitation to force the government to wipe out the big blackbird roosts along the lake. The Farm Bureau Federation, which welcomes controversial issues to sell memberships, jumped into the battle.

"We're out to clip their wings!" the Farm Bureau's monthly newsletter, *Fed-O-Gram*, announced. "We're going to put the heat on Congress to appropriate needed funds for the Department of Interior to go all out on a nationwide control program."

This sort of "heat" on the Fish and Wildlife Service has been building for some years, because the service is charged with regulating migratory birds (redwings among them). Some Ohio sportsmen, sensing an opening, have lobbied to transfer the redwing from a protected status to that of a gamebird. Since farmers are permitted, in any event, to kill "protected" birds in the act of destroying their crops, they have sought additional permission from their state legislature and the Fish and Wildlife Service to go into large roosts after the birds. That the farmers are indeed serious about their eradication campaign is clear from a request made of conservation leaders by the service in 1960.

The service "sounded all of us out," says Carl Buchheister, president emeritus of the National Audubon Society, "on the acceptability of changing their bird control policy to the extent of granting permission to 'accidentally kill' protected species while engaging in control operations against such species as starlings and blackbirds . . . We would oppose such a relaxation of policy simply because it would relieve the Fish and Wildlife Service of the responsibility it must now exercise in prosecuting for unwarranted or careless killing operations. None of us will file complaints if an occasional robin is killed when a blackbird flock is reduced, but we want the law to stand so that heedless killing can be controlled."

It is ironic that the Fish and Wildlife Service finds itself in this position. The problem, of course, was created by agricultural officials, who advised farmers to adopt methods of farming that invite environmental retaliation. Monoculture — or planting huge acreage to a single crop — encourages the growth of enormous pest-insect problems; while the presence of large animal feedlots, with tons of grain scattered about, encourages the growth of pest-bird problems. But since the Fish and Wildlife Service is "responsible" for the birds, the problems created by the agriculture people fall into its lap. Yet when Ohio farmers and their organizations prodded their Congressmen into action, the lawmakers, in turn, found that it was not easy to take drastic action against the birds.

"I don't mind telling you," said Congressman Clarence E. Miller of Ohio's 10th District to his farmer constituents, "that some members of Congress have already incurred the wrath of the women's garden club for attempting, mind you, to eliminate the problem of bird depredations . . . If you don't watch yourself, these flocks of elderly females, with all the charm of the vultures they lobby for, will swoop in to deny your right to improve your own place."

At the end of 1969 six Ohio Congressmen, with some of their constituents in tow, descended on the Fish and Wildlife Service in Washington, to make their wishes known. Confronting Dr. Leslie Glasgow, then Assistant Secretary of the Interior, Dr. John Gottschalk, then director of the Bureau of Sport Fisheries and Wildlife, and Jack Berryman, chief of the Division of Wildlife Services, the Congressmen demanded the development of a "lethal agent" to wipe out the blackbirds. Dr. Glasgow agreed to do what he could. Before leaving, the Ohio delegation also demanded that the service mute its opposition to the use of DDT and other chlorinated hydrocarbon pesticides used in agriculture.

The assault on blackbirds is now in full swing, implemented by a variety of methods. The scarecrow, of course, is one of man's earliest attempts to deal with pest birds. In most cases birds aren't fooled for long by a straw man dressed up in yesteryear's clothes. Modern man has tried to frighten away pest birds by sound rather than by sight; complicated batteries of fireworks and other explosives are set off in the fields at varying intervals.

These explosive devices have some effect on redwings because the birds' depredations occur during a short period in late summer. But problem birds are species well able to accommodate to man's activities, and, says John A. Kadlec, formerly of the Fish and Wildlife Service, "with remarkably few exceptions, we can assume that any species of bird which causes man problems is able to tolerate and profit from him."

The effectiveness of the devices can be reinforced by farmers who occasionally visit the fields with a shotgun to make "believers" of the birds with a few well-aimed volleys. "The value of any [scare] technique," Kadlec says, "can be increased if, occasionally, something disastrous does happen to a bird." One of the biggest drawbacks to this noisy assault on redwings, however, is that human neighbors often are offended by explosions or jeopardized by gunfire. Legal action is not uncommon.

Two quieter means of reducing pest bird populations are traps and chemosterilants. Birds can be lured by grain to large wood-and-wire traps, such as the "Australian crow trap," which the birds find easy to enter by folding their wings and dropping in through a small opening. Leaving the trap is a different matter. The birds try to fly out, but the opening is too small to allow passage when their wings are fully spread for flight. The birds are then driven to a killing chamber at one end of the trap and gassed.

Chemosterilants, which are mixed with grain, are much less effective against mobile populations than against static ones, such as pigeons. Since redwing damage is short-term, and the sterilants will not affect the population for some time, these chemicals do not provide the corn-growers with the drastic relief they call for.

The most popular weapon now used against redwings seems to be Avitrol, an unpleasant poison which its proponents describe euphemistically as a "fright-producing chemical." Avitrol cannot be bought and used by private individuals. It is applied by government workers, who spread the Avitrol-poisoned grain (one treated kernel to 99 untreated ones) on farmers' fields by planes or mechanical seeders.

"We keep the seeding to the center of the fields," a Fish and Wildlife Service official says, "so that other birds like pheasants aren't likely to pick it up. And even if a pheasant starts feeding on this grain he could eat ninety-nine kernels that are all right before he gets the treated one."

When a flock of redwings settles down to feed on the treated grain, some of them are in for a nasty surprise. The chemical takes three to five minutes to produce an effect on the unfortunate bird that swallows the treated kernel. Ed Hutchins of the Columbus *Dispatch* has described the result.

"It doesn't kill quickly," Hutchins writes. "Birds could die within 30 minutes, but they might not die for two days. Avitrol affects the body chemical that controls nerve synapses — much in the order of strychnine, but the purpose of Avitrol is to kill the bird slowly. And while it is dying, it flies out of control, is perhaps blinded, and its anguished screams are relatively effective in scaring away other birds."

A Fish and Wildlife Service biologist goes into a little more detail: "We observed that fields were cleared of blackbirds by affectation of about one percent of the population. Affected birds fly erratically in towering circles while emitting distress cries. After losing its flight capabilities, the affected bird continues to give visual and auditory stimuli while on the ground." The biologist also noted that "most landowners were satisfied with results of baiting, but the program would have been more successful had all the landowners in the area participated."

Studies remain vague about what effect this "fright-producing chemical" may have on nontarget species.

But farmers continue to put pressure on the Fish and Wildlife

Service for still more effective action. In the face of such pressure the service has experimented with dousing blackbird roosts in the South with detergents. Planes fly over wooded areas where redwings are known to roost, laying down a cloud of detergents. The attack must coincide with rain and a sudden drop in the temperature. If conditions are right, the birds' plumage, robbed of its insulation by the detergent, provides no defense against cold and wetness. Death follows comparatively quickly and humanely.

Some press reports have stirred the public to protest against these detergent raids. The specter of enormous bird kills, and the poisoning of streams, has been raised. To date, however, such has not been the case. The operations have been limited to small but troublesome roosts, and the infrequent raids apparently have not contributed significantly to the pollution of surrounding waterways.

At this point conservationists are not objecting to the detergent raids. If redwing control is really necessary, they prefer to see it carried out on a limited basis by Fish and Wildlife Service personnel, who are familiar with a broad area of environmental problems, rather than by agriculture officials, whose outlook is a good deal narrower. Choosing the least of several evils, ornithologists believe the detergents to be kinder to the redwings (freezing is among the less painful deaths) and kinder to the environment than broad-spectrum poisons.

There is no doubt, in any case, that many birds are being killed, whether by "approved" government methods, or by farmers who poison them illegally. But is the problem of redwing depredations being solved? Evidence gathered from bird-banding programs in northern Ohio suggests that the redwing population is comparatively unstable in the sense that the birds keep moving from one area to another in late summer. When large numbers of birds are killed in one area, a new wave is likely to enter the vacuum the next day.

Another obstacle to the success of the killing programs now under way is that a reduction of the birds' numbers in fall and winter is likely to *aid* the population in the long run. In England, for instance, ornithologists have noted that large populations of bullfinches tend to eat up all the available winter food in a short time and thus weaken the entire population. If the birds' numbers are reduced in the fall, their food supply lasts longer, and they enter the next nesting season in greater numbers and are able to produce a bumper crop of young birds.

"Taking the argument further," a British ornithologist says, "the most effective way to reduce a population between one breeding season and the next might not be to kill birds in autumn, but to release extra ones into the population then, thus increasing the competition for a limited food supply."

Some Ohio farmers and their spokesmen in state agricultural positions would take a different approach: they would kill so many redwings that the population would not be able to recover. And so we come to the ultimate point: is such a drastic step justified in order to rescue a few farmers who have chosen to plant the wrong crop — one that is environmentally vulnerable in that area?

Obviously a great many people think not. The economics of the redwing problem in Ohio has been greatly distorted. The redwings take some grain, and in localized areas it occasionally amounts to a significant portion of the "economic margin" of the crop. Inefficiency in modern agriculture, however, also wastes a significant portion of the crop. Several years ago an Illinois Agricultural Experiment Station studied the operation of 24 mechanical corn-picking machines. Each machine dropped at least five bushels of corn per acre, and some dropped as many as 25 of the 80 bushels raised in an acre. This sort of thing can be characterized as dollar efficient, perhaps, but it is also resource wasteful.

What we find in Ohio is that some farmers have chosen to fight the environment — to plant their acreage to corn, rather than to a less vulnerable crop, although they know by now that their land lies on the age-old migration route of a corn-eating wildlife species. The redwings are a limiting factor in the raising of corn, just as in other areas poor soils, a lack of moisture or too much of it, and a short growing season are recognized as limiting factors.

The farmers who continue to grow corn year after year while complaining of "unbearable losses" apparently also continue to make a good living — or else they would shift to a more profitable crop, as a few have done. And further, while working against nature, they demand that the public's taxes go toward subsidizing their operation. The taxpayers thus pay the bill for redwing control, as well as bear the less tangible costs occasioned by the loss of birds that are valuable and pleasing additions to the environment for the rest of the year.

When we justify large-scale control programs on the basis of "economic damage" we step onto shifting sands. It makes no sense to lump all bird damage in one category, because this damage varies from region to region and thus demands different remedies. The estimates of damages themselves are difficult to support, and generally shrink under scrutiny.

In any case, the farmer with his shotgun is usually preferable to the more extensive and complex control programs undertaken by most state and federal agencies. The law allows the farmer to proceed, within reason, to protect his crop against excessive wildlife damage. But the trouble with government control programs is that they tend to perpetuate themselves, as conservationists have seen in the case of the Department of the Interior's western "gopher chokers." When protection from pests is left to the individual, the main concern is that he be restrained from attacking the problem with dangerous chemicals.

Mankind should know by now, after the sad experience of recent years, that he cannot bend nature indiscriminately to his will without disastrous consequences.

"No real relief from crop damage can be obtained by anything less than the most drastic population reduction," says Roland C. Clement, vice-president of the National Audubon Society. "We must therefore concentrate on finding ways of preventing damage to particular crops during that brief season when they are vulnerable to damage. This is a cultural and technical problem, and we should stop calling it bird control because it is the prevention of crop damage by birds."

The problem here, as elsewhere, was created by man; or more specifically by the farmers' agricultural advisers — the Department of Agriculture's Extension Service and its experiment stations. Mechanical corn harvesting and inefficient feedlot operations bait the birds. Corn hybrids with short husks expose the ear and invite damage. Ecological land-use principles have been ignored, enabling huge cornfields to spring up in the most unsuitable areas.

With sounder agricultural advice the farmer will be better able to deal with these problems. But unless the redwings and other "pest birds" are extirpated from entire regions of the country, he will not be free from some damage. The social problem then becomes one of whether the taxpayer should compensate the farmer for this damage, or ask him to consider it a cost of production.

"Let us help the farmer but not sacrifice everything to his individual economic interests," Clement says. "The National

Audubon Society, representing long-run independent concern, agrees that some emergency control work may be necessary in many cases because we currently lack better methods. But it wants the job done right in the long run. Birds are not pests except locally and temporarily, and then usually because man has created undesirable conditions for all of us. There will be no shortage of corn because a few farmers are induced to adapt to reality by planting less vulnerable crops in a few places."

GEORGE LAYCOCK

Feed the Ducks
and Pass the Ammunition

IF A HUNTER WANTS to bring ducks into range so he can kill
a lot of them, and if he is willing to stoop to illegal means,
chances are he knows the fine points of a practice called baiting.
The idea is simple. The ducks are hungry and can be easily
lured with food. After several days of feeding they are condi-
tioned to the grain spread before a duck blind and have lost
much of their natural wariness. One morning the hunter goes
to the blind at dawn. As the ducks funnel into the shallow water,
where they expect that breakfast is waiting, the hunter stands
up and shoots them as fast as he can.

Though baiting has been prohibited by federal law since 1935,
it is still a way of life in some of America's most famous waterfowl
marshes and estuaries. State and federal agents may spend 100
hours a week during the waterfowl hunting season in an effort
to combat baiting, but they cannot halt it altogether. For instead
of taking a sporting chance like law-abiding hunters, the baiters
go to great lengths to kill more ducks than regulations allow.
Habitual baiters prefer to call it "feeding." When caught they
are likely to whimper some excuse to the effect that "if you
don't feed, you don't get any ducks."

Legitimate hunters disprove this argument every day of the
season. Instead of trying to beat the law, they rely on the skillful

use of decoys, calls, and knowledge of the outdoors to bring ducks
and geese within shotgun range.

If duck-baiting — a throwback to the infamous days of market-
hunting — were to become widespread again, "we could wipe
out the grain-eating ducks," I was told by John M. Anderson,
former biologist-manager of a large duck marsh on the shore
of Lake Erie and now director of the National Audubon Society's
Sanctuary Department. A few examples bear out that prediction.
On the border of Delta National Wildlife Refuge in Louisiana,
two gunners — shooting over bait — were arrested last season with
69 widgeon, 11 pintails, 3 gadwalls, and a mottled duck in their
possession. The 84 birds they had shot were 72 more than the
legal limit. Three other hunters were apprehended with a total
of 30 mallards, although each was allowed only two. In another
case, federal officers caught three gunners shooting over bait;
they already had killed 71 ducks.

And these cases of waterfowl slaughter are not uncommon.
After decades of market-hunting, pollution, and drainage of their
habitat, waterfowl face a dim future. Such illegal shooting is
an added pressure that they cannot withstand.

During the 1971 waterfowl hunting season I went into marshes
in two locales 1200 miles apart, accompanying federal and state
enforcement officers to see firsthand what progress they are
making in their efforts to curb the deadly practice of luring ducks
to the gun with food. Early in the season I joined federal game
management agent David L. Hall of the New Orleans office of
the Bureau of Sport Fisheries and Wildlife, whose area includes
the vast, remote marshlands of the Mississippi delta, the wintering
grounds for hundreds of thousands of waterfowl.

Hall had already done his groundwork. A few days before
the opening of the waterfowl season, pilot Joseph W. Perroux
arrived with the bureau helicopter. Flying at low altitudes,

The widgeon or baldpate is easily lured to the slaughter
by illegal baiting of waterfowl marshes

Perroux and Hall covered hundreds of miles of those flat and
beautiful marshlands. From the air, grain spread in the water
usually can be quickly spotted. Bait used in the Louisiana marshes
includes corn, rice, milo, and sweet potatoes.

Some of the shooting clubs in these marshes employ guards
to patrol the canals and warn the gunners when game officers
approach. Other clubs are arrogant and defiant and make little
effort to hide the 100-pound grain sacks around their camps.

Hall knows of one club that had 15 tons of grain stored and another that spread three tons of rice in the marsh in three applications. One officer told me he had watched a man scoop grain out of his pirogue and spread it in wide arcs over the water. When baiters are arrested they are likely to brag about it. What is needed, say the officers, is a firm law permitting them to close baited marshes to hunting.

By opening day, Hall and Perroux had pinpointed many baited shooting areas. One area particularly interested Hall, and we left a call at our motel for 3:30 A.M. so we could be on hand at dawn to check it out.

Working with Hall that day was one of his supervisors, Jack D. Frost, a veteran law enforcement agent and biologist from the bureau's regional office in Atlanta. We were joined later by two state officers and another federal agent, Sidney A. Woodson.

As we drove through the predawn blackness, Hall explained why he was surprised to find bait around the blinds of the camp. One year earlier he had apprehended the same group, and a court had convicted them of shooting over bait, shooting more than the limit of ducks, and using an unplugged gun with a capacity of more than three shells. "I didn't think they'd have the nerve to go back baiting this soon," Hall said.

An hour later Hall and I were in his boat, running along the twisting canals that reach into the heart of the marsh. Occasionally we stopped to listen. The law does not make it illegal to "feed" waterfowl, only to shoot over the bait once it is spread. So Hall must catch the hunters shooting over bait before he can make an arrest. Soon we heard the muffled reports of a shotgun off to the east. Hall started the motor, and we sped out of the canal into a broad pond. On the far edge of the pond stood a green boxlike house on stilts.

A few minutes later we eased to a stop beside a walkway that connected the house with a shed 75 feet away. An unsmiling man came out of the house, duck feathers sticking to his trousers. He informed Hall that we needed a search warrant. He also said his group had not been shooting. Then we heard more shots from a blind that was visible a quarter mile away. We watched three ducks fall from the sky. The camp owner volunteered that his son was in that blind and his grandson was occupying another blind farther out in the marsh. We lifted a pirogue off the outboard boat, settled ourselves carefully into the unstable shell, and began paddling out to the blind. By this time Woodson had joined us in his pirogue.

The shooting stopped as we came in sight, and a broad-shoul-dered young man stood up in the blind smiling sheepishly. We paddled about the lagoon, gathering the dead ducks that floated there. In our pirogue were 22 birds: 12 shovellers, 1 blue-winged teal, 1 green-winged teal, 2 mottled ducks, 1 pintail, 1 gadwall, 3 scaup, and 1 mallard. There were two guns in the blind. The second gun gave the hunter six shots without stopping to reload. Before we departed, the agents scooped up generous samples of milo and rice from the bait spread around the blind. These samples were photographed and labeled for use as evidence in court.

Duck-baiters have worked out devious methods of "feeding" the birds while fooling the agents. Some baits are more easily seen than others. Yellow corn is highly visible, especially from the air. Consequently, it may be spread a little at a time, leaving just as much grain as the ducks will clean up in a day. Sometimes corn is carefully dropped in footprints left in the mud, because it is less visible in these slight depressions. Milo, because it is darker in color than corn, is a favorite. In northern states, white corn is sometimes spread on snow to attract geese.

Grain buried in mud is out of sight, but ducks soon find it. A motorboat may be driven around a bay or marsh at high speed after grain is spread, stirring up mud that settles over the evidence. Experienced baiters know that corn should be soaked first because it becomes heavier and sinks better.

Duck-baiters must worry about not attracting attention in other ways. Heavy gunfire is a tip-off. Thus they try to kill as many ducks as possible with one shot. One way is to spread bait in a straight line leading toward the blind. Then, with the ducks lined up happily dabbling for the grain, the hunter pulls the trigger. There is none of that sophisticated sporting business of waiting until the ducks are on the wing. Instead, as they say in some quarters, "You Arkansas them ducks." Further translated into bayou language, that means, "Shoot 'em on the sit."

"We can tell where there is bait by the way the ducks act," Hall told me. "If I see them feeding in a straight line in front of the blind I wonder what makes them feed in such an orderly pattern. If the ducks concentrate around one blind I get curious."

One afternoon I flew over the marsh country to see what the game agents see when they check for bait. Before long I was able to pick out the places that probably were baited. The first sign is often a raft of ducks. "It's wonderful how these Cajuns can always build their blinds right in the places the ducks like," my pilot commented with some sarcasm. Blackbirds also are indicators; they pick up grain that spills in the drier places.

In 1971 federal game agents handled some 250 waterfowl cases in southeastern Louisiana, and a big percentage of the most flagrant violations involved baiting.

From Louisiana, I traveled to Maryland to join another federal game agent, Willie J. Parker, who is becoming a legend in his own time. From October until the end of the waterfowl season in mid-January, Parker spends from 100 to 110 hours a week in the marshes around Chesapeake Bay. He grew up during the depression years on a farm in northern Tennessee. "I've hunted all my life," he says, "and I still can't understand what drives people who try to kill all they can."

Parker spent his first eight years as a federal agent in Kentucky. "Down there you can do things differently," he recalls. "Catch a man with more than the limit and you can sit down on a log and talk things over. You say, 'Well, Hoss, looks like I got you cold on this one,' and he says, 'Reckon it does. What you figure it's gonna cost me?' You say, 'Looks like about a hundred dollars' worth to me. Anyhow, that's what I'm going to recommend to the judge.' Then he'll say, 'How about givin' me a week or so to raise the money?'"

When he moved to Maryland, Parker soon learned that duck-baiting is a deeply ingrained habit on Chesapeake Bay. "In eight years in Kentucky," he recalls, "I had fifteen baiting cases. But when I came up here, my education began. We had seventy-five cases the first day of the season." As we talked Parker and I were skirting the edge of a woods, observing two hunters in a distant blind that was known to be baited.

"Up here," he continued, "there's a world of difference. And you never know who you'll find in the next blind. It might be anybody from a U.S. senator to one of the sharpest lawyers in the world. Everything has to be at the highest professional level."

As violators have frequently learned, Parker's only interest is in catching the lawbreaker, no matter who he is or whom he knows. "I'm for the birds," he says. "The birds are having a rough time even if the laws are observed." He believes the season on the canvasback, historically the bird that made Chesapeake Bay hunting famous, should have been closed two years ago. And he adds that the redheads are also in trouble.

Not surprisingly, there are hunters who attempt to influence Parker. Many of those who have ended up in court on a waterfowl violation charge would like nothing better than to see him transferred to Alaska. "My first year in Maryland," Parker recalls, "I had a hundred and fifty-six invitations to shoot on private duck clubs. The next year the number dropped to fifty-three, and the third year there were only ten. Since then," he adds with some pride, "there haven't been any. But I've been on most of their clubs anyhow, and on most of them I've done business."

"Some of these folks hunting out here," added Edward Townsend, a Maryland wildlife officer who had joined us during the morning, "got enough money to burn forty wet mules, but you can't let that stop you." Frequently, when Parker apprehends a man for shooting over bait and over the limit, the offender will tell the agent what a conservationist he is and how many thousands of dollars he donates annually to the improvement of northern waterfowl nesting areas.

On rare occasions a gunner still may attempt the old and deadly practice of teaming live decoys with bait. Even the champion duck-caller from Stuttgart, Arkansas, can't touch the real thing when it comes to instilling confidence in ducks passing overhead and drawing them down out of the sky. Louisiana agents recall one case in 1961 involving a live decoy. The shooter had acquired a small mallard that had become a household pet.

When he went to his shooting blind, the owner would carry the little duck in the pocket of his hunting coat. Later, on the water, the pet duck would feed constantly while "talking" to wild ducks passing overhead. Sometimes it would even take to the air and lead a flight of ducks back to the master's gun. When the shooter was apprehended, the agents confiscated all of his hunting equipment — including the pet duck. In court the contrite shooter promised to reform for all time. "I'll do anything you say," he vowed, "but my wife won't let me come home if you don't give back her little duck."

Although not many modern duck hunters risk using live decoys, game agents know this is always a possibility. "I once drove past a bunch of decoys," one federal agent told me, "just as one of them turned its head and looked at me." As the agent wheeled around sharply to come back there was a shot from the blind. "He shot his decoy," the agent said, "but that gave him more ducks than he was supposed to have so I got him for being over the limit."

In the past, too many judges have treated waterfowl cases as a waste of their important time. But those days seem to be on the way out in some areas. Both Hall and Parker credit the courts with much of their success in combating waterfowl violations.

There can be little question that stiff penalties save ducks. On November 30, 1971, several of Hall's cases came before U.S. Magistrate Harry Lee in New Orleans. Lee and his fellow magistrates, Morey L. Sear and Ingard O. Johannesen, believe waterfowl violations are serious business and have little patience with repeaters. In one day, on cases brought in by Hall, Judge Lee handed out fines totaling $4825. Duck-baiters read this news in their local papers. Some weeks later Hall, after flying over the marshes again, could find only three places that had been baited.

If and when the pressure on the duck-baiters relaxes, the "feeding" will resume. All that stands between the dwindling populations of waterfowl and that fraction of the waterfowling fraternity willing to break the laws is a limited force of wildlife officers, in particular the federal agents, who refuse to relax. The Bureau of Sport Fisheries and Wildlife's Division of Manage-

ment and Enforcement has only 155 agents working the entire
country, and waterfowl violations are but one of the enforcement
jobs confronting them.

Meanwhile, the outlaws among the hunters continue to insist
that baiting should be legalized. Repeatedly they tell you this
is the only way they can get any ducks. What they really mean
is that only by baiting can they shoot great numbers of ducks.
Sometimes they find sympathy in public places. One parish
sheriff in Louisiana regularly provides waterfowl lawbreakers
transportation in his official car when they have to appear in
court in New Orleans.

Some duck-baiters are so defiant they still teach their children
the fine points of "feeding." These are the youngsters who, when
caught shooting illegally, are likely to tell Hall, "You can't do
me nothin'."

Both Hall and Parker believe we still may be a generation
away from breaking up the old duck-baiting syndrome in areas
where this is a hard-core way of waterfowling. Meanwhile, the
question is whether or not the ducks can hold out. To help assure
the birds a chance against the outlaw gunner, areas found to
be baited should be closed at once to all hunting, not just for
the remainder of the season, but for several years.

JOHN MADSON

They Haven't Danced
the Last Dance

For hundreds of miles inland from the Atlantic, the world's greatest
forest of oak, hickory, beech, and maple stretched across the
eastern fourth of the new country. It was an infinity of trees,
an ocean of trees that surged westward beyond the knowledge
of man, and was thought to go on unbroken and forever.

But as the vast forest approached the 90th meridian, it began
to show signs of wear. Past the western end of Lake Erie, gaps
and rents appeared in the great fabric of woodland as it was
invaded by meadows of tall grass. The forest still advanced
westward. But as rainfall diminished, the trees shrank away from
high ground and sought the hillsides and floodplains.

In parts of what would be western Indiana, Illinois, and
southern Michigan and Wisconsin, the world began to open into
a wilderness of light and sky. This was truly a new world, unlike
anything the early French and English had ever seen. It was
the beginning of prairie, the eastern edge of what would be
classically misnamed on later maps as "The Great American
Desert."

It was also the beginning of a whole new set of special
creatures — the prairie dog, prairie fox, prairie wolf, prairie falcon,
and a grouse that was so closely bound to this grassland that
it was called "prairie chicken" from the beginning.

We think of prairie chickens as birds of the West. But the pinnated grouse that we call "greater prairie chicken" will live almost anywhere that prairie extends, even east of the Mississippi.

Prairie chickens originally ranged right up to the wall of eastern forest into Indiana and Ohio. In early Michigan they prospered in the southern part of the state around marshes, open patches of prairie, and in some open hill country. The birds were plentiful in southern Wisconsin's open country, and the broad prairies of Illinois swarmed with pinnated grouse.

The bull-tongue plow that broke the prairie sod is said to have broken the prairie chicken as well. But up to a point, the prairie chicken prospered with cultivation. In Indiana, as forest was cleared to create cropland, the birds spread east and south into entirely new range. The same thing happened in Wisconsin and Michigan. The birds moved north with pioneer lumbermen, taking advantage of slash and grasslands that followed the cutting and burning of the original forest. Prairie chickens pioneered all the way into Michigan's Upper Peninsula — up to 300 miles north of their original prairie range.

On the rich Illinois and Indiana grasslands, prairie chickens flourished with early farming that created new cover types in the original unbroken prairie. The birds learned about corn and other small grains, and their food supplies expanded enormously. Yet enough native grassland remained for their courtship, nesting, and brood rearing.

When Abe Lincoln was learning to split rails, an Illinois hunter had to hustle to shoot a dozen chickens a day. Forty years later, in the 1870s, a hunter could kill up to a hundred chickens a day. Chokebored, breech-loading shotguns had a lot to do with that, but it's likely that there were just more prairie chickens.

The heyday was brief. In parts of Indiana, Wisconsin, and Michigan, forest succession began to choke some newly created prairie chicken range. Or settlers moved into cutover lands and started "stump farms." Prairie chickens lingered for years in eastern parts of Michigan's Upper Peninsula, but are now gone. The Illinois prairie chicken peak came shortly after 1860 with an optimum balance of prairie and cultivated land. But as cropland overwhelmed grassland, the prairie chicken began to fail. A few birds clung to some of the richest prairie until more than 85 percent of the land was broken into grainfields, surviving in small, isolated bands that eventually faded and vanished. Up into the early 1900s there were prairie chickens within the city limits of Chicago, and the birds lasted in parts of Cook County as late as the 1920s.

Remorseless cultivation, coupled with long, deadly hunting seasons, had a cumulative effect. When Ohio officially closed prairie chicken hunting in 1903 it was only a formality — the birds were gone.

Indiana ended its chicken hunting in 1909, when only a few birds remained along the Kankakee River. Protection helped, for a time. Indiana prairie chickens began to increase again, and by 1912 the state population was estimated at over 100,000 birds. That was the high-water mark of Hoosier prairie chickens. By 1941 they had dwindled to about a thousand birds. The old courting and nesting grounds were vanishing, and the birds with them. Where 21 booming grounds were in bluegrass in 1943, only one was still in grass ten years later. By 1951, Indiana prairie chickens survived in only three counties. One of the last strongholds, oddly enough, was within 50 miles of the Gary steel mills where an area held 99 booming males as late as 1950. But within five years all the dancing grounds had been put to the plow, and in 1955 only seven booming males could be heard. In the spring of 1972, there were still two or three booming male chickens in that corner of Indiana — but it was probably the last spring that Indiana prairie chickens would be heard.

Farther north, in central Michigan, a handful of prairie chickens

A booming prairie chicken cock on a Michigan dancing ground

survive on acquired range created by forest cutting, and here Michigan's remnant flocks are marooned with no southern Michigan grassland to return to. Until a few years ago some soil bank contracts were still in force and permanent grassland existed, especially in Missaukee County, but such grassland fades with government programs.

So Michigan prairie chickens are losing ground, literally and figuratively. Biologists reported 65 booming males on dancing grounds in 1966. By 1971 this had fallen to a new low of only 26 booming cocks. And in the front yard of a farmhouse near Gladwin, Michigan, one prairie chicken cock came each early-spring morning to boom a lonely, futile performance. There was not a hen nor was there another cock for many miles.

Wisconsin prairie chickens have been cut back to the central part of the state into the big Buena Vista and Leola marshes. These marshes have been partly drained in the usual abortive attempt to make money out of marshland, but farming failed for several reasons, not the least of which was the fact that the big marsh basins turned out to be frost pockets. There is some plowland, woods, brush, and wet marsh remaining, but the key to this chicken range has been the bluegrass raised there as a cash crop. A combination of unusual factors held prairie chickens in this part of Wisconsin after the birds were long gone from other sections of the state.

Back in 1948, biologist Wallace Grange predicted that the Wisconsin prairie chicken would be extinct by 1967. He had good reasons for that prediction, and he might have been right if it hadn't been for dedicated biologists like Fred and Frances Hamerstrom, a remarkable couple who learned what Wisconsin prairie chickens needed and then worked to provide it. The Hamerstroms, the Buena Vista and Leola marshes, and a handful of citizen naturalists combined to save the Wisconsin prairie chicken. In 1954 there wasn't an acre in the state being managed for prairie chickens. Today nearly 11,000 acres are under management and more is being added. In the spring of 1971 there were 204 booming prairie chickens on the Buena Vista Marsh — indicating a total of some 400 birds. This is a decline from the 1950 high of 550 cocks on Buena Vista, but it is a big improvement on Grange's grim prediction.

Commercial bluegrass was one of the things that saved the Wisconsin prairie chicken. Several hundred miles away, in southeastern Illinois, commercial redtop grass was doing the same thing.

Southeastern Illinois is prairie, but not the heavy black prairie found farther north. This is gray prairie that was created by earlier glaciers than the black, it is less fertile and more acid, and better adapted to redtop grass than to corn. Redtop is second only to bluegrass as prime pasturage, and has been a specialty of southern Illinois since 1875. In the 1930s, 95 percent of the nation's redtop seed was produced in a dozen southeastern Illinois counties. Farming had taken the gray prairie out of one type of grass production and put it into another. And since redtop is not harvested until July or even August, the nesting and brood-rearing habitat of the prairie chicken survived the change. The bird adapted easily to a redtop grass culture that was an oasis in a desert of corn and small grain.

The zenith of redtop production was reached in 1940 when more than 300,000 acres of redtop were harvested in southern Illinois. This also saw the last real abundance of Illinois prairie chickens, whose fortunes were now entirely invested in the redtop market.

"Then," as the late late movie would put it, "came Pearl Harbor."

It wasn't the first time that the prairie chicken had been a civilian casualty of our great wars. The Civil War had been a turning point in Midwestern agriculture and marked the real end of the prairie frontier. It was also the beginning of a new agriculture that was powered by an industrial revolution.

World War I needed grain in huge amounts, and we drained countless Midwestern potholes and broke up the largest surviving blocks of native prairie to raise that grain. When my father marched away from an Iowa farm in 1917, there were still many prairie chickens. When he returned after the Armistice he found that prairie chickens had gone to wherever it is that natural resources — including the illusions of gassed farm boys — are banished by war. In an attempt to make the world safe for democracy, the world was made distinctly unsafe for prairie chickens.

Yet, in southeastern Illinois, life ran blithely on for the pinnated grouse. The redtop industry was prospering, and the row-crop doom of the northern prairie chickens had not yet hit the birds on the gray prairies of "down home" Illinois.

World War II settled that. There was a new intensification of land use, and a new land technology. The acid gray-prairie soils were sweetened with lime, bankrolled with federal subsidies, and put into small grains. The gray prairies, last real refuge of the Illinois prairie chicken, were being farmed almost as intensively as the black soils farther north. Going into World War II, there were tens of thousands of Illinois prairie chickens. By 1955, about 2000 remained. In 1961 there were about 1000. In 1957 there were a few birds still surviving in northern and western Illinois, but these are gone now. The only survivors are on the gray prairies of southeastern Illinois. In spring 1971 there were about 450 birds in 9 flocks.

These, then, are the three remaining outposts on the eastern frontier of the greater prairie chicken: Michigan, Wisconsin, and Illinois, with a total of something fewer than 700 surviving booming males that are as out-of-place as wampum on Wall Street. They are relics that have long outlived the original prairies that brought them into being. Now they exist on artificial prairies that are the final strongholds east of the Mississippi — three reliquaries of flocks that once spanned the prairie horizons.

On the face of it, no one has seemed to care much. Landowners are committed to a financial course and most of them look at the land in the usual terms of cash crops. Most hunters have felt the same way, but in terms of huntable crops.

Then, about a decade ago, there appeared a handful of diehards who had the temerity to flout economics and reserve a few scraps of land for a dying species with no market value. In 1958 the Prairie Chicken Foundation was organized in Wisconsin. In 1959 the Prairie Chicken Foundation of Illinois was formed. Two years later, in Wisconsin, there appeared the Society of Tympanuchus Cupido Pinnatus, Ltd., with its publication *BOOM!*

Don't let the ponderous title throw you. The society is about as ponderous as a professor heaving a custard pie at the dean. The group is committed to a solemn job and takes its prairie chickens seriously enough, but it grins as it works. This is a welcome switch — too many conservationists are joyless bores who, to the public eye, are self-anointed pallbearers for our natural resources. The society includes some of the nation's most eminent conservationists and businessmen — none of whom is above a few laughs. But behind the laughter is action.

The Illinois Prairie Chicken Foundation is an alloy of dedicated biologists and fired-up citizens that includes such unusual bedfellows as the Illinois Audubon Society, the Illinois Federation of Sportsmen's Clubs, the Illinois chapter of the Nature Conservancy, the Illinois division of the Izaak Walton League, and the Field Trial Clubs of Illinois. Allied with these are the Illinois Conservation Department and the doughty Illinois Natural History Survey.

Taking a cue from the Hamerstroms' work in Wisconsin, the Illinois group set its goal: a checkerboard of 20- to 40-acre refuges of permanent grassland covering about a fourth of an area four miles square. This would be the minimum to assure prairie chicken survival in any area. It was a tough project. Some key lands were not for sale, and all land values were soaring. Much of the Buena Vista Marsh had been bought for $25 an acre or less. The Illinois land was $500 per acre or more.

Habitat improvement is the most effective way to manage wildlife, and also the most impractical. But in the case of the Illinois prairie chicken, there is no alternative. With redtop grass going out of the picture, there is no choice but to buy land and deed it to the prairie chicken. This is not an impossible goal, however, for the bird can be managed with success even on high-production farmlands. Its entire range needn't be grassland, and as little as 20 percent grassland within the bird's total range can be enough to bring it through.

The Illinois foundation decided to concentrate on an area near Bogota, particularly on a long glacial moraine about a mile wide and ten miles long. Prairie chickens dote on this high, well-drained grassland, and it is home ground for at least one-fourth of the birds remaining in Illinois.

Then began the hat-in-hand appeal to clubs, corporations, state agencies, prominent sportsmen and naturalists, and foundations. Plans and revenue had to keep pace with rising land prices, and it takes a lot of hats in a lot of hands to buy much land at $500 per acre. But as of last summer, the Prairie Chicken Foundation of Illinois, together with the Prairie Grouse Committee of the Nature Conservancy, had bought or leased 1322 acres.

At the same time, state agencies came through with technical help. The prairie chicken has never had a greater ally than Dr. Ralph Yeatter of the Illinois Natural History Survey. Biologist Ron Westemeier of the survey began full-time research on prairie chickens, backed with Pittman-Robertson funds from the Department of Conservation. Biologist John Slachter of the department has spent at least a fourth of his time on prairie chicken work. The department is also leasing small satellite grasslands around the refuge areas being bought by the Prairie Chicken Foundation.

In the matter of prairie chickens, let it be understood that the Illinois Department of Conservation is damned if it does and damned if it doesn't. It tries to compromise by providing token aid to keep the prairie chicken people placated, but not enough to arouse hunters who don't want their money spent on nongame species.

In Illinois, as everywhere else, the hunter pays for game management programs with funds that are earmarked for the improvement of hunting. This may rankle the nonhunting naturalist who would like a slice of this money, but there it is. The Illinois Audubon Society, by the way, has been refused $50,000 in game management funds for allocation to prairie chicken preservation in Illinois.

It's a fact of life that the hunter holds wildlife conservation's purse strings — and the average Illinois hunter cares little about prairie chickens and their problems. The man on the street cares even less, and his politicians know it. Former Governor Otto Kerner, asked about money from the general fund for prairie chicken preservation, said that he would veto any prairie chicken appropriations that came across his desk, for he felt that he could not justify this to the taxpayer.

That taxpayer might ask: "Why spend money on prairie chickens? What are they good for? We can't hunt them, and we can't see them in the backyard."

It is unlikely that prairie chickens will ever be hunted again east of the Mississippi — or seen in the backyard. But the very rareness that precludes hunting should also establish special value. A rare animal or bird should be cherished simply because it is too scarce to be used in any way except to have.

Besides, there's something appealing about having a few living remnants of the old time here today. In our desert of soybeans and corn, a reserve of original ecology will survive. Some of the new refuges in Illinois will be managed for redtop grass and even some row crops, for prairie chickens like variety as much as the next critter. But some areas will be seeded to original prairie and allowed to happily relax au naturel. In a thoroughly cowed, plowed, and commercialized landscape, it's good to see a few areas that don't serve commerce. There will be big bluestem, yellow star grass, and rattlesnake master. And prairie grouse strutting through the cold spring dawn, their hollow, haunting *ooooh-ooh-ooohm* drifting across the prairie.

This is some of the finest live theater in the American outdoors. As such, it is a trump card of the prairie chicken people. Illinois has several large blinds from which courting grouse can be watched at close range, and a contributor may be wrapped up and sold before the sun has cleared the horizon. My friend Joe Galbreath does his best to lure prospective angels into the big blind on the Bogota area. ("If we can once get a prospect into a prairie chicken blind and let him watch a spring courtship display, sometimes from only a few feet away, we've got him hooked!")

In the false dawn of an April morning, this show has an unreal quality. The birds materialize from nowhere onto a dancing ground that they may have used for lovemaking for centuries. They are indistinct, and their booming has a muted quality that stands strange and distant on the ear. It is one of those things that can be instantly sensed as an authentic part of the old time. There is nothing contemporary about it. It gives the uneasy impression that you're out of sync with your time warp — something like hearing the echo of a Sioux courting flute in Central Park.

Although these Illinois birds have shown recent declines, it is felt that the Bogota flock has been saved. The threshold habitat has been secured, although more land is needed to clinch the security of the birds during cyclic lows. The prairie chicken is tough and persistent — but so are agricultural economics. Off the Bogota area, the issue of the few other Illinois prairie chickens is in doubt. It is astonishing that some of these birds — like the ones in Indiana — still survive at all. They are, as Joe puts it, birds of wonderful integrity, but they haven't a prayer without land of their own. ,

Cynics have observed that even though the greater prairie

chicken may vanish from Illinois and Wisconsin, it will not be extinct. The species is not on the national endangered list, and is even hunted in some states at the western edge of its range.

Dr. Fred Hamerstrom points out, however, that the prairie chicken's eastern and western ranges each have a fatal flaw. The bird's eastern frontier is optimum range, but total land use there has almost evicted the bird. Farther west there is more room for prairie chickens and land use is not as intensive, but it may be more hostile range with greater environmental resistance. If a lethal combination of weather conditions and land use should decimate the western prairie chicken, and if the eastern flocks have been dispossessed, the thin reserves of the greater prairie chicken would be exhausted.

And although Kansas prairie chickens may be the same species as our Illinois and Wisconsin birds, they just aren't "home folks." Having a few Kansas imports in the Lincoln Park Zoo is a pale substitute for having some original prairie chickens still living free where they have always been.

People like Ralph Yeatter and Joe Galbreath are pretty unreasonable like this. They don't take any comfort in knowing that everything is O.K. with the chickens out in Kansas's Flint Hills, or some other place on the far side of the sunset that they and their grandchildren may never see. To paraphrase Aldo Leopold, relegating prairie chickens to Kansas is about like relegating happiness to heaven; one may never get there.

It is better to keep the prairie chickens that we already have, at home where they belong, now and tomorrow.

C. E. GILLHAM

Tomorrow's Critters

YEARS AGO the federal government, in all its power and wisdom, formally labeled me as a biologist.

This accrued from the fact that I had trapped wolves and chased dickeybirds and waterfowl through the Arctic for Uncle Samuel. And although it was something like a ward heeler getting an honorary Ph.D. for having finished grammar school, I accepted the new title (and the new civil service rating) with modesty. The only reason I mention it now is to present my credentials, for I am about to describe some new species of wildlife that are beginning to evolve.

Evolution is speeding up, like everything else. It has to: if creatures are going to adjust to environmental pollution they'd better change their way of living, and quick.

We already have examples of swift evolutionary change. Take quail, for example. You can get out of your car in northern Iowa, slam the door, and flush a covey of roadside quail that will fly across the state line into Minnesota and instantly evolve from gamebirds to songbirds, by virtue of Minnesota statute.

Those quail may show other changes, too. Suppose, for example, they should fly as far as Minneapolis. A big change from an Iowa cornfield. The quail would develop sinus trouble, and their eyes would be constantly filled with tears from sulfur dioxide.

Because of the carbon monoxide around the Twin Cities' Beltline, a quail's red blood corpuscles would lose their ability to hold iron. As a result, the iron in the birds' systems would be secreted through the tear ducts, staining the quail's cheek feathers. This could result in an entirely new subspecies of songbird called the *rusty-cheeked weeper.*

That's how this evolution thing works.

And unless I miss my guess, it will produce some strange critters. I'm going to dispense with their scientific names because I got a D in Latin in high school — and that was back in the days when Latin was a lot more common than it is now. So I shall stick to what will undoubtedly be the common names of some typical future species:

Berkanbok. A hybrid mammal, a cross between a white-tailed deer and a billy goat. Its name is a corruption of "beer-can buck," because it eats beer cans. These creatures will have complete protection on all the freeways and will act as scavengers, cleaning up cans and billboards — same as crows and buzzards formerly cleaned up dead rabbits and skunks when there were rabbits and skunks. The berkanbok will be the fastest animal afoot in the world — the first Mach IV mammal. His illegal flesh will have a tinny taste. If used, it should be marinated overnight in a 50-50 solution of sulfuric acid and 100-proof vodka. A sprinkling of roadside marijuana leaves will add zest but is optional.

Oilslick brant. A subspecies of the Atlantic or white-breasted brant. It will be found also on the southern California coast in the vicinity of oil rigs, where it has learned to digest crude oil in much the same way that catalytic heaters digest white gas. This fowl has lost its migratory instincts and now follows tankers as gulls pursue fishing fleets. The flesh of the oilslick brant has an aroma of a Texas pipeline and should be thoroughly washed in hi-test gasoline and dried. Parboil in a good detergent, rinse and dry again. Bake breast up and garnish with eelgrass — if you can find it. Serve on a clean sand beach — if you can find one.

Sooty smog grouse. A new species. Probably a descendant of the blue grouse which was driven by brush fires into the Los Angeles vicinity ages ago. Unlike other gallinaceous grouse this one has developed webbed feet so that it can walk across mud slides that result from erosion that results from California brush fires. Unable to scratch for a living, its food habits were drastically changed. It is believed this bird now lives chiefly on smog and vapors from chili parlors and taco joints. I offer no cooking directions because they wouldn't do much good, anyway.

Silt hen. A new species. The ancestors of this bird may have belonged to the family of herons, shorebirds, or the cranes. Its habitat is confined exclusively to silt basins created by river dams. Future Army Engineers will honor this bird on their shoulder patches. The Bureau of Reclamation and the Soil Conservation Service also deserve to share the honor. The silt hen spends its life walking across mud flats caused by drawdowns, picking at mud-filled beer cans, rusty tackle boxes, and drowned cats in rotting burlap bags. The main food is garbage. The only diversion they have is watching the dredges pumping silt. Don't eat them. They are poisonous.

Dryland alligator. A subspecies of the common 'gator. Found only in the vicinity of Greater Miami Jetport. With the encroachment of landfills in the Everglades the dryland alligator had time to evolve. First he fed on walking catfish and as they disappeared from the drying landscape he moved in beside the jetport's runways where he subsists on the leftover desserts from airlines' lunches. He is no longer in danger of extermination for his skin resembles the crust of an airline's pie and has no value whatever. His feet will change with further evolution and will probably develop Neolite soles for oily runways. He will have no voice, for an alligator's bellow can't be heard over the roar of jets. And he will carry his tail over his back as it is easier than dragging it over the tarmac.

Gray-shafted freeway flicker. Another new species. Probably the ancestor of this bird was the ivory-billed woodpecker. With the logging off of Southern forests and the coming of the freeways, a transition took place. Always powerful of bill, the woodpecker developed into a concrete-pecking bird. By close association with concrete overpasses the feathers have become gray. The jack-hammer staccato of their pecking will be forever with us for overpasses will soon dominate half the land area of our country.

Junk-car hare. A subspecies that hasn't changed a great deal from its ancestor, the cottontail rabbit, except for habitat and food. Thousands of our roadside junkyards are infested with these animals which nest in old upholstery and live chiefly on stale lollipops, popcorn, and potato chips that have slipped down behind the seats. Their legs have become extremely short and may grow even shorter, for these animals must crawl around under modern cars that have only three inches of road clearance. They will be as permanent as the junkyards and will be with us forever. They should not be hunted in their prime habitat because of the danger of ricochets.

Long-haired eagle. A new species because of appearance, food habits, and habitat. The extinct bald eagle may be a distant relative of this bird. When the coho salmon and other freshwater fishes became loaded with DDT, the bald eagle was hard put to reproduce its kind. Their eggshells became thin and would break during incubation. Quickly the eagles shifted to other food. Most mammals were gone so they carried off long-haired kids. After centuries this bird has developed a long-haired head instead of a short-feathered bald one. Their contribution in keeping down the population explosion has been great. They are sometimes called the "beatle eagle." They roost on high TV antennae and freeway signs. Because it is illegal to own rifles, they are never destroyed and should survive the ages.

Whispering crane. A subspecies. This giant black bird is a direct descendant of the extinct whooping crane. The latter had a melodious voice that could be heard for miles. Often they flew so high that it was barely possible to see them in the stratosphere. With the coming of jetplanes they evolved. Their once white plumage gradually darkened until it became black. The long coiled windpipe in the sternum of the bird that produced deep, sonorous trumpeting became clogged with soot from the burning kerosene of the jets. Finally the crane could barely speak above a whisper. The black skies that darkened his feathers will ever conceal him in flight. He may need to evolve again to survive.

Pipeline caribou. A descendant of the Barren Ground caribou that once roamed all the Arctic tundra. This animal will differ a bit from his ancestral relatives. His hoofs will be black and shiny from wading through pools of leaking crude oil and his nose will be black to his eyes from grazing on oil-soaked lichens. His rack of horns will shrink so that he may crawl beneath huge pipelines where they cross canyons and washes. His legs will become longer so that he can jump over huge conduits and not be fenced in behind the Brooks Range when he wishes to migrate to Mount McKinley. Around the oil camps where lichens no

The pipeline caribou — oil-era descendant of the
barren ground caribou?

longer grow, his diet is discarded *Playboy* magazines and the
Dacron batting of old insulated underwear. This species should
survive as long as the oil depletion allowance.

Desert dipper. A subspecies of the ancient roadrunner of the
Southwest. The once-famous chaparral cock that vanished as
the chaparral was replaced by golf courses, drag strips, and atomic
test sites. This new subspecies is found around the only existing
water in today's desert — backyard swimming pools. It no longer
runs, for there is no room left for running nor any coyotes to
run from. This species builds its nest from old Kleenex tissues
and subsists on barbecue sauce spilled on patios. Its flesh is edible,
but has a slight taste of suntan lotion. Was recently adopted
as the Official Bird of the Tucson Suburban League.

Flak-jacketed honker. A new and almost indestructible species. No doubt its ancestors were Canada geese. These birds were once heavily hunted and game departments enticed them into shooting areas with yellow corn and made a once wily bird a complete damned fool. They did learn to stay within their refuges and only sally forth when the corn became scarce or they needed sand in their gizzards to grind the stuff up. They learned to fly higher over the pit blinds. Man increased his ordnance. Made longer-range shotguns and used bigger shot that had shorter shot strings. Biologists fluoroscoped captured birds and determined that 60 percent were carrying ingested shot in their bodies. But evolution was taking place. The flak-jacketed honker became a reality. Scar tissue on the birds' breasts became so common that it became hereditary, and evolved into a horny covering similar to the shell of a sea tortoise. Heavy shot could not penetrate this armor and frequently ricocheted back into the pit blinds below, injuring gunners, and local safety councils eventually succeeded in prohibiting this dangerous sport.

The big question is: how will man evolve?

I predict that he will become hairier as he becomes hippier. His forehead will grow low and slanting, for a more streamlined effect in sport convertibles. He will slowly develop a tail for swinging through trees, for the flat surface of the Earth will be entirely converted to a parking lot. Since he is walking very little, if any, his legs will become shorter. All in all, he'll end up looking just about the same as when he started.

The trouble is — his world won't.

A katydid sings under a full autumn moon

HAL BORLAND

A Quiet in the Night

HARD FROST HAS COME and there is a quiet in the night, at last,
that has not been there since the hylas began to yelp last April.
The fiddlers and scratchers, the hummers and the buzzers, have
lived their lives, left their hostages to fortune in egg and pupa,
and died of old age and cold nights. Only an occasional indoor
cricket will be heard from now on. The rhythm enters another
beat. Winter comes, and after the equinox next March we will
approach another spring, the quickening of life again. But there
is no real ending even now, any more than there is an ending
with sunset. There are only varying aspects of the continuous,
of nature.

The words we use so readily are vague. We talk of nature
and what we mean is life, the whole life principle. We too
often think of nature, and even of life, as apart from ourselves.
Biologically we are animals, capable of procreation, needing food
and drink, tolerant of a relatively narrow range of temperature
and humidity, physical weaklings subject to injury and disease,
organisms that eventually wear out and hence of limited life-span.
Yet we talk of "the animals" apart from ourselves, and of
"nature" as apart from this environment where we live. Actually,
nature is you and me and the air and water around us, wherever
we are, and the soil underfoot. Nature is a mouse, a rat, a bear,

an earthworm, a louse, a flock of geese, a child and its parents.

I suspect that we set ourselves apart because nature is so unforgivably impartial — nature is no more concerned with the welfare of mankind than with that of rabbits or snapping turtles or periodic locusts. So far as dispassionate inquiry has yet determined, nature is a complexity of impersonal forces and materials whose only purpose is to sustain and perpetuate life on this planet. Not one particular form of life, but the basic life-force whether expressed in algae or slime mold or daffodils or buzzards or tigers. There are countless life-forms, from microscopic bacteria to elephants and whales and giant redwoods. And men. Man just happens to be one of those forms, a relatively minor one and a conspicuous physical weakling at that. Man is bigger than a fox, smaller than a cow, lacks fangs, claws, horns, and poisonous saliva, is so naked of skin that he sunburns in summer, is frostbitten in winter, and is an open feast for fleas, gnats, mosquitoes, and all manner of hungry insects.

And man is a newcomer, an upstart. Nature got along without him for a long time. The better estimates set the Earth's age at around five billion years. By anthropologic and geologic reckoning, man, *Homo sapiens,* is less than two *million* years old. Man's rise has been meteoric. It is quite possible that he is a sport or a biological accident. Even without his own ingenuity, he might be disposed of and dispensed with, as were the giant lizards which preceded him. There is evidence that other sports and biological accidents were destroyed when they proved intolerable in their environment or were a menace to the total life-force.

Thus far it seems that man has persisted and even become dominant, despite his handicaps and shortcomings, because he had more brain capacity than any known creature that preceded him. He had the urge to think. He invented speech, a means of shaping ideas and communicating them. When he began to talk and think about matters beyond his own rather limited self he soon outdistanced all other forms of life around him. He thus became a creature with a dual nature — he was an animal who still needed food and shelter, but he was also a thinking, emotional being with the urge to know and the capacity to remember, to imagine, to share ideas. And he began to dominate the conditions of life around him. Somewhere along the way, and quite early, he evolved the idea that it was his destiny, even his duty, to dominate, to dictate to nature itself.

Until man evolved, life was primarily a matter of survival, and change was largely limited to accident and evolution. Man has altered that somewhat, particularly with relation to his own kind and to those forms of life on which he is dependent or which he thinks threaten his comfort or security. But mostly man has changed himself and his immediate environment as he moved from the trees to the caves, from the caves to the river valleys, from the valleys onto the open plain, and thence out across the whole of the land until every habitable part of the world became known to him.

Man has done remarkable things but he has never escaped his link with nature and the basic rhythms. He never will. What he has accomplished has been within the framework of those natural laws, and his primary achievements have been in the study and use of those laws. But he still must live in the environment to which he was born — on this planet, this Earth. He has discovered means of exploring space, including the moon, at enormous financial cost and at yet unknown physical and social cost; but even his plans for that venture were based on the fundamentals of nature, the rhythms and the certainties of the planetary system centered on the sun. The rhythms and conditions with which man has learned to live here on Earth —

such matters as gravity, light, sound, time, atomic motion. And all this is limited by that mysterious rhythmic capacity in us, the power of thought.

Our lives are completely dominated by the fundamental rhythms. My breathing, my pulse, my unconscious processes of digestion, my hearing, my eyesight, my sense of touch, my speech, my thought — all are matters of rhythm. Life is governed by the rhythms. The female animal has rhythmic periods of fertility. The sex act of fertilization is rhythmic. Birth is accomplished in rhythmic labor. And all the rhythmic processes in us, pulse to speech, are a part of growth, maturity, life's continuation. When they cease, a unit of life has come to its physical end. When my pulse stops, I die. But my progeny, in whom the rhythm continues, live on, the next step, the next beat, in the rhythm of life.

The disturbing element here is man's tendency to drift or stray from the basic elements of his environment, the fundamental rhythms of life. As he has evolved complexities of living which he calls civilization, he has repeatedly lost perspective of himself and his cosmos. Surrounded by institutions he evolved and structures he created, he too often believes that he can ignore or repeal the most enduring fundamental of all — cause and effect. And he tends to minimize the importance of life itself — not his own life, perhaps, but the great stream of life, the whole life principle of this Earth of which he is a part. His tendency to dominate becomes a belief in his own omniscience and omnipotence.

We see this every day, hear about it every hour. A crew with bulldozers must move mountains because some man wants the mountains moved to build a factory, to strip a seam of ore. A crew with chain saws must cut down a forest because some man wants more paper, more plywood, more timbers to build a rustic bridge. A crew of dam-builders must build a dam because some city wants more electricity to run mechanical toothbrushes, can openers, artificial climate-makers, more water to wash more automobiles, to flush its filthy streets.

It is of no consequence that a mountain is an entity, with its own place in the scheme of the land, or that a tree is a living thing that grows slowly, year by year, or that a river is not only water but fish and fowl and a whole spectrum of aquatic life. It is important only that "the plan" be carried out, even a plan made without knowledge or accounting of the whole consequence.

Sometimes we talk of protecting such elements of life and the environment. And too much of the talk is as arrogant as the destruction itself. It assumes that man is the sole judge of what should be saved, that he can save what is an essential part of nature and thus control nature itself. But what we are dealing with is not really at man's command, and that is the life-force, the total which is nature itself. What we really should be saying, and believing, is that we will respect life, all life. That is the essential — the respect that comes from understanding, the respect that leads to a sense of proportion and a proper sense of humility. Man is not a god. He cannot create new rhythms in nature or long disrupt the old, eternal rhythms. Man is a tenant here on sufferance, not the proprietor. He can conserve what he has, he can control his own actions, but the environment does not belong to him. It belongs to the whole of life, and there is little doubt that if he too long or too completely abuses it he will be eliminated from it, or at the very least reduced to a minor element in the whole spectrum of life.

As I was saying, hard frost has brought quiet to the night again. The stridulating insects have lived their lives, left their heritage for another summer, and perished. I live on, a sentient man in a shelter that protects me from the killing frost. I live here only because I have made my compromises with the life around me, with this environment, and I can continue to live here in relative comfort and safety only so long as I continue to make those compromises. I am both wiser and more adaptable than the field cricket or the katydid. Or am I, after all? They have been here at least a hundred times as long as my own kind. In terms of life, they are a success. Perhaps it is too soon to know about man.

Oh, but the crickets and katydids cannot think! They cannot dream and plan as my kind can!

Is that the difference, then? Is the dreaming and planning important if it does not recognize the whole life-scheme? After all, I, too, am a part of that, a part of all the life we know, of the very fundamentals of life. If there are answers, that must be the one that endures, year after year after year.

II. The Assault
on Originality

The bucket of a 50-ton dragline gouges a straight new channel for a once wild and lovely Tennessee creek

JOHN MADSON

A Plague on All Your Rivers

WE GREW UP ON THE BEST PART of the river, where the North Fork of the Skunk, also called the Cha-Ca-Gua, began to break out of the terminal moraine of the last glacial advance into central Iowa.

The little river had a good gradient there, and as prairie streams go, it went pretty good. Down a rather narrow valley, flanked with low ridges of bur oak and pasture, the Skunk sauntered along through groves of ash, elm, and cottonwood — as unhurried and independent as its namesake.

There were a few places, our favorites, where it flowed beside limestone ledges fed from deep springs, or over sheets of bedrock used as wagon fords. It slid past loam cutbanks and clay cliffs where it dug holes almost as deep as the river was wide, under log drifts where big catfish lay, across flats of bright sand with their schools of redhorse suckers, and then ran off down sloping floors of glacial pebbles, ankle-deep and laughing. On the inside of each deep bend was a sandbar — and to country boys, deep water shoaling into sand can mean only one thing. For three months of the year those sandbars were peopled with small boys — naked, raucous, undisciplined, and wonderfully free boys with sun-bleached hair and skins burned dark except where overall straps crossed their shoulders. We had Barebutt Beach #1 at Maxwell's Bend; up near Olsen's Farm was Barebutt Beach

#2. I was always partial to #1, myself. It was near a melon patch.

South of there a few miles, the valley widened as the Skunk entered a much older bed. In times past, that broader valley had been an impassable bog of quicksand and prairie sloughs. Tile drains solved the slough problem, but there were still those June floods when the river came swelling up out of its channel and over the floodplain to reclaim its own.

That part of the Skunk was channelized and tamed before I was born, which is getting to be a few years ago, now.

Draglines had cut a long, straight channel and deepened it; spoil was heaped high on the banks for levees. Bends, deep holes, riffles, sandbars, log drifts — all normal river features vanished. The channel was now deep and straight, and high water sped down it like a sluiceway. The river lost its identity as a river, and no longer held interest for man, boy, or fish. I cannot recall anyone ever condemning that barren stretch of river or the process that made it what it was — it simply did not exist for us. No one trapped, fished, or swam there. It was tacitly regarded as the lower limit of the real river, as if the Skunk had suddenly drained into a blankness.

And so we grew up with the images of two rivers in our heads. One was as vivid and real and young as we were. The lower river was a ghost. No, it was less than that, for a ghost would have held some interest for us. It was just a place that had stopped being. A rural gutter, as functional as any other and just as drab.

I can still recall my intense surprise years later, as a budding limnologist, when I learned of an old record of muskellunge in the river before it had been gutterized. Only then did I have an inkling of what had been lost.

o   o   o

By any name — channelization, canalization, or gutterizing — it is a classic engineering method for taming wild streams.

It consists of deepening, straightening, and completely clearing a natural channel to hasten runoff, removing water as quickly as possible to reduce chances of overflow. A natural channel, during peak flows, offers a damming effect. Snags, drifts, shallows, and sharp bends all impede a strong head of water. Slowed by such natural features, the waters rise over the streambanks into the floodplain. Remove all natural stream features, and the high water hurries away.

Rechanneling a natural drainage to hasten runoff is as old as the shovel — and until not long ago, it was almost as limited. With the teams and scrapers of the last century, the most economical drainage ditch was only about five feet deep and seldom more than four feet wide at the bottom. Then, in 1906, the dragline excavator appeared, and it has been in general use ever since. Efficient and economical, there is a dragline for almost any size of ditch — from three feet deep to twenty feet.

Still, for many years channelizing was a piecemeal effort by scattered farmers who clawed away at small stream channels with little real or lasting effect. The real bite began when big federal agencies started to throw dollars and draglines into the act.

Until the mid-1930s, federal assistance in drainage had been largely limited to research and planning by the U.S. Department of Agriculture. The Flood Control Act of 1936 jelled national flood control policy and recognized the importance of managing the watersheds — which is where floods are born — as well as controlling those floods in the main stream channels. The responsibility for protecting watersheds was given to the USDA and its brand-new Soil Conservation Service.

In 1944 the Flood Control Act was amended to involve the

U.S. Army Corps of Engineers in major drainage programs. That was the first time the Corps had been instructed to engage in drainage work for flood control, rather than limiting its flood control effort to levees and dams. At the same time, Congress authorized the USDA to carry out drainage improvement programs in eleven watersheds — flood protection work that included some stream channelization.

It was becoming more apparent that such channel work was a useful part of "land-use adjustment." Stabilizing a watershed is no guarantee against lowland flooding; even when virgin forests and grasslands covered our watersheds, there were severe floods. (Two of the three greatest floods on record at Pittsburgh occurred in 1762 and 1763, and Hernando de Soto may have seen one of the all-time great floods on the Mississippi.) Knowing this, watershed engineers sought to minimize the effects of flood situations by increasing the capacities of natural stream channels. This opened up a whole new vista of public works whose goal was to protect or create agricultural lands on the floodplains. The fact that it wrought terrible destruction on the streams' ecosystems was a point of little importance.

The decade of 1944 to 1954 saw the Corps of Engineers marching boldly into new campaigns against natural streams and bottomland forests, while the Soil Conservation Service watched from the watersheds. At the time, the Corps was in an entirely different flood control league from the SCS. The Corps had immense power and funds; the Soil Conservation Service was a staid conservation agency of excellent reputation but limited political and economic resources.

The SCS had been formed in 1935 in a desperate reaction to the ravages of the Dust Bowl. It was one of the New Deal alphabet agencies that survived, and for good reason: it was a solid, land-wise conservation body that did a job that had long wanted doing. One of its mandates was to "hold the raindrop where it falls" (or thereabouts) through careful watershed management that included contour farming, grassed waterways, farm ponds, crop rotation, and erosion control plantings. All were essential, but all shared the basic drawback of most fine conservation programs: they just weren't good show biz. As the American landowner's official conscience, the SCS was woefully lacking in political clout and juicy appropriations. It was in a rut, with narrow political horizons. And then, in the mid-1950s, the horizons broadened.

The Watershed Protection and Flood Prevention Act of 1954 put the SCS in the same pork barrel league as the Army Engineers. This act, known as Public Law 566, authorized the USDA to help local groups plan and carry out programs of flood control and drainage. To prevent duplication of effort with the Corps — which was busy building larger dams and digging larger stream channels — the SCS flood control projects were limited to watersheds not exceeding 250,000 acres, and to reservoirs storing not more than 25,000 acre-feet of water.

Many of us resource biologists were enthusiastic about P.L. 566. The new act promised to greatly modify many project watersheds in favor of fish and wildlife. But P.L. 566 had a hidden thorn: the cost of such flood control practices as stream channelization may be paid by Uncle Sam in full, but only half of any game and fish habitat enhancement is paid with federal funds. Landowners go for the biggest possible slice of federal subsidy (especially if it results in more tillable land) and ignore those parts of a multiple-use plan for which they must pay half. The promising new law made fish and wildlife destruction far more attractive than fish and wildlife conservation.

Technically, any damage done to fish and wildlife in the course of drainage or channelization is supposed to be mitigated by the agency responsible. That doesn't mean much. An agency may agree to mitigation, but mitigation funds require separate appropriations that may never be made. During its years of resource rapine in eastern Arkansas, for example, the Corps of Engineers has rarely paid for any of the deadly damage it has done to fish and wildlife habitat. Even when mitigation is made, it is a salvage effort that may have little real value.

So, armed with P.L. 566, the Soil Conservation Service began to gird for action. Through the Eisenhower years of the 1950s, with relatively tight reins on federal spending, the SCS did its homework and made plans. But beginning with President Kennedy and Secretary of Agriculture Orville Freeman, federal purse strings loosened and the draglines roared into action on the watersheds.

The SCS may protest at this point, reminding us that flood control and drainage projects are initiated by local people and that the SCS enters the picture only after due supplication by honest grangers.

But according to Peter Harnick of *Environmental Action:*

"Although there's plenty of chance to put on political or financial pressure at the congressional level, the real boondoggle of stream channelization takes place at the earlier stages, at the local level. There, according to the SCS, 'local landowners get together, decide that they need the protection of channelization, and in the best tradition of local level decision-making, form a conservation district and request federal assistance for their project.'

"In actual fact, the landowners are generally coaxed into the endeavor every step of the way by the National Association of Conservation Districts, a lobby group, and its backers, the local construction and development companies.

"For each successful effort, the local district rises in stature, the construction company gets a contract, and the developers get a chance to build on formerly marshy, useless land. The farmers rarely fight the proceedings since they incur relatively few costs and stand to pick up more acreage of cultivated land. The only losers are those without a voice — the taxpayers and wildlife and streams."

In all this, certain checks and balances are supposed to operate. First, any stream channelization project must be supported by a favorable cost-benefit ratio in which gains substantially exceed losses. It isn't hard to conjure up such a ratio, and the Corps and the SCS have grown adept at fiscal sleight of hand. It is especially easy in situations where the major losses are in terms of fish, wildlife, and scenery — whose total values are extremely difficult to measure — while the benefits are stated as full market values of crops grown on drained floodplains. The fact that fish and wildlife are dwindling commodities of increasing worth, while the crops are likely to be surplus commodities, seems to make little difference.

Second, an environmental impact statement for each channelization project must be filed in compliance with the National Environmental Policy Act. This requirement is even easier for the channelizers to handle: they may simply ignore it. The SCS contends the act does not apply to projects approved before 1969, and may refuse to file impact statements on such projects even though they are just now beginning. As a substitute for environmental impact statements on such older projects, the SCS has whipped up its own balm for growing public irritation — a 1971 document known as Watershed Memorandum 108. Under this memo, which was written by the SCS to itself, the field staff was charged to review every channelization plan and put it into one of three categories: group 1 for minor environmental impact, group 2 for adverse environmental impact, and group 3 for seriously adverse impact.

Memo 108 did not have the full soothing effect that was hoped for, and an April 6, 1972, memo from SCS Administrator Kenneth Grant directed environmental impact statements to be prepared for all channelization projects that would use fiscal year 1973 funds, as well as any projects judged by a reviewing agency to have adverse environmental impact.

Although the public would have little chance to comment on Memo 108 reviews, the SCS had assured the federal Bureau of Sport Fisheries and Wildlife that it would see those reviews and that the bureau's comments would be sought. But the federal fish and wildlife people say this has seldom happened. Many such reviews are simply sent to Washington without first being submitted for comment to the Bureau of Sport Fisheries and Wildlife.

Early this year the bureau wrote a hot report, charging that the SCS has classed 4000 miles of impending stream channelization in group 1, of "minor environmental impact," but that the bureau had rated those works as destructive. Furthermore, the SCS had not consulted the bureau on half of the 83 environmental impact statements that the SCS has filed with the Council of Environmental Quality — the White House environmental advisory body. Nathaniel Reed, Assistant Secretary of the Interior for Fish and Wildlife and Parks, drew a bead on both the SCS and CEQ: "The bureau believes that 45 of the environmental statements filed should have been rejected by the Council of Environmental Quality as not being in compliance with the law or with CEQ guidelines."

The CEQ and SCS quickly acted to pull the teeth from the bureau report, "requesting" the bureau to delete the list of projects with which it found fault. Former Secretary of the Interior Stewart Udall suggests this is a White House effort to keep in the good graces of wealthy farmers who benefit from drainage, and certain southern Congressmen.

This has not been lost on other members of the Congress. Last summer Representative Henry Reuss of Wisconsin held a Congressional hearing on channelization — and the 2788 pages of testimony and exhibits add up to a damning indictment of stream channelization by the foremost conservationists in the nation. Reuss's proposed amendment to the USDA appropriations bill, setting a year's moratorium on channelization while a more thorough environmental review could be made, was at odds with the Nixon Administration's support of the SCS — and the amendment was beaten 278 to 129.

It is the golden age of the dragline. To date, over 8000 miles of living streambeds in more than 40 states have been gutterized; 13,000 miles more have been scheduled for "improvement." Planning beyond that, SCS leaders estimate that 175,000 miles of streams — 5 percent of our national total — need "channel improvement."

So much for the small streams, and "holding the raindrop where it falls." Farther down the watersheds, at the downstream limits of the SCS channels, the Corps of Engineers takes over. So much for the larger streams, too.

A lake is a fine place with much to offer, but there is a certain sadness in it, too, for it is a prisoner that must lie helpless in its basin as the invading land slowly chokes and buries it. From the moment a lake is born, it begins to die. Not so with a river. From the moment a river is born it begins to grow and travel, working and moving on, changing the land and giving it the features that make country worth living in.

I know many wild lakes that are splendid places — no doubt of that. But to me, they aren't a patch on the rivers that feed and drain them. That's where the action is — the life, the movement and changing. I'd infinitely rather fish or canoe in a stream than a lake. Which isn't to say that I don't respect lakes. But while an engineer may build a lake that's a fair imitation of the real thing, I've never known of anyone building a good stream.

There are many kinds of good streams. Any stream is good if it's allowed to keep some of its integrity. It needn't be a snow-fed mountain creek with waterfalls and all. It can be a big, brown river like the Missouri or Mississippi; a mature river, solid and strong, wandering through a broad floodplain that it began carving in its youth eons ago. A grandfather river. I like to go out on the great heavy rivers and set hoop nets and basket traps, snooping around such backwaters as Jug Handle Slough and the Butterfly Chute, poling through green caverns out into vast beds of lotus, heady with fragrance and ablaze with sunlight.

I also like to ride on the little limestone rivers of the Ozarks — rivers that may be almost as old as the Mississippi but which have kept their youth. Bright, laughing streams, moving over their gravel beds and drowned ledges, fed by watercress springs from beneath towering walls. The Mississippi and our other senior rivers are very solemn, and take themselves very seriously. Little limestone rivers are never solemn. They move with soft laughter and subtle music; they dance with your canoe, teasing it and running lightly beside it, cool and sweet, with the caprice and innocence of Indian girls.

Some of the best streams of all are the small farmland rivers. Modest places, rarely spectacular, but lending a measure of freedom and wildness to landscapes that are thoroughly plowed, cowed, and put to cash grain. In many parts of our Midwest, South, and Southeast — rich humid regions that are intensely cultivated — such streams are some of the best escape routes from the soul-bruising press of modern living.

The best of these are bordered with greenbelts of timber that persist because the shoulders of the river valley are too steep to farm, or the floodplain too subject to overflow. It is possible to float for days with walls of forest slipping past on each side, and a sandbar at every bend for your evening camp. The farms just beyond the trees are forgotten, and the highway bridges are quickly left behind. There are purists who demean such experience as only an illusion of real wildness and freedom — but they're wrong. Wildness and freedom, like other types of beauty, are relative qualities. Someday, maybe, you and I will really canoe the Coppermine or Mackenzie and go adventuring into regions "where nameless men by nameless rivers wander." And maybe we won't. Until then, let no one demean our mini-adventures on the rivers of home, for even a mini-adventure assumes remarkable proportions when compared with the sterility of television and air-conditioned suburbs.

Then there are the least of rivers — the little farm creeks that poke along through woodlots and pastures, replete with a few somnolent cows, punkinseed sunfish, feist dogs, and small, noisy farm boys. Sun-dappled creeks with shaded pools under the root masses of great cottonwoods and soft maples, and maybe grapevines to climb and leap from. When such creeks run out into open fields, their inner bends are often shaggy with grasses and coarse weeds where the tractors cannot reach — the only real wildlife cover in some totally cultivated farmscapes. This is where the quail covey will be, and perhaps a deer, and muskrat and coon trails through the grass between cornfield and creek, haunted by mink and red fox. Exciting places to the naturalist, but the river-wreckers are very businesslike about such things. Their draglines feed on the farm creeks and streams, their dredges wait to devour the Mississippi backwaters, and their dams have stilled little limestone rivers.

Not far from my home in western Illinois is a small river called Shoal Creek. In normal flow it probably averages less than 40 feet wide, wandering down its wooded valley between deserts of corn and soybeans. A hard-bottomed, productive little stream, much of it is overhung with soft maples that shade and cool the water, their twisted root wads anchoring the banks. Deep bends alternate with shallow riffles. The adjacent woodlands are some of the best deer range left in the county, and there are long, canopied sloughs that produce countless wood ducks. Last year, fisheries biologists rotenoned a hundred-yard stretch of Shoal Creek that ended in a log drift. The hole under the drift, only 52 inches deep, produced a number of flathead catfish weighing up to 12 pounds, and many channel catfish, crappies, and sunfish. The biologists estimated that this one pocket of Shoal Creek held the equivalent of 700 pounds of catchable fish per river acre — a fantastic standing fishery.

A good place, but not good enough for the Soil Conservation Service and the Army Corps of Engineers. Three years ago the SCS channelized the upper end of Shoal Creek for twenty miles. The Corps wanted to channelize much of the rest, killing the stream on the way to its union with the Kaskaskia, but they were stopped — for the time being.

Thousands of such creeks and rivers have caught the eyes of the SCS and the Corps, and are scheduled for treatment. It is brutal treatment, ruthless and efficient, converting natural streams like Shoal Creek into straight, featureless, high-banked drainage ditches.

I have heard colonels of the Army Engineers speak glibly of the quality recreation provided by their works — of the advantages of damming natural streams and exchanging canoes for speedboats, and smallmouth bass for water-skiing. Kenneth Grant, chief of the Soil Conservation Service, has noted that channel improvement "has very little adverse impact" on recreation within a watershed, and that stream channelization can actually benefit fishing, hunting, boating, and canoeing.

He didn't say how. And the boys up there along the headwaters of Shoal Creek would like to know.

As resource engineering, stream channelization may be doing far more long-range damage than short-term good, and in some cases it isn't even competent civil engineering.

The Blackwater River in western Missouri was channelized sixty years ago, and today presents an interesting picture of an engineering project gone wrong. Geologist John Emerson of Central Missouri State College recently studied the Blackwater and published his gloomy findings in *Science*.

The subject portion of the Blackwater was originally 54 kilometers long, meandering through rolling countryside an hour's drive east of Kansas City. In 1910 a new channel was dredged, shortening the old channel by 50 percent. With the channel only half as long, the stream gradient became twice as steep — and the water really tore out of there.

A host of variables attends the erosive action of water in a streambed, and most of the minus ones were at work in the new channel of the Blackwater. At first the new channel was nine meters wide at the top, one meter wide at the bottom, and 3.8 meters deep — for a cross-sectional channel area of 38 square meters. That didn't last long. With bank cover stripped away, and stream velocity accelerated, severe erosion began. Today the cross-sectional area of the Blackwater ranges as high as 484 square meters — an increase of 1173 percent. The same thing happened in some of the Blackwater's channelized tributaries. Honey Creek's channel has increased from a newly dredged cross-sectional area of 12 square meters to a modern 255 square meters. Higher on the hillsides, there was also an increase of headward erosion of gullies that led to the tributaries.

The "improved" channel has eaten bridges as well, undermining their approaches until they crash into the river. Professor Emerson cites a chain bridge built by local farmers in 1930, replacing the original structure that had collapsed. The new bridge was 27 meters long. It was replaced in 1942 and again in 1947. The last version of that bridge was 70 meters long — over twice as long as the original — and it too has collapsed.

On top of all that, the channelized Blackwater is still flooding its valley.

Downstream from the channelized part of the river, limestone formations made further dredging impossible and the river resumes its traditional, unhurried way. The abrupt decrease in cross-sectional area between the channelized stretch and the natural streambed presents a distinct bottleneck — and floodwaters surge up out of the "improved" stream channel. There are long-time residents who can remember no extensive flooding before their sections of the Blackwater were channelized. But since then, in at least one area, two successive generations of fence posts have been buried beneath flood silt.

Finally, the fisheries resource in the channelized part of the Blackwater is only about one-fifth that of the unchannelized portion: 51 kilograms of fish per acre versus 256 kilograms per acre. It could have been worse. In some streams, biologists have found that channelization has reduced fish populations by over 90 percent.

Channelizers often claim they do no permanent damage and that a stream will restore itself to its original condition if it is not maintained, recutting its meanders and reshaping its bottom features if debris is not removed. This has not happened on the Blackwater, whose dredged channel has shown no tendency

to resume meandering although it has had a man's lifetime to
do so. Obviously, any altered stream will eventually regain
natural equilibrium if left to itself. The question is: how long
will it take? And one recurring answer is: not in our lifetime.

The sort of havoc wrought 60 years ago on the Blackwater
has become more universal and efficient. There is great political
and economic impetus to national channelization today, and it
is being executed with modern equipment. We are channelizing
on a broad front, in many types of streams and wetlands.

Within 25 miles of downtown Atlanta is the headwaters of
a little flowage known as the Alcovy River. It is one of the
finest surviving river swamps in the Southeast, a brooding wilderness of tupelo gum that is mirrored in water like polished slate.
Yet this dark, tannin-dyed water is pure and potable, the result
of remarkable filtering action by a virgin hardwood swamp. It
is the haunt of swamp deer, and the big "canecutter" swamp
rabbits that are twice as big as cottontails, and it is the last
good spawning stream for the runs of white bass out of Jackson
Lake. The SCS hopes to channelize the Alcovy — a process that
would inevitably result in swamp drainage and clearing of the
bottomland forests. Fierce resistance from state and local conservation groups stopped the SCS for the time being, and the Alcovy
is officially "in limbo." Maybe the Alcovy River swamps have
been saved — but I wouldn't bet on it.

In western Tennessee, the Obion River meanders through dense
bottomland forests toward the Mississippi. There are places
where the fabled Obion Bottoms are miles wide — alluvial forests
that are frequently flooded and are as forbidding to agriculture
as they are inviting to wildlife. The floodplain of the Obion
included some of the wildest pockets left in western Tennessee —
until the Corps of Engineers came. The Obion River today is
a barren shadow of what it was; much of the river is sterile,

sand-choked ditch, and its broad forests are melting away into soybean fields.

The Corps and the SCS, let it be understood, undertake such projects in the interests of flood control and not to create new croplands. But as the river is straightened and deepened, adjacent landowners can dig lateral canals to lower the water table and drain marshy bottoms. It is then a matter of clear-cutting the bottomland forests and *voilà*! Instant soybeans.

Across the Mississippi, the Corps has fought a long and success-ful campaign against the virgin cypress swamps of the eastern Arkansas flatlands. A few scraps still linger, however, and the Corps has planned a mopping-up action. In the threatened Cache River basin of northeastern Arkansas — considered the only part of eastern Arkansas with any important remaining wildlife habi-tat — it is estimated that a proposed Corps channelization scheme will doom 60 percent of the furbearers in the basin, 75 percent of all small game, and 79 percent of the big game.

Farther south, in the famed Atchafalaya basin of southern Louisiana, a Corps drainage project is cutting the heart out of 1300 square miles of prime fish and wildlife habitat. Larger than the Okefenokee Swamp of Georgia, the 'Chafalaya basin is a southern swamp wilderness surpassed only by the Everglades.

About 70 percent of all stream channelization work is being done in the flat, humid Southeast. However, rivers are even being channelized in the Southwestern desert, where such major streams as the Gila, San Pedro, and Lower Colorado are being dredged, straightened, and stripped of their bank cover.

But one of the deadliest projects has been planned for north-eastern North Dakota.

It is a region of prairie marshes, potholes, and little lakes known officially as the Starkweather Watershed, a rolling, glacier-carved sweep of high prairie that is poorly drained by an outlet system that is not really a stream at all, but shallow coulees and long swales. As a flood relief channel, it's something that the SCS wants to improve.

The Starkweather Project is a boondoggle whose tasteless bungling approaches art — a sort of agricultural Mount Rushmore.

The 246,477-acre Starkweather Watershed still has about 18,400 acres of native wetlands. Adjoining this is the 247,000-acre Edmore Watershed, which holds about 30,000 acres of wetlands. Lying between the Starkweather and Edmore is a 25,000-acre strip of land that forms parts of both watersheds. In its plan, the SCS has blocked out this portion of the two watersheds, since its inclusion would boost both watersheds over the 250,000-acre legal limit of the Small Watershed Act. This strip is known in the Bureau of Sport Fisheries and Wildlife as "the dead area," and it's a well-chosen term. It holds about 5000 acres of fine prairie wetlands that are doomed.

In the SCS environmental impact statement on the Starkweather Project we can find no mention of the Edmore Watershed. Yet when the main Starkweather ditch is completed into Dry Lake, the Edmore Watershed will be hooked up with the Starkweather by a new ditch of its own. This isn't just speculation; the Starkweather outlet has been overdesigned to accommodate the Edmore flow, and landowners in the Edmore Watershed are being assessed for part of the construction of the Starkweather drainage.

The Starkweather, the Edmore, and their "dead area" hold about 50,000 acres of the finest prairie wetlands and waterfowl habitat left in North America. A couple of years ago, one 18,000-acre section produced about 75,000 ducklings. Since current SCS channelization plans threaten as much as 40,000 acres of wetlands in and around the Starkweather, it could add up to an annual loss of hundreds of thousands of waterfowl. Our federal government, our gravely concerned-with-environment federal government, will foot 80 percent of the bill.

It's too bad that the statistics of channelization don't flow onto paper with the life and color of the native wetlands that they represent. But labor as we will at typewriter and offset press, we can never swim a brood of teal ducklings across this page, nor slide a Cajun pirogue through these lines of type with any of the grace that it has on an Atchafalaya bayou. For that, we tender apologies.

A basic flaw in our technology is the fact that engineering usually precedes biology. Alterations of our world are invariably done in terms of engineering feasibility, and the biology of the matter is ignored.

This flaw is exemplified by irresponsible canalization. Such "channel improvement," in the view of the SCS engineer, is a classic exercise in simplification. A natural watercourse is simplified to ruthless efficiency by a precisely engineered ditch executing the swiftest discharge, stripped of all biotic frills.

The ecologic brutality of this is shown by the fact that the biologist holds an exactly opposite view of "channel improvement." In his view, a stream's quality is directly related to the complexity of its channel. A simple, clean, ditchlike streambed is anathema to fish and wildlife, and fisheries managers employ stream improvement structures such as boulder retards, wing deflectors, digger logs, Deibler dams, and other devices to force a stream to run slow, run fast, dig, and aerate. At the same time, riparian vegetation is protected to stabilize the banks and to cool and shade the water.

So the term "stream improvement" to the SCS engineer and the fisheries biologist entails two diametrically opposed principles. It is ironic that biologists play second fiddle in the SCS — an agency mandated to protect our most basic biological resource. Still, there it is. The engineers have carried the day, and the biologists languish.

Recently the National Audubon Society's Charles Callison told a Congressional hearing: "Gradually, the SCS built up its staff of civil engineers, and somewhere along the line — I guess after the enactment of Public Law 566 — the cocky voices of the engineers began to drown out the cautious warnings of the ecologists. Laying out terraces and contour lines for strip cropping seemed penny-ante stuff, hardly worthy monuments to graduates of the nation's leading engineering schools."

Charlie Callison is sort of rough on the SCS engineers, there. But he's got their number.

The engineer is a product of the same technology that he helps produce, and is often locked into a cycle from which he cannot escape. Like some scientists, many engineers reject moral responsibility for their acts, insisting that they be held accountable only for the professional quality of their work.

I have known few engineers who really grasped the land ethic, and they were usually engineers within state game and fish departments. Such men make up the Association of Conservation Engineers — a professional society dedicated to applying good engineering to environmental ends. As a point of interest, no federal engineer may be an active member of that association.

I know something of the engineering mind, having started out in civil engineering. Years ago, I worked for an engineering firm that specialized in airfields. One of our jobs was to lay out a naval air station on some of the best cropland in the Midwest. Farms were bought, families displaced, and by mid-June we had made our establishing shots and were running levels through deserted barnyards and young cropfields.

My survey party was sitting one noon on the front stoop of a vacant farmhouse, eating lunch and looking out over rich fields that would soon be runways and perimeter tracks. Our chief engineer had joined us, and I commented that it was rather a shame to slather all that fine farmland with tarmac. He turned to me slowly, a slight look of distaste on his face, and said:

"Listen, son. You just glue your eye to that transit and to hell with the land. It's the project that counts!"

Moral: one of the gravest problems besetting our nation today may not be the number of certain engineers that are unemployed, but the number that are still at work.

One more thing.

When my bunch got into conservation work over twenty years ago, we had a lot going for us. Not money, nor great expectations. Then, as now, the trained conservationist began and ended in obscurity.

But though we had few prospects for money or acclaim, we knew what we had to do as wildlife biologists, or fisheries men, or soils men. We had professional pride and purpose, and each other, and that was enough.

The "state boys" and "the feds" — how we've scrapped among ourselves! But they were family fights, mostly, and against raids by spoilers and partisan politics we would close ranks. We almost always got whipped — but we got whipped together and were never ashamed of it. Our wounds were all on the front of us.

The Soil Conservation Service field men were part of that. Underpaid, fighting uphill, and browbeaten by their bureaucrats just as we wildlifers were, but pure professionals trying to spread the gospel among cash-grain farmers and stockmen. Maybe they weren't the smartest guys in the world. Maybe none of us was. If we had been, maybe we'd have gone with the smart money, with the engineers. But the veteran SCS field men I've known were working toward something great, plodding doggedly toward a vision shown them by their old boss, Hugh Bennett, something that no one who has not seen a Depression Dust Bowl can really understand.

I do not know who is responsible for this stream channelization adventure. But it is wrecking more than just some good little flowages. It is heaping dishonor upon an honorable service. It is degrading professionals — men with long careers of quiet service, some now nearing retirement in shame and bitterness. I am angry about that, for it has hurt some of my friends as well as my rivers. Thus, the cruelty and waste of a rampant, arrogant bureaucracy, sacrificing the reputations of its career men and the cream of its civil servants to political opportunism and the folly of expansionist policy.

The environmental outcry against the Soil Conservation Service is especially bitter because it smacks of betrayal. One can expect despoliation from the civil works of the Corps of Engineers. The Corps, to any real conservationist, is a legion of rascals. But the SCS? That agency may have been as literal an expression of faith, hope, and charity as one is likely to find in big government. Now the faith and hope are fading with our native streams, and the charity is reserved for a few riparian landowners and contractors.

A misty morning on a woodland lake in the Big Thicket wilderness

EDWIN WAY TEALE

The Big Thicket —
Crossroads of Nature

As OUR LIGHT PLANE swung toward the sun its shadow curved in a great arc across the varied landscape below. It raced over brown bayous and cypress sloughs gray with Spanish moss, over the infinitely diversified greens of the forest, over backcountry roads of pale sand and red clay. In its swift advance, it traced a path across the heart of an area unlike any other in North America, a unique remnant of the original wilderness, the Big Thicket of East Texas.

North of Beaumont and just over the line from Louisiana, the Big Thicket once embraced an area of more than 3 million acres. In a rough triangle, it extended across the basins of three rivers, the Sabine, the Neches, and the Trinity. Even as late as the 1930s, there remained nearly 1 million acres. Today, after generations of exploitation and abuse, it has been reduced to hardly more than 300,000 acres, less than one-tenth its initial size. Yet this shrunken fragment of the great wilderness still contains green solitudes and untamed beauty and regions that are remote and mysterious, filled with contrast and surprise.

For the Big Thicket has well been called "The Biological Crossroads of North America." It is a meeting and mixing place for the fauna and flora of North and South, East and West. It contains, according to a National Park Service report, "elements common to the Florida Everglades, the Okefenokee Swamp, the Appalachians region, the Piedmont forests, and the open woodlands of the coastal plains."

Trees of the North, elm and beech, sugar maple and shagbark hickory, grow here as well as species of the South, cypress and magnolia, sparkleberry and two-wing silverbell. Deep sphagnum bogs, such as are characteristic of far-northern regions, are a feature of the area. Among the Big Thicket's 26 species of ferns are the sensitive fern, the royal fern, the New York fern, the Christmas fern, the ebony spleenwort, the cut-leaved grape fern, the cinnamon fern, and the bracken, all common to New England. Here you find the wood thrush, associated with damp northern forests, and the roadrunner, familiar to the dry desert country of the Southwest. Trillium, grass-of-Parnassus, and Jack-in-the-pulpit bloom where also grow the western tumbleweed and mesquite, the palmetto, yucca, and several species of cactus.

On that spring morning of our aerial reconnaissance — at times flying high with the Thicket outspread below us and horizons far off, at other times slipping down for a nearer view in low-level flight — my wife, Nellie, and I ranged over all the amazing diversity of this land of orchids and will-o'-the-wisps and "wood rooters" — long-snouted hogs whose ancestors escaped into the wilderness generations ago. The first oil well in Texas was sunk in the Big Thicket in the 1860s. Pre–Civil War "dogtrot" cabins are still in use. And in its depths backwoods dwellers continue to embrace the culture of Elizabethan England.

On later days, for the better part of a week, we became acquainted with it on the ground, close-up, following its trails, its dirt roads, its bayous and streams. They carried us through a region of giant trees, champions of their kind. For the Big Thicket and its immediate vicinity contains not only the world's largest American holly and the world's highest cypress, but the world's largest red bay, yaupon, sweetleaf, planertree, black hickory, two-wing silverbell, sparkleberry, and eastern red cedar.

In all probability no other area of similar size in North America has so great a botanical diversity. Here are found four of America's five kinds of carnivorous plants and more than forty kinds of orchids and more than 1000 kinds of fungi. Because many of the plants have reached the limit of their range, they tend to differ from others of their kind growing elsewhere. Such changes are sometimes sufficient to warrant classifying variant plants as new species. Botanists refer to an area of the kind where evolution is meeting the challenge of environment as "a region of critical speciation." As such the Big Thicket is of immense interest to science.

In spite of the great fascination of the area for scientists and nature observers in general, parts of it remain surprisingly un-known. Although it reaches almost to Beaumont and extends to within fifty miles of Houston, it is considered inaccessible and remote. Those who follow the few hardtop roads which traverse it see only commonplace second-growth woodland and keep asking: "Where is the Big Thicket?"

When old-timers speak of the Big Thicket they refer to the heart of this wilderness which is confined largely to the watershed of Pine Island Bayou. This is the traditional Big Thicket, the Big Thicket of ballad and legend. But there is a more modern concept — the ecological Big Thicket. This grew from the work of a survey team sent out in 1936 by the Texas Academy of Sciences. Its conclusion, based largely on indicator species of plants, was that the original area of more than 3 million acres had possessed similar characteristics and similar plant and animal life. The wilderness, however, was never uniform. Different areas exhibit different conditions, elevations, types of soil, and amounts of water. Rather than one unique area, the Big Thicket is an assemblage of unique areas. Variety is the key word in considering the overall character of the region. Its habitats range from open beech woods of the higher land to the dense baygalls, swampy and low-lying.

Diaries dating from the early Spanish missions tell how all the trails skirted around the Big Thicket. Later, pioneers traveling west through the region were turned aside by this "impenetrable wood." Over a span of three centuries the Big Thicket provided a hideout, first for Indians and later for outlaws, runaway slaves, and army deserters. Sam Houston, during the Texas Revolution, planned, if he lost the Battle of San Jacinto, to disappear with his army into this wild sanctuary. In the time of the Civil War, whole families of Southern pacifists, who owned no slaves and refused to fight to preserve slavery, hid in the Big Thicket. Living largely on game and wild honey, they took up stands on remote islands of higher ground deep in the lush and tangled vegetation.

Why is this growth so lush? What accounts for the unusual character of this particular portion of Texas?

Along its northern border runs a range of low hills. To the south of this ridge the Miocene rock slopes down to form a titanic basin filled to a depth of as much as 30,000 feet with rich soil, much of it deep, fine sandy loams deposited in the Pleistocene Period. The water table is high. Rainfall in the region is heavy, about 60 inches a year. The elevation of the land is low, between 100 and 400 feet above sea level. Winds from the Gulf maintain the moderate climate. The result is an area characterized by dense growth and an unusual variety of species.

Among the innumerable wildflowers of the Big Thicket, more than 400 species have been studied while in bloom by the artist and botanist Geraldine Watson, of Silsbee. Although she is only in her forties, Mrs. Watson's memory spans many of the changes that have overtaken the region. As a child, she recalls walking among the spring flowers of the open forests of longleaf pine near Woodville and later going that way and seeing only miles of blackened stumps left in the wake of lumbermen. With this knowledgeable and dedicated conservationist as our guide, we wandered day after day through the Big Thicket in its varied forms.

At times we found ourselves among palmettos that here grow high enough to hide a man on horseback. At other times we were in open woodland or among wet meadows dotted with the slender trumpets and yellow flowers of pitcher plants or in arid stretches where sand verbenas bloomed. Again we edged our way around dense baygalls, areas new to us, where sweet bay and gallberry holly are the dominant trees and where acid bogs are deep with sphagnum moss and cinnamon ferns lift six feet into the air. Most of these swampy, moccasin-haunted baygalls are surrounded by tangled vegetation, dense green walls of intertwining laurel-leaf smilax, poison ivy, and muscadine grape vines. They comprise some of the most impenetrable thickets of the Big Thicket.

One afternoon we followed a moist trail where "cut-ants" in a long procession were carrying bits of yaupon leaves to their nests. The trail ended at the top of an ancient plank stairway that dropped in an almost vertical descent. At the bottom of its fifty-six mossy steps we entered a secluded and magic place beside a forest stream.

Immense cypresses, sweet gums, and water tupelos lifted their tops far above a woodland floor blue with violets. Tree frogs called from among the resurrection ferns massed in the crotches and along the moss-covered limbs above us. This tract by Village Creek — a name derived from a long-ago Indian village on its bank — is one of the few, if not the only remaining fragment of the virgin forest. Often our path was white with the fallen bracts of flowering dogwood and the moist air was filled with a strange, sweet perfume, the fragrance of the tiny flowers of the holly trees. And all along the sunlit winding flow of Village Creek, from bushes and trees bordering its course, came the wild music of nesting songbirds.

For the Big Thicket is a meeting place for birds as well as for plants. The great Mississippi Flyway and the flyway along the Gulf Coast into Mexico intersect in its vicinity. Spring and fall, a host of migrants stream through, joining for a time the more than 300 species of resident birds. The latter include such rarities as the Swainson's warbler and the red-cockaded woodpecker. The ivory-billed woodpecker, given up for extinct by many ornithologists, has been reported here. Among the mammals, in remote portions of the Thicket the black bear and panther have made their last stands in eastern Texas. As late as the 1930s the jaguar and the Mexican ocelot were numbered among the inhabitants of the area. And here occasionally still is sighted the rare red wolf, a mammal close to extinction.

Fifteen hundred feet in the air, when we had flown down the Neches and were nearing Evadale, we had suddenly been enveloped in the sickish sweet stench of a vast pulp-paper mill. To local people this is "the sweet smell of money." This tells much about the attitude of the region. The main sources of employment here are associated with the destruction, rather than the preservation, of the Big Thicket. Most of the remaining acreage is in the possession of lumber companies — particularly such giants as the Kirby Lumber Company, owned almost entirely by the Atcheson, Topeka and Santa Fe Railroad, and the Southwest Timber Company, a division of Eastex, Inc., a subsidiary of Time, Inc. Many of the people of the region have become convinced that their welfare is dependent on maintaining the status quo, that any effort to preserve any substantial portion of the area is a threat to their livelihood and that any movement to halt the destruction of the Big Thicket would affect them adversely through lost jobs and raised taxes.

Let us consider taxes first. In the year before our visit, the timberland of the big corporations was valued at $83.37 per acre in Hardin County, where figures are typical. The tax assessment rate was 20 percent, giving a tax assessment of $16.68 per acre against which to apply a county tax of 42 cents per hundred dollars. At this rate, the total tax loss from removing even 65,000 acres from the tax rolls of the seven counties involved would average less than $7,000 per county. This total, in counties where the budgets run in the millions, is an insignificant amount.

Even the favorable tax situation they had so long enjoyed was not enough to satisfy the timbermen. Before the 1970 elections, a heavily financed TV campaign urged at thirty-minute intervals the adoption of a constitutional amendment. It would have changed the method of taxing so the timber corporations in East Texas would have paid taxes only on the production value of land being used. In a prevalent local method of harvesting, larger trees are cut out at intervals of about twenty years. All the rest of the time, between such harvesting, immense tracts of timber company land could have been tax-free. The blitz campaign failed and the amendment was defeated at the polls.

Ralph Nader, the consumer crusader, recently reported that millions of dollars had been lost to East Texas through special tax treatment for timber interests. As little as one-fifth the amount of taxes that should have been paid, based on market value in comparison to other properties, he pointed out, was being paid by timber companies of the area. Any loss of taxes resulting from setting aside part of the Big Thicket for all the people would be mere peanuts compared to what has been lost and is now being lost through special tax consideration for the large timber owners of the area.

As far as ultimate loss of jobs is concerned, innumerable instances have shown that, on the contrary, preserving the best of the remaining Big Thicket as a nationally protected area would bring to the region an income from tourism far greater than is derived from the present sources. And that income would be spread out to more people. It would provide more diversified forms of employment. The economy of the region would not rise and fall with one or two industries.

Such arguments have been used for years by the Big Thicket Association, whose membership has grown to more than 5000. Ideas are slowly changing in the region and, as Justice William O. Douglas points out in his *Farewell to Texas,* there is hope that with increasing education "a new generation will realize the awful destruction which the lumber companies, the oil companies, the real estate developers, the road builders and the poachers have wreaked on one of the loveliest areas with which God had blessed this nation."

We saw this loveliness from a new angle during the day we drifted down the winding miles of the upper Neches. This wilderness stream, with its chain of gleaming white sandbars that extend out from the inner curve of every loop of its serpentine advance, was to the Indians "The Snow River." You can float with its unpolluted flow for three days and never see a community of any kind. We came to no bridges. The only human being we encountered that day was a backwoodsman out with his horn calling a lost hound.

To reach the river at Timber Slough and launch our twelve-foot, flat-bottomed float boat, we bumped over eleven miles of dirt roads after we left the hard-top. When we pushed out into the current, I sat in the squared-off stern, Nellie sat in the middle, and Geraldine Watson, by paddling on either side of the narrowed, also squared-off bow, guided us around snags and fallen trees. In long arcs we swept around the curves on a current surprisingly strong for a stream so serpentine.

In high green walls, the Big Thicket pressed close on either hand. Often it was so dense our eyes could penetrate no more than a few feet. Vines clambered over the bushes or dangled from the trees — the heavy ropes of the muscadine grapes, the slenderer coils of the pepper vines, and wild wisteria with massed blooms descending in cascades of purple. From time to time, over the river, from wall to wall, the white wings of common egrets and the slaty-blue wings of Louisiana herons passed in steady, silent flight.

We seemed a thousand miles from smoke and noise and pollution. Each curve brought some fresh enjoyment. The most unexpected of them all, and the most ethereally beautiful, was the sudden appearance of a moth of the night, a pale-green luna. Shimmering and luminous in the backlighting of the midday sun, it fluttered above us over the river and into a clump of willows.

Except for the splash of leaping mullet and the plop of turtles dropping into the water from sunning-logs, almost the sum total of the sound we heard came from the spring music of the birds. For miles we were accompanied by the singing of prothonotary warblers. We could see them flitting from willow to willow along the sandbars. Back in the river-bottom forest we could hear the calling of pileated woodpeckers, the singing of parula warblers, tufted titmice, and white-eyed vireos. The Neches, that day, was a river of birdsong.

Sometimes only a foot of water — stained the color of tea by swamp leachings — lay beneath us as we skirted some bar of pure white sand. At other times, the depth increased to forty feet or more when we were carried by the river's flow close to the steep face of the outer bank where the current had scoured deeply. Along the lower reaches of the Neches, which Mrs. Cleve Bachman, of Beaumont, showed us on another day, the sandbars are gone and the wide, dark river, nearing sea level, mirrors the blue and yellow of wild iris and the massed white of spider lilies. But all along the upper stream, each curve brings its shining sandbar, some shaped like gigantic white clamshells, others like scimitars pointing downstream. When we pulled up on one at noon to eat our lunch, tiger beetles, glittering in metallic colors, darted away ahead of us. And as we ate, a large dragonfly in a sudden swoop a dozen feet away snatched a painted lady butterfly from the air. Entomologists have hardly touched the fertile field of the Big Thicket. Everywhere we saw the richness of insect life. In fact, it is the emergence of insects of the evening, clouds of hungry mosquitoes, that reminds a visitor that the Big Thicket is not a paradise unalloyed. However, those who find in this remnant of the wilderness only "mud, moccasins, and mosquitoes" are missing much.

Often that day we had the sensation of drifting on the current in another century. But, as we rounded one wide curve, we were jerked back to the present literally with a bang. In quick succession, like two blasts of dynamite, the sonic boom of high-flying military planes struck us and reverberated over the river. We were back in the twentieth century. It had caught up with us even on this remote wilderness stream.

Toward the end of that day, I remember, we swung to shore from time to time and gathered handfuls of the fruit of the mayhaw hanging on bushes like tiny red apples. Drifting on, we enjoyed their tart, unfamiliar flavor, so prized in that famous dish of the Big Thicket, hot biscuits and mayhaw jelly. When at last we hauled our flat-bottomed boat out at a landing where another dirt road wandered out through the forest, we rested for a time, watching the river flow away downstream. That passing water would follow the windings of the Neches for a full two days more before it reached and passed the first community below us.

Such scenes as these come first to mind when I recall the Big Thicket. But there are also memories of other surroundings, vastly different. We saw them from the air; we visited them on the ground — areas raw and wrecked by man's exploitation and abuse. The pressure of destruction increases yearly. Like spreading sores, bare, sterile patches — some as much as 500 acres in extent — stand out in the green landscape. They record where saltwater, flowing from oil-drilling operations, has killed each stem and leaf and root. We passed through areas pockmarked with water-filled holes where pine stumps had been blasted from the ground for their turpentine. Oil pipelines crisscross the region, each gashing the width of its right-of-way. Land speculators are clearing choice sites to subdivide for small vacation homes. Drainage plans have been advanced that would alter the whole ecology of the region. And always across vast stretches first the ax and then the power saw have laid waste the forest. The Big Thicket, this irreplaceable sanctuary for rare species of plant and animal life, is shrinking in a destruction that, year by year, is speeded up through the newest advances of technology.

Probably the most serious threat the Big Thicket faces has developed in recent decades. This is the wiping out of the forest completely and replacing it with pine plantations. These regimented rows of trees, largely slash pine, grow rapidly and produce greater income for the forest products industry. In the wake of immense machines that trample down, crush, and bury vegetation several feet beneath the ground, only bare, cleared land remains. Here pines, and nothing but pines, are permitted to grow. Herbicides sprayed from tractor rigs kill every hardwood seedling, and more chemicals are used to control weeds and fungi.

The result is very nearly a biological desert. It is an area devoid of trees which provide nesting holes for birds, without underbrush for cover, without the necessary variety of habitat for food supply. In these areas, streams of the forest are turned from shaded, winding watercourses into bare drainage ditches bulldozed up to the bank on either side.

Each such operation, wiping out the growth that has characterized the Big Thicket for thousands of years and substituting artificial conditions maintained by chemical spraying, means that, in such places, the Thicket will disappear forever. A cutover forest, if left to itself, eventually will restore itself. But a forest that is wiped out and replaced with entirely new conditions, conditions that will change even the character of the soil, is a forest lost. In flying over the Big Thicket we saw below us large squares and rectangles of such cleared land. We saw other areas ribbed with the lines of planted trees. I was told that, according to present plans, the forest products industry will transform 35,000 acres each year from diversified forest into such tracts devoted to pines alone.

For decades plans have been advanced to preserve part of the Big Thicket before it is too late. Hopes ran high a few years ago when the Big Thicket Association interested a governor of the state. He flew to East Texas to make an on-the-spot personal inspection. But the hopes evaporated. Nothing happened — a result that might have been predicted from the fact that he arrived for his inspection tour in the private plane of one of the largest of the timber corporations.

When a National Park Service study team first investigated the area in 1938, preservation of a portion of the Big Thicket was highly recommended. Lack of funds and the Second World

War caused the proposal to be shelved. In the postwar building boom, the cutting of the forest was accelerated. During the years 1965 and 1966, the Park Service again made first a "preliminary reconnaissance" and then an intensive study of the area. The conclusion: "The scientific and recreational values of the Big Thicket are so outstanding in quality and importance, and their threatened loss to the nation so grave, that their preservation by the Federal Government for the enjoyment, education, and inspiration of all the people is imperative."

In making its recommendation, this study group suggested that "unique specimen areas," outstanding features of the Big Thicket, might be preserved, and at the same time have the least adverse effect on the economy of the region, by setting aside nine units, ranging in size from 18,180 acres to 50 acres with a total of 35,500 acres. This plan became known as the "String of Pearls" concept. This was an important step forward. Every one of the "specimen areas" well deserves to be preserved. And certainly saving 35,500 acres is better than saving nothing.

But the problem, as it was soon pointed out, would be to keep the pearls from becoming unstrung. No strong connection would combine the separate parts into a larger unit. The portion of the Big Thicket that would be preserved would be fragmented. The protection of nine relatively small, disconnected tracts could easily become an administrative nightmare.

Early in 1967 this recommendation of the study group appeared under the heading: "A Study of Alternatives." Later that same year, the Dallas attorney Edward C. Fritz, of the Texas Committee on Natural Resources, proposed a variant of the "String of Pearls" idea. This was to connect the major units with environmental corridors at least half a mile wide to produce a continuous wheel or double-circle, running up the Neches and curving down to Pine Island Bayou, with another connection the length of

Village Creek. Such a "Green Wheel" would have the administrative advantage of continuity of territory; it would supply a
web of trails more than a hundred miles in length; and it would
provide wildlife with uninterrupted protection. The corridor
concept has been strongly urged by the Sierra Club and has been
backed by more than fifty conservation organizations in Texas.

During several sessions of Congress, former Senator Ralph
Yarborough introduced bills proposing the saving of as much as
100,000 acres of the Big Thicket. Although no action was taken
on these bills, by the time Senator Alan Bible's Parks and
Recreation Subcommittee held hearings in Beaumont last June,
all witnesses agreed the Big Thicket is unique; none opposed
the idea of preservation completely; testimony dealt almost
exclusively with different ideas about the size and character of
the area to be saved.

Even the timber companies have recently assumed a new
stance. Over the years, with lobbying, propaganda, fear campaigns, they have been the most bitter opponents of every effort
to withdraw from cutting any part of the Big Thicket. This former
attitude was exemplified by the reply of one corporation official
to a question about setting aside a relatively small area of his
timberlands. That, he said, was "sort of like asking someone
if they can get by without their little finger." But more recently,
through a change of heart or the recognition of an idea whose
time has come, the organization of the Big Thicket timbermen,
the Texas Forestry Association, has been urging people to "have
a part in preserving the best of the Big Thicket for everyone."

This assuredly is a step in the right direction. However, what
support is solicited for is the minimum proposal, the one least
feasible administratively, the one least likely to be effective, the
35,500-acre "String of Pearls." It seems rather apparent that
this is accentuating the positive to achieve the negative, that

by pushing for the smallest acreage proposed — about the equivalent of the area the forest products corporations plan to destroy with pine plantations each year — it is hoped to undercut efforts to achieve more effective and substantial preservation. The industry's speakers, color films, and a beautifully printed, full-color brochure called "Stewards of the Land," all urge garden clubs and other groups to work for this minimum proposal.

Inasmuch as "Stewards of the Land" is the designation the timbermen of the Big Thicket have chosen for themselves, it is fair to ask: What kinds of stewards have they been? A comparison of words and deeds will indicate the answer.

The initial paragraph of the brochure states: "Much of the forest land is owned by timber producers whose production practices specifically include preservation of unusual plant life and the protection of birds and other forms of animal life." Because of this, it continues, the forests of East Texas contain the orchids, trees, shrubs, and birds now found there. On the contrary, their timbering operations continue to destroy orchids, azaleas, and other native species of flowers and shrubs. They continue to wipe out rare plants by draining acid bogs to improve growing conditions for their pine plantations. They continue to reduce the habitats of many birds. In truth, what remains today of wild nature that characterized the Big Thicket before the first ax fell is there largely in spite of, rather than because of, the practices of the East Texas timbermen.

How concerned have they really been over the preservation of unusual plant life?

Dr. Clarence Cottam, director of the Welder Wildlife Foundation and former assistant director of the U.S. Fish and Wildlife Service, told me of visiting the Big Thicket when magnolias were in bloom. For miles along the land of one timber company all these magnificent trees within sight of the road had been felled and left to rot. This destructive effort appeared to have as its only aim reducing the beauty and attractiveness of the landscape. Justice William O. Douglas reports a similar instance of wanton destruction. Many conservationists in the region are convinced that the timber interests of the Big Thicket have been engaged in a calculated program of making the area less attractive to the public by destroying the beautiful and the unusual, by eliminating what might attract tourists and encourage the establishment of a large federally administered area set aside for the use and enjoyment of all the people.

In Tight-Eye, an area so dense "you can't walk with your eyes open," three Texas counties, Hardin, Polk, and Liberty, meet. From the time of the earliest pioneers, at this meeting place stood an immense magnolia famed as The Witness Tree. For, it is believed, as long as ten centuries, this landmark, the oldest known individual of its species, had put forth its richly glossy leaves. Then in 1966 the leaves were gone. The ancient tree was dead. But it had died in no natural accident. It had been deliberately poisoned. Five holes had been bored into its trunk, filled with arsenate of lead, and stopped up with wooden pegs. Who was responsible for this seemingly senseless act is so far unknown. But it may be significant that the tree stood in one of the areas considered for preservation.

And what of the timber interests' concern for the welfare of birds?

Not long before his death in the spring of 1970, Lance Rosier, the self-taught authority on the Big Thicket and steadfast advocate of its preservation through the years, visited an extensive rookery he had known for decades. It was inhabited by anhingas, herons, roseate spoonbills, and egrets. As part of a national preserve such a rookery would have been a special attraction for many visitors. Rosier found everything changed. Silence had replaced the sound and animation of the past. Except for three birds, all the hundreds of inhabitants of the rookery, young and old, were dead. All around was evidence that heavy aerial spraying had drenched the area with chemicals. The whole colony of nesting birds, easily recognized from the air, had been wiped out in what appeared to Rosier to be a deliberate act by the lumber company that owned the land.

So the past has demonstrated the kind of preservation the forest and its inhabitants can expect from these "Stewards of the Land." For so many decades have the timber interests of the Big Thicket dominated the politics and enjoyed special consideration in the courts and the tax offices of the region that they view with hostility any new departure that might loosen the hold of their entrenched power. They fear even tourism as a competitor. If anything beyond the mere minimum is to be saved in the Big Thicket, the effective change must come from federal action rather than on the local level.

About 55 percent of the area that would be included in the "String of Pearls" is owned by major lumber companies. A large number of smaller companies hold title to the rest. So far, the major companies apparently have observed a self-imposed moratorium on logging in these areas. But some of the smaller companies have continued cutting. The National Park Service reports that in the beautiful Beech Creek Unit, with its superb grove of immense beech trees, nearly one-tenth of the tract has been felled since it was listed as a "unique specimen area" especially deserving protection. And in the proposed "environmental corridors" cutting by all companies continues.

Each year there is less of the Big Thicket left for saving. Time is on the side of the lumbermen, the pipeline operators, the oil-well drillers, the land speculators. Every two days there are 100 fewer acres to save. While various proposals are debated, the bulldozer and the power saw continue their work of destruction. Give the despoilers enough time and there will be little of any importance to save. As Dr. Claude A. McLeod, biologist and authority on the region, writes in *The Big Thicket of East Texas:* "Hopes for the preservation of any sizable part of the Big Thicket forest in its pristine naturalness become less tenable yearly." A lumber company executive put it more succinctly. He is reported to have said: "What Big Thicket? In a few years there won't be any Big Thicket!" Whatever delays action, whatever obstructs prompt decision, whatever confuses or divides conservationists, these form the most potent weapons in the hands of the opponents of effective preservation.

In this whole country — Alaska and Hawaii included — there is only one Big Thicket. If it is destroyed, an area unduplicated in America will be lost forever. We can rebuild an Empire State Building or an Eiffel Tower but not a Big Thicket. In the time that is left before all is gone, a time that is steadily decreasing, as much as possible should be preserved of this beautiful, vulnerable, unique, and irreplaceable remnant of the American wilderness.

SIGURD F. OLSON

Wilderness Besieged

GRAND PORTAGE extended from the north shore of Lake Superior around the wild rapids of the Pigeon River. It was the gateway to the fabulous lake region now known as the Quetico-Superior Country extending north and west for about two hundred miles along the Minnesota-Ontario border. That carry was as brutal a stretch of packing as there was on the continent.

Here the boys were separated from the men. To say "I made Grand Portage" was to set a voyageur apart, for he was judged in those early days by the way he took that trail. Two 90-pound packets were the normal load, and anyone who could not take the grueling punishment was not worthy of the name. Some carried even bigger loads across the long trail, such as the great Jean Bonga who carried five packets, 450 pounds all told, a feat talked about with awe at campfires along the three thousand-mile Voyageurs' Highway from Montreal into the far Northwest.

Today modern voyageurs again strain muscles and sinews in this land of the fur trade, and cruise through the same delightful waterways along the international border. They, too, love this country for the beauty of its lakes and rivers, its clean glaciated campsites, plunging rapids, and fascinating vistas. What they see is the old wilderness, but most do not know of the sixty years of effort it has taken to keep it that way, or of the new threat now looming over the Boundary Waters Canoe Area on the United States side of the border.

I first made the famous Grand Portage some thirty years ago, the same nine-mile trail the voyageurs knew, its hills and muskegs, treacherous boulders and windfalls, its deerflies, mosquitoes, and no-see-ums. After the rugged climb from the lakeshore to the top of the great ridge, I looked back at the sparkling expanses of Lake Superior.

Off in the far distance, almost obscured in the morning mist, lay the huge mass of Isle Royale; just outside the bay, Gagnon's Island, and to the left Hat Point, with its gnarled and twisted cedar known as the Witches' Tree, the place where brigades stopped to prepare themselves for the grand entry into Grand Portage Post. It was not hard to imagine a scene of two hundred years before, the gaily decorated Montreal canoes, red-tipped paddles flashing in the sunlight, French chansons drifting across the water, the beach alive with activity in preparation for the landing, a pageant the world would never see again.

That day I thought of the ancient voyageur who said, "I could carry, paddle, walk and sing with any man I ever saw. I have been twenty-four years a canoe man and forty-one years in the service; no portage was ever too long for me. Fifty songs could I sing. I have saved the lives of ten voyageurs, have had twelve wives and six running dogs. I spent all my money in pleasure. Were I young again, I should spend my life the same way over. There is no life so happy as a voyageur's life."

Times have changed in the famous canoe country, but the spirit of exploration and adventure is still there. Despite logging, fires, and three centuries of exploitation, it is surpassingly beautiful, a wilderness where one can hear the calling of the loons and the slap of a beaver's tail at dusk. White-throated sparrows still utter clear plaintive notes and hermit thrushes play their violins until dark. In the morning eagles and ospreys soar and scream over the high ridges. Around the campsites, chickadees and whisky jacks make themselves at home.

At night when the new explorers sit arount their campfires, the spirits of the great ones of the past are with them — Radisson and Groseilliers, who saw it first in 1659, Vérendrye, who passed through in 1731, Alexander Mackenzie on his way to the western seas — and a host of others who left their names on the waterways, Lac la Croix, Deux Rivières, Lac des Mille Lacs, and Maligne. So conscious are they of those days of old, they can almost hear voices across the water, and when firelight flickers along some dark shore, they are sure a brigade has landed for the night.

The effort to preserve this historic area began almost three-quarters of a century ago when Canadians watched with misgiving the illegal killing of moose and other game by hunters and trappers from the American side of the border. Loggers, too, had a way of confusing timber stands, not knowing exactly where the border lay. To stop such piracy, W. A. Preston, a member of Parliament from Rainy Lake, proposed the establishment of a preserve on the Canadian side. Because of his work, Quetico Provincial Park was finally established in April 1909, followed a few weeks later by President Theodore Roosevelt's creation of the Superior National Forest. It was recognized even then that the Quetico-Superior Region, as it then became known, was a geographical and historic unit which should have common administrative protection.

Since that time there has been a constant effort to keep the two adjacent areas along the Minnesota-Ontario border intact, with the wilderness unchanged. The long struggle is a remarkable story of loyalty and dedication by thousands of people of both countries, for this wilderness has always been besieged by those who coveted its fur, timber, minerals, hydro potential, and resort possibilities. The threats have been many, any one of which if successful would have meant complete destruction of the area's wilderness character.

In the early 1920s, when roads were proposed into the heart of what is now the Boundary Waters Canoe Area and federal funds were already appropriated, conservationists and canoemen — with strong support from the U.S. Forest Service — won a five-year fight for the creation of the first Superior Primitive Area.

Before this issue was concluded, however, a proposal was made to create a gigantic hydropower complex along the border with seven high dams which would have impounded some of the lakes as high as eighty feet, flooding river systems, submerging countless islands, campsites, rapids, and beaches, changing the country into a morass of dead snags and stagnant water. An organization then known as the Quetico-Superior Council proposed a long-range plan of land management based on sound policies of balanced use and zoning which would perpetuate all resources, and above all preserve the character of the region on both sides of the border.

For nine long years this organization fought the hydro proposal, until in 1934 the International Joint Commission denied the pending application for power development, and advised both countries that "The boundary waters referred to . . . are of matchless scenic beauty and of inestimable value. The Commission takes the position that nothing should mar the beauty of this last great wilderness."

Before this decision, in 1931, Congress passed the Shipstead-Newton-Nolan Act which protects a large part of the Superior National Forest from logging of shorelines or raising of water levels, followed in 1933 by similar action by the Minnesota Legislature covering state lands within the same area.

President Franklin D. Roosevelt, now aware of the national

A rocky promontory offers an ideal campsite in the
canoe country wilderness of northern Minnesota

interest in the Quetico-Superior region, appointed the first President's Quetico-Superior Committee to work toward a program
of protection, zoning, and proper resource use. The committee
has been reappointed by five different administrations, the most
recent that of President Richard M. Nixon.

Such actions made it appear the canoe country was safe for
all time. But new threats developed after World War II when
airplane pilots discovered the country had hundreds of landing
areas for float planes and was riddled by thousands of acres of
private land ideal for summer homes and fly-in resorts. This

triggered a bonanza in private development which threatened to undo all the good that had been accomplished. Ely, Minnesota, became known as the biggest seaplane base in America, with planes flying in from such major cities as Minneapolis and St. Paul, Chicago and Milwaukee, Cleveland, Detroit, and St. Louis.

So swift was this development and so intense the traffic that the U.S. Forest Service and the President's Quetico-Superior Committee, backed by all major conservation groups, urged the establishment of an airspace reservation over the area. President Truman signed the Executive Order in 1949, the first airspace reservation ever established for the protection of wilderness. There were violations immediately, but the District Court, the Circuit Court of Appeals, and finally the U.S. Supreme Court upheld the order.

After that it was necessary to purchase the private homes and resorts built all over the area, including lands not yet in government ownership. Congress was asked for funds, and the Thye-Blatnik Act of 1948 provided $500,000, later increased by $2 million. The Izaak Walton League, with thousands of citizen contributions, raised a revolving fund of $100,000 to speed the work along, purchasing more than 7000 acres of land, which was transferred to the government. By direct purchase, plus exchanges of lands inside the Boundary Waters Canoe Area for holdings outside, the vast bulk of the land went into federal ownership, with 103,000 acres still held by the state.

In the meantime the original Superior Primitive Area had become the Roadless Areas of the Superior National Forest, and finally the Boundary Waters Canoe Area, occupying over a million acres of land and water with a core of 360,000 in the heart of it set aside as a no-cut area. On the Canadian side and adjacent to the Boundary Waters Canoe Area lies the Quetico of approximately the same size, the two areas making more than two million acres of lake country dedicated to wilderness use. Cooperating with the U.S. Forest Service, the Ontario Department of Lands and Forests established its own airspace reservation, eliminated all private structures, banned mining in all provincial parks, and in administrative procedures maintained its side of the border through a sound program of protection.

But with increasing visitation by canoeists, there has been a rising criticism of motor and snowmobile use on major canoe routes and of the logging which continues on both sides of the border. While shorelines are protected, the feeling is growing that the harvesting of timber with its all-weather logging roads is a violation of the wilderness concept, and that both areas should eventually become the wilderness originally intended. Conservation groups were encouraged by the appointment of a special committee to study the area and their proposals. Chaired by Dr. George Selke, former conservation commissioner of Minnesota and consultant at the time to Secretary of Agriculture Orville Freeman, the committee in 1965 urged enlargement of the no-cut zone in the canoe area, severe limitation of logging, and the setting aside of certain routes for motor and snowmobile use and others for canoes only. As a result, the interior no-cut zone was increased to 568,000 acres, and a portal zone in which logging would be permitted to 494,000 acres, with a total size for the Boundary Waters Canoe Area of 1,063,000 acres. The hope of no logging in the area and the prohibition of all mechanized travel seemed closer than ever before, and the ideal everyone had dreamed of within reach for the first time.

(The Minnesota Public Interest Research Group has recently filed suit against the U.S. Forest Service, requesting a moratorium on all logging within the entire Boundary Waters Canoe Area until a satisfactory environmental impact statement has been made as required by federal law.)

Then in 1969 a new threat crashed into the complacency of all who thought the country was safe. George St. Clair and Thomas Yawkey of New York announced that they intended to prospect for copper-nickel in the very heart of the canoe area — indeed in one of its choicest areas of wilderness, the Gabemichigami country. They declared this could be done legally under an old mining law of 1872 which allowed anyone holding mineral rights, even though they did not own the surface, to enter any area for prospecting and mining.

Stating they had acquired the subsurface mineral rights to some 30,000 acres of land owned by the federal government, they were confident and determined. While the U.S. Forest Service will use every possible legal device to stop this mining group from coming in with heavy equipment, it is handicapped by the cold fact that such an invasion is legal under present laws.

In view of this situation, the Izaak Walton League of America, which had committed itself half a century before to the protection of the lake country, filed suit in the U.S. District Court to enjoin mineral exploration and mining by private interests in the Boundary Waters Canoe Area, maintaining that federal, state, and local laws, Presidential and departmental executive orders, decisions of courts and international government commissions, administrative practices, decrees, and wide public support had indisputedly zoned the canoe area as a wilderness. The Multiple Use Act of 1960 made it plain that economic value alone was not to be the overriding factor in making multiple use judgments in national forests, while the Wilderness Act of 1964 gave official sanction to the public desire that the Boundary Waters Canoe Area be preserved as a wilderness.

On January 5, 1973, in a landmark decision, the U.S. District Court did indeed ban all prospecting and mining within the Boundary Waters Canoe Area. If the ruling is upheld in the appeals that seem almost certain to come, it will be a precedent-setting decision on federal laws governing wilderness areas. For it sets forth the principle that the protection of those areas from commercial development supersedes the mineral claims allegedly held by individuals.

While the current court case will temporarily shelve the threat of immediate prospecting and mining, permanent protection must be sought. It is well to remember that during the last decade several large mining companies have been busy prospecting the Superior National Forest outside the canoe area — International Nickel, Kennecott Copper, Bear Creek Mining, and others. While reports indicate nothing has been found with higher percentages than three-quarters of one percent combined copper-nickel, with new technology in the refinement of low-grade ores there is always a possibility of development.

The President's Quetico-Superior Committee advised President Eisenhower as long ago as in 1953 that "If mineral deposits of major value are found, the public welfare must be the deciding factor in their use and development. If it cannot be demonstrated that their commercial use is of greater value than the wilderness that will be destroyed, such use should be prohibited."

And so after six decades of continual effort by federal and state governments, national conservation organizations, and hundreds of thousands of individuals from coast to coast, this beautiful wilderness of lakes, rivers, and forests, the only area of its kind in the United States, is again threatened by the demands of technology and our affluent society. Today, when environmental problems are on everyone's mind and it is recognized by all that the quality of life in America is deteriorating, it is inconceivable that because of an ancient, outmoded statute, this land we have learned to cherish can be taken from us.

Do we have to sacrifice the Boundary Waters Canoe Area

for minerals when there is no national need? Must we again make the same shortsighted judgments of the past, destroying a wilderness and leaving scars which will take thousands of years to heal? Do all decisions have to be made now?

The real bonanzas in our ravished environment today are not new mineral discoveries, but the existence of such wilderness regions. These belong to us all, reminders of what America was like when we found it long before pollution, desecration, and waste were even thought of. Now, more than ever, we need the assurance, spiritual rejuvenation, and perspective they can give us. They are ours. We must keep them forever.

ARCHIE CARR

Black Water, Green Light

IT WAS THE END OF WINTER when first I went into Four Holes
Swamp. We paddled out among the big trees in a little two-place
kayak and kept going till the outside light faded behind us and
the bare limbs of the cypress trees made a fretted dome against
the sky. Then we stopped paddling, and the little boat slipped
along like a blown leaf across the slow drift of the black
water. When it squeezed to a stop between two cypress knees
we sat there soaking in the feel of the first uncut forest of bald
cypress and tupelo gum I had seen since childhood. The dim
green light, the cool, clean-smelling air, the vaulted spaces
flanked by tapering trunks of big gum trees and cypresses rising
out of clear black water made a magic that is almost lost from
the cypress country.

Down in northern Florida, where I live, you are never far
from cypress swamp, but it is all either cutover bald cypress,
or pole-sized pond cypress in lens-shaped stands in pine flatwoods.
There has been some regeneration in the bald cypress stands
that remain undrained, but none gives you the old sense of being
inside a majestic edifice, with tapered columns rising from floors
of liquid obsidian and holding up translucent domes.

Farley Smith was showing my wife and me the swamp. Farley
was environmental editor of the Charleston *News and Courier*.

Lord knows how many visitors he has taken into Four Holes since the campaign to save the place began. Driving out from Charleston he had talked hard about the wonders of the swamp, but once we got inside it he eased away in his sliver of a kayak and lost himself down a twist of the channel, leaving us to savor the tranquillity of the place. So we sat quietly and did that, for a long time only floated there on the black-glass water in the primal serenity of the world's last fragment of an enchanted kind of landscape. The water crept past too slowly to lap a whisper from the pliant skin of the boat, and the only sure sign of current was a chartreuse crescent of pollen rimmed by a drifted row of bright red smilax berries that stood out from the upstream side of a moss-covered log.

It was too early in the year for treefrogs to trill or for big bullfrogs to talk, and a misting rain had quieted most of the between-season birds. I heard a few prothonotary warblers and a lot of the little sizzling ditties that blue-gray gnatcatchers sing. There were other desultory warbler airs I didn't know, and out through the swamp a barred owl rendered a single eight-note stanza and then fell silent, as if recalling that owls don't sing by day. For a while there were only those few sounds to abridge the silence of the place.

Then, suddenly, the hunting-horn cry of a pileated woodpecker exploded in the swamp, and the ranting staccato went echoing down the water lanes in a way that took me back through time to south Georgia, to days when tupelo–cypress forest stood in the Ogeechee bottomland there. It was not the great-god's song itself that took me back, but the bounding echoes of it in the aisles and rooms of the forest, conjuring back late afternoons when black Ogeechee boatmen paddled cypress dugouts up the river from downstream farm plots or fishing places. As they moved along upstream a bend or more apart, they used to call to one another in fantastic yodeling melodies, artfully devised to careen about in the echo-breeding spaces of the swamp. It was strange, lovely Afro-Geechee song talk, and it kept a long file of separate travelers in social contact through their twilight journey; and for me, on evenings when squirrels were shy and red-breasted bream were slow to bite, there was always that enchanted yodeling to hear. While the call of the Four Holes great-god was nothing like those boat songs, it set the forest ringing with echoes I had thought were gone forever.

The barely saved relic of a forest that now is the Four Holes Swamp sanctuary is located in the South Carolina coastal plain 35 miles northwest of Charleston, between the towns of Harley-ville and Holly Hill. It is the only uncut remnant of a long sinuous swamp–stream system that arises in Orangeburg County near the Congaree River Valley, winds through the Low Country for 65 miles, and joins the Edisto River a few miles northwest of Summerville.

The origin of the name Four Holes Swamp seems to be lost in time. No one is sure whether it applies to four springs or deep places somewhere along its course, or perhaps instead to four holes *through* the swamp, four passes by which a traveler could cross it on foot, on a horse, or in a wagon. The name recurs in accounts of pre-Revolutionary Indian troubles, and the area was important terrain in the Revolutionary campaigns against the British in the Low Country. In 1844 a band of Natchez Indians that had settled in Four Holes was offered Pollowanny Island, near Port Royal, as a new reservation. In much of the early writing the name appears in the plural: Four Holes Swamp; on later maps the singular, Four Hole Swamp, is used.

On a contour map the swamp has a puzzling look — to a person like me, at least, who had only elementary geology in school. It is contained in a broad trough bounded by scarplike bluffs that look as if they should be confining some fast-moving stream that is cutting its way through high country, instead of a raveled-out complex of interconnected channels and quiet lagoons. Another curious feature of the system is a sudden right angle in its lower reaches, where instead of continuing its southeastward course to the sea it turns southwestward and runs parallel with the coastline, joining the Edisto just northwest of Givhans Ferry. After puzzling over this for a while I decided that Four Holes had undergone two classic geologic processes: block faulting and stream piracy. Actually, it had undergone neither. I was set right by Dr. Donald J. Colquhoun, professor of geology at the University of South Carolina, who told me that the swamp probably got its scarplike borders at a time when the seas were higher and the valley was an estuarine arm of the pre-Pleistocene Atlantic, which sculptured the bluff-shored look with its tidal flow and wave action. The hard-right turn is not a sign of stream piracy, he said, but the work of currents that built an offshore bar, which deflected the lower reach of the old Four Holes river into its present southwesterly course.

Besides its diffusely continuous flow from upstream sources, the swamp — which nobody calls a river because it has no identifiable mother channel — is fed by myriad springs along its course. Within the sanctuary the flow condenses in two fairly well-defined streams. These are interconnected by some 40 miles of waterways.

The land in the sanctuary purchase comprises 3415 acres. There are 1783 acres in the virgin tract, which forms a rough triangle, about four and a half miles long and from a half mile to a mile and a half wide. The sanctuary is bounded on two sides by high bluffs and elsewhere by cutover swamp. The most recent timbering occurred in 1969, but cutting began long before that, and the purchase includes regenerating areas of various ages.

Some of the cutover blocks seem to have been mainly hardwoods to start with, and these are now almost pure stands of big black gums and tupelos. A broad spectrum of successional stages and variants is thus represented in the tract. But the unique treasure at Four Holes is the undisturbed forest in which ancient bald cypress trees as tall as ten-story buildings spread a canopy over a high understory of big gum trees.

One reason why old cypress has been almost completely lost is simply that the wood is very good — easy to work, durable, and resistant to insects. Though somewhat soft and not very strong, the heartwood lasts practically forever, especially underwater or in mud, where it would probably fossilize before it rotted. The Florida State Museum has a hall full of ancient Indian dugout cypress canoes that were fished up out of Florida lakes and sinkholes. Fortunes have been made salvaging drowned cypress logs fifty years after the timbering operations that lost them; and other fortunes are still down there in the mud. Because of its durability when wet, the wood is in great demand for building tanks, and until lately was widely used to make separators for storage batteries. One of the sad changes in the look of the Southeastern countryside came when they stopped roofing farmhouses with cypress shingles. Around the edges of the uncut Four Holes block of forest you can find the occasional moldering stump of a big old tree cut long ago to be split into shingles.

The 1800 acres of old-growth timber in the Four Holes sanctuary contain the highest-quality, cleanest, straightest cypress still standing anywhere, as well as several million feet of top-quality pine, oak, tupelo, and black gum. At current prices this represents a formidable sum. To save anything so negotiable took vision, work, and power. It is hard enough nowadays just to save plain land, let alone land with a gold mine on it. The power in this case eventually came from a coalition of the Nature Conservancy,

Next page: The black-water swamp called Four Holes

which by charter is dedicated to such preservation, and the National Audubon Society, which already had the Corkscrew Swamp Sanctuary in Florida to its credit and has been leaning increasingly toward landscape preservation as the surest way to save species. These two organizations had worked together before, but never on a project of the stature of the Four Holes Swamp sanctuary.

As with most important feats of landscape preservation, this was accomplished by the efforts of a few energetic and dedicated people. The swamp was part of much larger holdings owned by the Francis Beidler estate of Chicago. The last virgin timber in it was scheduled to be cut when its existence and its looming fate became known to Peter Manigault, president of the Charleston *News and Courier* and a director of the National Audubon Society, and to Farley Smith. These two were soon joined by State Representative Julian Sidi Limehouse III, and by H. Exo Hilton, who lives near the swamp, had hunting rights in it, and brought to the campaign a great store of information on the area. Other members of the original team included Mrs. Dielle Fleischmann of Washington, D.C., also a National Audubon Society director, a strong proponent of wilderness preservation, and a special champion of swamplands; and William P. Baldwin of Summerville, South Carolina, an alumnus of the U.S. Fish and Wildlife Service who is now a private consultant in the joint management of timber and wildlife.

Robert F. Knoth of Charleston, consulting forester and South Carolina representative for the Beidler estate, provided highly professional maps and timber-cruise data, a friendly and uncomplicated channel of communications with the owners, and a sympathetic understanding of the philosophies and goals of the prospective purchasers. The Beidler family, although obliged to regard the tract as a market value asset of the estate, facilitated frank and friendly negotiations. Members of a forest products family that dates back to the early days of Midwestern white pine, and later became involved with Southeastern cypress, they have also shown a knowledgeable interest in plans for the use and interpretation of the sanctuary. The Georgia-Pacific Corporation, which had recently acquired several large lumbermills in South Carolina, had already made a bid on the uncut portions of the Beidler tract. When told of Audubon–Nature Conservancy plans, its regional vice-president, H. S. Mersereau of Augusta, Georgia, recognized the value of setting aside a representative remnant of the once extensive cypress resource, and he agreed to hold off as long as there was a chance that the two conservation groups would meet a price satisfactory to the owners.

After an intensive campaign of divulgence and persuasion, and considerable preliminary negotiation, these people were rewarded by the formal coming together of the National Audubon Society and the Nature Conservancy to stand behind the purchase of the swamp. Representative Limehouse had arranged tax exemption for the tract, and on February 17, 1971, he introduced before the state legislature a concurrent resolution "expressing the appreciation of the General Assembly to the National Audubon Society and the Nature Conservancy for preserving this last great stand of virgin cypress which is in South Carolina."

So Four Holes is going to be saved, and that is cause for rejoicing. But mixed in with the joy there is no escaping a little shame at the cliff-hanging character of the action. Why does such saving have to wait till destruction is almost total? Why is it so often left to a handful of people to make the world see that some last fragment of a primeval landscape is about to disappear forever — or if not forever, then for so many centuries of careful tending back that the new folk, corrupted by the heritage of wreckage we are leaving them, may never have heart for the tending?

Part of the problem is ignorance; but another part is greed:

the morbid insistence on assessing all worth as short-term worth in dollars. Or lira, or yen. The definitive long-range value of a Four Holes Swamp could not possibly be reckoned. You can come up with figures that show some of the material worth involved by simply itemizing the demonstrable practical assets and adding up their separate values. You can point out that swamps store water, filter and purify water, and impede the dangerous rush of water; that they are refuges for endangered wildlife; and that they are laboratories for the teaching and research necessary for the advancement of environmental technology. But once you have assigned the corresponding dollar values and added them up you will still hardly have begun to assess the total value of the asset. The total worth of wild landscape is not just the sum of different separate values, because these interact and augment each other in endless ways. And in any case, there remains unitemized the absolutely incalculable practical value of wild, green spaces left intact where mistakes we don't even know we have made can later be corrected. Besides all that, the dwindling hoard of places such as Four Holes Swamp is in another, more intangible but nonetheless vital way a strategic resource. They sustain the nostalgia for unruined nature that has got to be kept alive if we are to keep on struggling against the destruction of the world or the turning of it into a termite mound.

During the Cross-Florida Barge Canal controversy the group of superannuated politicians, land speculators, and compulsive channelizers that set out to sacrifice the Oklawaha River and its bottomland forests for their own commercial and political advantage used to smoke-screen their motivation with strangely phrased invective against anyone who opposed their mischief. They spoke a very peculiar language. "Impractical, visionary people," they called anybody who questioned their scheme to trade a public heritage for quick profit. And, "You can't stand in the way of progress," they would say — by progress meaning, evidently, not so much progress toward the kind of chaos their works are building as simply a more direct movement into reaching distance of the pork barrel. Another favored term of opprobrium of theirs was *preservationist:* "Just a bunch of god-damn preservationists," they would say derisively of any group of people who set out to save unsquandered space for their children's world. There was also the utterly devastating adjective *emotional.* Whenever the canal people got really indignant they would call the river people emotional. Just thinking about that made them very emotional indeed. And then there was the sort of eerie way they used the word *fad.* Repeatedly they would point out: "It's only a fad, anyway, all this concern about the environment — it will all be over in a little while." No translation I have tried for that makes any sense at all.

And so on — they used a lot of words like that, in curious obsolescent ways. It was a sort of old-fashioned, pork-chop dialect they spoke, very quaint and interesting. It is dying out now, and it ought to be saved on tape. But that kind of mentality persists in lingering infections all around the country, and it has seemed to some people only good sense to combat it by working up price sheets for some of the more obvious usefulness of aboriginal nature. Some impressive conversion schemes have recently been devised. One of these, specifically designed for swamps, was calculated by Dr. Charles Wharton and his col-leagues at Georgia State University. What Dr. Wharton set out to show was how much the state of Georgia would lose financially if it should authorize the proposed channelization of the 2300-acre Alcovy River Swamp, thirty miles southeast of Atlanta. Reckon-ing all the kinds of useful yields of the swamp to the people of the Atlanta area — recreation, education, water quality, water quantity, and general harvestable production — he calculated a total annual value of $7,189,103 and a 100-year value of $403,019,333.

If the Alcovy is ultimately saved, Dr. Wharton's price list will no doubt have weighed heavily in the decision to save it. In fact, it may turn out to have been the only thing that would have worked at all. Nevertheless, having to resort to that kind of ammunition to save original landscape is not very different from trying to cope with a chap who has gone into the British Museum with a hammer and aims to bash up the Elgin Marbles by waving a price list at him and saying. "Look here, this Elgin Marble is worth ten thousand dollars, and that one over there would bring at least twice that," and so on. You might stop the man that way, but it would be a very saddening, roundabout way to have to go about it.

One of the subsidiary obstacles to saving swamps is simple-minded prejudice. A principal cause of this is the black water that some swamps have. People who have known wild water only in a mountain trout stream or a Minnesota lake usually recoil when they see the black water of a bayhead or cypress swamp. In a field course in ecology that I teach we go to several such places every year, and each time we stop at our first black-water stream somebody says look how dirty the water is, and instantly gets jumped on by others to whom swamp water is lovely potable stuff in which red-breasted bream, redfin pike, otters, and wood ducks abide.

One way to relieve that particular prejudice is to make the biased person stick his face down into the water and suck up a long drink of it. He won't want to do this, perhaps; and he may not be immediately carried away with the taste of the drink, either, because it is just weak leaf tea, really, without lemon or sugar. But the astounding harmlessness of the draught is bound to be a salutary revelation. Since childhood I have drunk black water whenever I got thirsty in a swamp, providing the place was far from the haunts of man; and while I am no physical paragon, I have no ailments that could possibly be laid to drinking black swamp water.

Nevertheless, one prevalent hang-up that modern city dwellers have in regard to swamps is fear of the diseases they believe you get there. Blackwater fever, for example. A lot of them fear that, and not without cause; because blackwater fever is bad, practically terminal; and because it actually *is* instigated by mosquitoes; and because mosquitoes do, in the public eye, arise almost abiogenetically from swamps. But two rank injustices result from putting those facts together in that way. In the first place, fever-causing mosquitoes are not inhabitants of swamps but of man-made ruins of swamps — of ditches, canals, drained or flooded places, cutover country, and poisoned-out marshes. And as for blackwater fever, it is not, as the name sounds, a fever derived from the black water of virgin swamps, which is pure, clear, and beautiful, but is instead a malady that makes a person urinate black because the hemoglobin of his blood has been let out of the red cells by a lot of little animals introduced into him by mosquitoes that were born, not in black swamp water, but in old tin cans and coconut shells, or in ruined pools where some idiot poisoned off all the killifishes that eat mosquito wigglers.

Anyway, one of the special obstacles to saving swamps is simple-minded prejudice. In fact, next to atavistic greed and the restlessness of the Army Corps of Engineers, silly prejudice has probably done more to lose valuable swampland than anything else. And the sad thing is, I am pretty sure that if you could get a man who habitually deprecates swamps to go out into one — on a spring morning, say, when the place was entirely free of poisonous miasmas — and would comfortably ensconce him in a steady boat and make him safe from snakes and leeches, and then persuade him to sit quietly and listen, look, and meditate, I swear that if he had even bat brains he would go away ashamed that he had feared or hated swamps — or insisted on assessing their worth in dollars.

When Charles Wharton made his calculations of the money value of the Alcovy Swamp, he rated the educational assets of the place at about $1,250,000 a year. This seems very conservative. When you try to think through all the interrelated teaching, learning, and research opportunities that they afford, swamps begin to seem a resource of major, long-range importance. For instance, there is a desperate shortage nowadays of students trained in environmental science and management. Much of their training can be done by means of lectures, laboratories, textbooks, and computers; but eventually you have simply got to get students into the field. Every year it is becoming more difficult to reinforce theoretical discussions of ecologic principles with fieldwork in an undisturbed landscape. In a course in community ecology that I have taught for several years, we spend a good deal of time talking about ecologic succession — the process by which natural communities mature, or regain complex organization, after being destroyed or disturbed. In North Florida nowadays the complete loss of virgin climax forest communities in which a student can see what succession is leading to is a dismal handicap. Four Holes Swamp is not merely the world's only remaining tract of virgin tupelo–cypress swamp — it is one of the very last scraps of aboriginal forest of any kind between Charleston and Miami. So when I took some students up there last spring, over and above their reaction to the beauty of the swamp, they were pushovers for its impact as an intact biological landscape.

Black-water cypress swamps were all lost before it was even learned whether they are successional stages, destined to be replaced in due course by some other community of the region, or are held steady in a subclimax state by the flushing away of detritus and nutrients during floodtime. A pond cypress head or dome in a Florida flatwoods is clearly destined to fill in, with time, and to become a low hammock of bay trees and maples; and after that to change into some even less swamplike forest. But what is the ultimate fate of a bald cypress–tupelo forest such as Four Holes, with moving water around its feet? Will it hold on forever, or will it, too, slowly change?

One of the practical reasons for trying to understand swamp succession is the potential role of swamps in fighting two human ills: floods and water pollution. The importance of river swamps and marshes as both buffers for floods and filters to take up and recycle excess nutrients is now widely recognized. Clearing floodplain forests accelerates flow and increases damage downstream. A river that can spread into a floodplain swamp is more continent and less dangerous to people in its lower reaches, and to the extent that it spreads through bottomland forest is sure to have much of its load of pollution converted into biological growth. For these reasons alone it is good sense to keep swamps, and to learn how to predict what they will do and what will happen inside them under various kinds of use. At Four Holes there is, besides the virgin tract, a surrounding zone of cutover country in various stages of regenerative growth. These cutover tracts not only shield the virgin ecosystem but also furnish a field laboratory in which the natural processes by which disrupted riverine landscape restores itself can be observed.

I am not suggesting that Four Holes be used as an experimental plot. What I am saying is that it is one of the few remaining places in which the natural organization of a virgin black-water

tree swamp can be studied. With every passing year the need
to understand such organization becomes more urgent, if we are
to stem the loss of open green spaces and to husband them in
ways that will keep life feasible and pleasant for generations
to come.

On my visits to Four Holes I have more or less consciously
tallied points of comparison with Corkscrew Swamp, the National
Audubon Society sanctuary down in the Big Cypress, northwest
of the Florida Everglades. Corkscrew is the only virgin tract
of bald cypress left in Florida, and the only continuous stand
of any size from there to Four Holes. When the Audubon Society
established the sanctuary a boardwalk more than a mile long
was built into its interior, and now the place is visited by
thousands of people every year. When the effort to save Four
Holes began, a querulous party used to ask why we needed
another cypress swamp when we already had Corkscrew. It
seemed about like asking why you need a book when you already
have one; but I remembered the question, and it helped motivate
me to compare the more obvious features of the two swamps.
It goes without saying that even if Four Holes and Corkscrew
were identical both would still have to be saved, simply because
one is not enough. Two are not enough, really. These two
priceless fragments of primeval organization, of a kind that once
was widespread but now has been almost completely scraped
away or dried out, would not, for many reasons, be nearly enough
for security and pride. And actually, though both are forests
dominated by bald cypress, they are vastly different places.

The similarities are mainly hydrological. Both are black-water
swamps in limestone country; and neither is a true river-bottom
forest, occupying the floodplain of a stream that runs in a clear-cut
bed. Instead, both stand in clear, coffee-colored water that moves
slowly downhill toward the sea. In Corkscrew the flow is an
almost imperceptible drift across the slightly tilted tip of the

Florida peninsula. The Four Holes water moves a little faster, but not much so, because it keeps constantly braiding out into side channels or spreading in little pools or long lagoons. In those ways the two swamps are alike.

Biologically, however, they are very different. In Four Holes the understory trees — if you can call gum trees that go up seventy-five feet an *understory* — are mainly tupelo and black gum. At Corkscrew they are custard apple, red bay, swamp maple, and pop ash. A conspicuous difference is the profuse drapery of gray moss that hangs from the trees in Corkscrew and is almost wholly lacking in Four Holes. At first I thought this difference might have been caused by the moss disease that recently swept up from Florida and into the Southeast. But it seems more likely that the Four Holes canopy is simply too high and tight to let in the light that Spanish moss must have to flourish.

The Corkscrew Swamp Sanctuary is more open country than Four Holes, with water-lettuce lakes, duckweed pools, patches of saw grass, or pickerelweed and arrowhead marshes. There is a diverse epiphytic flora of bromeliads and orchids there, and many of the trees are laced about with strangler fig. It gets too cold for most of these at Four Holes, where the only conspicuous epiphytes are luxuriant mats of mosses and lichens that clothe the trunks of some of the cypresses. The last time I saw Corkscrew the spider lilies and scarlet mallows were in bloom, while up at Four Holes last May every little pool and lagoon where good light came in was rimmed with golden ragwort flowers.

On my last walk down the Corkscrew boardwalk, vireos, wrens, cardinals, and red-winged blackbirds made most of the music, while Four Holes I recall as a woods full of parula and prothonotary warblers. In both places blue-gray gnatcatchers sing their heads off.

As for snakes, the prevalent Four Holes species is the brown

water snake, *Natrix taxispilota*, while down at Corkscrew you
see mainly green and banded water snakes. In both swamps
skinks and anoles are the abundant lizards, and on fair warm
days, at least, they are perhaps the most conspicuous wild
creatures of any kind. The Corkscrew and Four Holes skinks
are different species of the same genus, *Eumeces*. The anole,
or "chameleon," is nominally the same in both places, but at
Four Holes it seems half again heavier in body weight than down
in Florida. The breeding males that I saw were real old bulls,
much longer and probably twice as heavy as any I had ever
seen in Florida. They set me to wondering why a tropical reptile
should grow so much bigger in the northern edge of its range.
The big frog voice at Four Holes is that of *Rana catesbeiana*,
the common bullfrog, and the brief, whistled trill of *Hyla
versicolor* is the treefrog song you hear. At Corkscrew the
drumming call of the southern bullfrog echoes about the woods,
and the usual treefrog call is the yelp of the green treefrog, *Hyla
cinerea*.

In both swamps, if you go out at night with a strong light
and play the beam about, you shine the eyes of alligators, and
those of big spread-out spiders that live on the trunks of the
trees. At Four Holes there is a noble big crayfish that glows
in a flashlight beam like a chunk of red coral. At Corkscrew
there are crayfish too, but they are small, dun-colored, and meek.

A conspicuous difference in the internal structure of the two
swamps is the conformation of the buttresses and knees of the
bald cypress trees. Both seem higher and more gently tapered
down in Corkscrew. The buttresses of the Four Holes cypresses
are less deeply fluted than those of Big Cypress trees, and the
knees are more blunt and ponderous. I don't know why this
should be. In fact, I don't know for sure what functions buttresses
and knees serve. The obvious duty of a buttress would be to
support a tree on unstable ground, and the knees are said by

some to be respiratory organs. But plant ecologists bicker about this, and look insecure when you ask them direct questions about the matter. In any case, the shape of the knees and buttresses of the bald cypress trees is noticeably different in the Four Holes and Corkscrew swamps.

A peculiarity of Four Holes is the perching of its deer on the panel buttresses of the cypress trees. On our first trip into the swamp my wife and I had paddled only a short way when we began to notice that the sides and upper edges of the thin flying buttresses that jutted out from some of the cypress trunks were unaccountably worn and scratched. When I called ahead to Farley to ask why, he said that foraging deer occasionally use the panels to rest on when they get tired from swimming and sloshing about between patches of blue-stem palm hammock. Even during times of high water deer go out into the depths of the swamp to browse on smilax and other delicacies. At such times the only dry perches within reach of a whitetail are the occasional panel buttresses of the cypress trees. These seem unlikely rest stations for any ungulate short of a klipspringer, but the Four Holes deer must find them a comfort, because every flat-topped prop-panel that we came upon showed signs that deer had draped themselves across it.

The cypress knees and spreading bases of the gums and cypress trees are islands of refuge for various other inhabitants of both swamps. Big glistening green or blue dragonflies perch on the peaks of knees during their aerial contests with fellows over territory. Debris lodged at the bases and in the flutings is used as a nesting medium by turtles: the Florida mud turtle and striped mud turtle at Corkscrew; and at Four Holes, the common musk turtle and common mud turtle. At Corkscrew the sides of the knees are often beaded with patches of pearly-white eggs the size of BB shot. These are left there by apple snails to get them away from stumpknockers and bream. I have seen no apple snail eggs at Four Holes, and this may be why we heard no limpkins there. Limpkins are inveterate snail eaters and in Florida are partial to apple snails. An unexpected inhabitant of Four Holes cypress knees was a summer tanager my son Stephen found nesting in a little chamber made by three knees growing close together. If you scratch about in the moist debris in the grooved knees and bases of the Four Holes trees you often scratch out dusky salamanders. These I have not found at Corkscrew, where the same refuge is more likely to yield an amphiuma or a red-bellied mud snake.

One of the striking points of divergence between the two swamps that my visits have revealed is the abundance and trusting nature of the Four Holes turtles. There are at least half a dozen kinds of turtles in both places — probably more. At Corkscrew the two most often seen are the chicken turtle and red-bellied turtle. At Four Holes the most conspicuous turtles are two species of the genus *Chrysemys*. One is C. *scripta scripta*, the yellow-bellied turtle, and the other is C. *floridana floridana*, the Florida cooter.

To be able to show students live species of any vertebrate animal in an undisturbed natural setting has become so difficult nowadays that finding these two closely related cooters living together in populous harmony at Four Holes was a privilege. To me it was particularly gratifying, because there was a time when I fancied myself a cooter man. Years ago I undertook the job of learning how many different species and subspecies of this particular genus of hard-shelled turtles there were in the world. When sea turtles finally distracted me from the problem there remained a frustrating gap in the zoogeographic picture in South Carolina between the cooter in the Piedmont streams and the related kind in the lower coastal plain. It still troubles me that nobody ever found out what happens when the two

South Carolina turtles meet in the upper coastal plain. I had never seen *floridana* anywhere except very near the coast, and only a few old museum specimens from there. At Four Holes it is all over the place. While finding it there shed no light on the question of whether it and the Piedmont race interbreed when their ranges come together a little farther inland, at least it cut down the gap in the geography of the genus by a small bit.

There was nothing particularly surprising about finding the yellow-bellied turtle at Four Holes, but to see it so closely associated with the Florida cooter was of interest. Along the lagoon shores any half-sunk log was likely to be covered with more or less hat-sized turtles, and these were always about half yellow-bellies and half Florida cooters. The yearlings and hatchlings of both perch about on half-sunk brush-tops and floating pads of spatterdock.

Even more agreeable than finding these two species so numerous was finding the younger ones so tame you could sometimes pick them up with your hand. I spent a while paddling about from one patch of spatterdock to another, trying to make out whether the two species chose different basking sites, and whether they behaved differently before the approach of the boat. What I found was that the Florida cooters usually rested at lower levels, often out at the edge of a leaf, with their bellies in the water; while the yellow-belly yearlings more often climbed onto the humped center of a leaf, or perched high up among the twigs of brush. Both species were more numerous on the lagoon shore and around the more open pools than in deep swamp. Back in the shaded forest, where no spatterdock grew, I found very few turtles, although even there a few yellow-bellies were basking in the scattered sunlit brush-tops, and one was high up in a crown of poison ivy that stood out around the top of a

cypress knee. Most of the young yellow-bellies were very small —
only an inch and a half or so in shell length — while the yearling
cooters were mostly two to four inches in length; and I was
not able to decide what the nesting schedules were that produced
the disparity. But it was, as I said, very pleasant to see turtles
so numerous and serene, yearlings and old mossbacks of two
different kinds, all living together in the quiet of Four Holes
Swamp.

One could go on and on nosing out little differences between
Four Holes and Corkscrew. But the most fundamental difference
is in the light that gets inside them. It is strange to find two
forests so similar in basic composition so different in their internal
illumination. The Four Holes interior is uncluttered, spacious,
and serene to the point of austerity, with the clean-boled cypresses
rising out of sight through a secondary canopy spread by massive,
buttressed gum trees. The Corkscrew cypress forest is open and
light-filled. The understory of ash, maple, and custard apple is
low and ragged, and there is a wildly diverse flora of emergent
and semiaquatic herbaceous plants, such as pickerelweed, arrowhead, fire-flag, and mallows, as well as a welter of kinds of ferns.
The ponderous old cypresses there are mostly truncate and are
set far apart, leaving unused space that the lower-story trees
only partly fill. It is as if once each century a powerful hurricane
had come through this part of the Big Cypress, weeding out
all but the staunchest trees, and knocking the tops out of the
others. At Four Holes the interior is all dim-green, windless,
pillared space, with the feel of a finished landscape, and of one
that might stand unchanged in quiet peace forever.

The Carolina Low Country shares many kinds of animals with
North Florida, and for me one of the private joys of Four Holes
Swamp was finding familiar species looking or acting in ways
that seemed slightly out of character. To my ear, for instance,

the quail in the Indian field beside the swamp had a perfectly
stentorian bobwhite call, so gross I thought one of our party
was out there trying unsuccessfully to sound like a quail. Another
surprise was finding a common musk turtle basking on the apex
of a cypress knee. At home I never saw this species bask at
all. One afternoon in the swamp, schools of small fish kept
knocking out splashes of spray along the edges of the spatterdock
beds. The fish seemed to be schooling there, and their striking
seemed all wrong for freshwater and reminded me of skipjacks
or little mackerel in the sea. I went away wondering what they
were. Later on I heard from Farley that one clear day when
the sun had slanted right he had sneaked up close and found
them to be little gars.

The familiar Four Holes creature that surprised me most was
the brown water snake, *Natrix taxispilota*, a big, very aquatic,
rough-scaled snake that is light brown in color and decorated
with square chocolate blotches. It has a long, deep-sided, lance-
shaped head, and it scares timid people badly. In North Florida
the brown water snake lives mainly along rivers, but for some
reason has in late years grown abundant on the shores of Newnans
Lake, a cypress-bordered lake near Gainesville. The fishermen
complain about this, taking it as another sign of the degradation
of the world; but at the University of Florida the coming of
the brown water snakes gratified a lot of people. They are good
snakes, really. Don Goodman of the University of Florida did
his doctoral research on the physiological ecology of the population out at the lake and learned some engrossing things.

There are other aquatic snakes at Four Holes, of course — I
have seen several banded water snakes, and other kinds are bound
to turn up as the place becomes better known. On a chilly March
day we came upon a lovely big cottonmouth moccasin laid out
in the half-submerged trench of a split log, vainly feeling for

a little warmth through a thin rain. But cottonmouths are scarce there, compared to other places; and so are banded water snakes. The predominant snake is *taxispilota*, and it abounds. On the single day of full sun that I spent in the swamp there was probably more overt serpentine traffic there than I had ever seen anywhere. It would have jolted Don Goodman to witness the activity, because back home he had found that the Newnans Lake snakes are mainly nocturnal. Those at Four Holes, on the other hand — on the day I spoke of — were in a perfect sweat of locomotion all day long. Some were cruising along the lagoon margins or among the bases of the trees; but mostly they were swimming back and forth across Mallard Lake, purposefully and on clearly oriented courses, straight across a hundred yards of clear black water — some going, some coming, and to no discernible end. There was hardly a moment during that day when no gleaming V of serpent wake engraved the surface of the water.

That afternoon I was standing by the boat landing on the lagoon when a thin, rustic man drove up in a pickup truck. He got out and walked down to the boat landing, having obviously come to see whether the rain the night before had filled up his bateau. The boat was a moss-bottomed cypress heirloom of a johnboat, with heavy caulking at the bow held in by two old car license plates. I said hello, and we started talking about the rain the day before; and then I asked about fishing, and the man said it was good in the lake. He was a bream fisherman, he said; and after talking some more I found that he meant not just bluegill bream but redbreasts and stumpknockers too. He went on to say he loved that place, and it was a damn shame it was such a bad place for moccasins. He meant such a *good* place for moccasins, but I understood him, being myself a mixture of cracker and reptile man.

I told him I had seen only one moccasin there, and that one away back in March; but he said that hell, all them snakes swimming around out there back and forth across the lake was moccasins. "There is days they about ruin the place," he said. "Fer wimmin, specially, but fer everybody, really." I said I had caught one of the moccasins to photograph, and it was not the poisonous kind at all; but he went right on talking about how bad it was when a lot of snakes come out like that and keep swimming by your boat, and the sides of it so low and all. On a misguided impulse I picked up my snake bag and took out the snake I had there; and because *taxispilota* is on first acquaintance short-tempered, this one struck and snagged its teeth in the muslin bag; and the man said godalmighty and went right up to his pickup and drove away. I yelled that it was true what I was telling him, that that kind of snake never hurt anybody; but it didn't do any good. He went on away.

I stood there with mixed feelings, sorry I had offended him, but at the same time pondering that water snakes are a two-edged sword in a way, because they both help to save wet country from invasion, by scaring people off to safer sites of outdoor recreation; and give heart to mindless or mercenary men who call swamps useless places, or fetid quagmires rife with venomous snakes and disease-carrying mosquitoes, and so persuade the public to let them dig canals.

But the main point is, those Four Holes brown water snakes were tearing around all over the place in the middle of the day, whereas only the week before I had been reading in Don Goodman's dissertation that brown water snakes fish at night and spend the days basking. And actually, I can't remember seeing them go anywhere by day in Florida, or do anything much except drowse on limbs over the water. A few of the Four Holes snakes were basking, too. My son Chuck caught a big one that was sunning itself in a brush-top. Later on it threw up a big eel, which must have been caught the night before. So at least one Four Holes water snake had done its hunting at night; and this made me wonder whether the heavy traffic during the day might not have been exceptional restlessness generated by the frog-choking rain that had hit the place the night before.

One of the very specialized attractions of Four Holes is the semilegendary *Chologaster*, the rice-field fish. Of the students who went there with me, none had ever seen one of these fish, and I had never seen one alive. We had talked about *Chologaster* in class when we considered the adaptations of cave animals — both the preadaptations that lead them into caves, and the subsequent adaptive changes that come with cave dwelling. When such talk is going on, *Amblyopsis*, the blind, white fish of the Kentucky caverns, is likely to come up, and to lead into speculation about what kind of ancestor it came from. This turns out to have been some little, cylindrical, small-eyed fish, obviously quite like the rice-field fish. The Four Holes *Chologaster* duly revealed the preadaptations — the tiny eyes, and habit of groping about dark and secret places — that qualified its forebears for invading caves and for founding the line of the cave fishes.

I realize that ancestral cave fishes and a lot of snakes doing things that violate generalizations in a doctoral dissertation might not vastly enhance a layman's appreciation of the value of swamps. But then neither should the mouthings of some fat cat drooling to make a pile out of drained-land real estate count much either; nor should the Army Corps's clamoring to keep its machinery at work count for anything at all. It's all where you see the burden of proof to be. To me it rests with people who aim to do the devastating. And if snakes are not admissible evidence of the value of wilderness, then they at least shouldn't count as grounds for wrecking it.

The last time I went into Four Holes Swamp it was springtime, and I went alone in a little one-man kayak. I paddled down to the end of Mallard Lake and took one of the main water trails that lead out into the old-growth block. I pushed along against the slow drift of the current till the sounds of the camp were out of hearing, and the magic of the big wet woods was coming on me. To heighten the feeling, I left the main trail and clawed the boat down a half-open byway that threaded among mossy buttresses of gum and cypress trees. I moved out that way until the enchantment of the place was reinforced by a sense of being a little lost. When the thin bow of the boat wedged between two tupelo trees and stopped, I shipped the double-bladed paddle and sat there for a long time in the soft, cool air and in a kind of light not exactly duplicated anywhere else on Earth.

The swamp seemed an endless array of free-form rooms and corridors under a ceiling of glowing green. I had stopped in one of these serene chambers, beside a gleaming pool flanked by the tapered trunks of massive gum trees. On beyond the near columns, other gums and colossal cypresses were set out in endless other ways around countless other little pools and braiding waterways; and smaller trees, mostly tupelo gum, ash, and water oak, rose for a way and spread their limbs beneath the main ceiling. It was May, and the trees were in full foliage. The sunlight filtering in was submarine green, except where separate beams broke through and splashed on the mossy trunks or shone gold and black on the glossy water.

It was ten in the morning, and many of the swamp animals were out in the patches of sunlight basking back to whatever body temperature they enjoy. In a little arm of the central pool three feet away from the side of my boat, there was a little flood of sun, and a host of small mellow bugs — whirligig beetles

— had gathered there. There were hundreds of them, in a square-yard patch of sunlight, grouped almost shoulder to shoulder in a tranquil host, separated by only the space each needed to keep up a slow, meditative circling. None floated wholly still, but none, on the other hand, skidded and swirled in the frenetic way of their kind. Each seemed content to idle in small arcs with a thousand fellows. Farther out in the open water there were bigger mellow bugs, and these were not basking but raced incontinently about in the usual way of whirling beetles, as if chasing fleet, invisible rabbits. Once in a while one of these big ones would streak through the aggregation of smaller beetles and they would open silently before the wild career, then calmly close again and resume their peaceful gliding.

I idly tried to draw some small moral from this, and found there was none; but it was good to watch the mellow bugs, anyway.

For a long time I just sat there pondering the fantastic tranquillity of the swamp. After a while a gnatcatcher sizzled on a sour-gum limb above the pool, and trying to find him I got sidetracked wondering whether tupelo fruits, or Geechee limes, as they are called in Georgia, got ripe at Four Holes in October and floated in the black water as they did along the Ogeechee River in Octobers long ago. The Ogeechee people made marmalade of them; and here in Four Holes Swamp, back before vitamins were known by name — in the old days when the ivorybills chopped and little parrots streaked shrieking through the trees and turkey gobblers shouted together at the dawn — Marion's men may have kept their teeth tighter in their heads and more ably harassed the British regulars with will-o'-the-wisp forays when gum fruits fell in October. And long before the Swamp Fox fought, the Yamasee squaws — if Yamasee is what they were, over in the town beside the swamp, where cotton now grows among potsherds and flint flakes — must have cruised the swamp in scooped-out cypress logs, and dipped up baskets of Geechee limes for relishes and ades.

Thinking back I recalled the small sour shock it was when, to ease the tedium between the times the float on my redbreast line went down, I fished a lime out of the water and bit down on it. I felt an urge to come back to Four Holes in October and add that taste to the sight of soaring cypress columns and shining black water and the running echoes of the great-god's song. As I mused that way a treefrog trilled, and across the pool on a sunlit twig an anole lizard bobbed and spread his pink throat fan, took a few steps forward along the twig, then stopped and bobbed and spread his fan again. On a limb low over the water trail a black-crowned night heron muttered and settled back on the nest she had left when I passed beneath it. From a near jut of swampside hammock the woodwind song of a thrush came floating out among the trees, and his liquid piping told more of the wonder of the place than any words will tell.

The high-rises of Brooklyn loom in the smoggy background as waterfowl gather in the protection of Jamaica Bay Wildlife Refuge

FRANK GRAHAM, JR.

Sanctuary on the Subway

JAMAICA BAY, the wildlife refuge on the subway, has turned New York City's nature study partly in upon itself. Some years ago I rode the Independent subway there from midtown Manhattan to get my first glimpse of a white pelican in the wild. Today, metropolitan birders, many of their favorite outlying woods and beaches progressively overwhelmed by urban sprawl, are turning to this unique and flourishing sanctuary to add birds to their life lists — and perhaps a little time to their carbon monoxide-smothered lives.

Jamaica Bay Wildlife Refuge endures, under the roar of the jets and in the shadow of skyscrapers and within reach of those who would do it in, as a monument to the man who fashioned it out of the misused bay. Herbert Johnson is that rare man — a public employee who has devoted his life to nurturing public property, overcoming by initiative and persistence the usual obstacles which tend to dampen the enthusiasm of workers low on the administrative ladder. Because it bears Johnson's imprint, Jamaica Bay is like no other refuge in the world.

"He's done an incredible job," says Richard Edes "Rikki" Harrison, New York cartographer and naturalist-conservationist. "When the Parks Department wouldn't give him the money to plant young Japanese pines, Johnson went over to Jacob Riis Park on his day off and collected all the pine cones he could find lying on the ground. Then he took them back to Jamaica Bay and raised his own trees. *That's* initiative."

The results are there to be wondered at. It is a great deal easier to live in New York City (and even to visit there) when one knows that, almost in its heart, nest such species as the snowy egret, Louisiana heron, American bittern, glossy ibis, wood duck, marsh hawk, sora rail, and piping plover. The miracle of the Mets pales to insignificance beside that of Herbert Johnson.

Look at a map of the city. Jamaica Bay is a large body of water, eight miles long and four miles wide, lying between the boroughs of Brooklyn and Queens. The bay is part of the residue of the great glacier which covered the region ten thousand years ago. Streams from the melting glacier made their erratic way to the sea, dropping their burden of sand to build beaches just offshore. These beaches protect the bay and its many small islands from the open ocean.

For thousands of years this region of brackish water, salt marshes, and grassy islands has formed an incubator for marine life. It is estimated that as much as 60 percent of the thriving fisheries of Coney Island and the Rockaways are produced in Jamaica Bay. Fish and shellfish prosper here. Waterfowl, shorebirds, gulls, and terns, and a variety of other species come to feed on the teeming life of the bay. But as New York grew, the bay began to suffer. Man poured his wastes into it and dredged sand from its bottom for his own uses. Jamaica Bay became something of an urban wasteland.

Yet the birds never completely deserted it. Jamaica Bay lies on the Atlantic Flyway, and they were still able to feed on the clams and other organisms considered too tainted for human consumption. An occasional birder poked about among the channels and marshes, uncovering rarities which inured him to the enveloping blight and stench.

The future of Jamaica Bay apparently had been determined after World War I when the city zoned it for industrial and waterfront development. Unrevised maps still carry the bulkhead lines dividing the bay into large basins, in the manner of Newark Bay. City fathers planned eventually to dredge the basins and build, on "made" land, the various warehouses, factories, and processing plants that would turn the bay into something "useful."

"I've been a great critic of Robert Moses because he's destroyed so much of what is good in our parks," Rikki Harrison says, "but you have to give him credit for Jamaica Bay. I always believed the story that Fairfield Osborn was the one who originally suggested, just after World War II, that the city make this a sanctuary and recreational area. But one day I unearthed an old slick pamphlet — true Robert Moses style — dated 1938, which proposed that the bay be set aside for recreation and natural areas."

World War II intervened before any progress was made on the plan. But after the war, Moses invited wildlife management experts, including Clarence Cottam, from the U.S. Fish and Wildlife Service to make suggestions for a refuge in the bay. Cottam and his associates toured the region by boat and plane. They suggested building dikes to form the two freshwater ponds that are the central feature of the present refuge.

"Then there was a tremendous stroke of luck," Harrison says. "Or maybe it was good sense — let's give them credit. The Parks Department picked Herb Johnson to be the superintendent of the new refuge."

One recent day I made the now familiar trip by subway from Manhattan to Jamaica Bay to talk to Herb Johnson. I took the Independent line which passes Aqueduct Race Track ("The Big A") and then sets out on a causeway across the bay to the

Rockaways. There is a stop at Broad Channel in the middle of the bay, where I got off.

Branded a slum by Robert Moses, who would like to bulldoze it into the bay, Broad Channel is a dollhouse community originally built on city land by squatters. Its present inhabitants live behind neat lawns and gardens in small houses that often stand a foot or two above high water, thereby presenting sewage disposal problems, as well as something of a target for the flooding that accompanies hurricane winds. From Broad Channel I walked north on Cross Bay Boulevard to the refuge.

Herb Johnson was waiting for me at the refuge headquarters, a small building just off the boulevard. (Johnson lives with his wife and daughter in a house provided by the Parks Department at the northern end of the refuge.) I could see small flocks of ducks dropping into West Pond. Beyond, looming incongruously in the distance across the bay, was the silhouette of lower Manhattan. A giant airliner, which had just taken off from John F. Kennedy International Airport behind us, strung its stream of pollution in a rising line against the sky.

"I tell the school kids who come out here that those are *gashawks.*" Johnson grinned. "They get a kick out of that."

Johnson himself gets a kick out of escorting the visiting teachers and their classes around the refuge. It is a source of much satisfaction to him that the Board of Education, through its Children's Natural Science Workshop, has taken an increasing interest in Jamaica Bay; most of the teachers connected with the project are graduates of Audubon Camps in Connecticut and Maine. On many days during the school year, Johnson can be seen leading one of these groups on the path around West Pond, pointing out a flock of ducks or a lone grebe in his enthusiastic, heavily New York flavored voice.

Johnson and I walked along the path until we came to a wooden bench from which a sweep of open land led down toward the pond. Ducks were feeding in the shallows at its edge, and a snowy egret could be seen moving purposefully behind a screen of grasses. We sat down to watch.

"There's nothing fancy out here," Johnson said almost apologetically, running his hand over the bench. "We made these benches out of utility poles that cars have knocked down out on the parkways."

Johnson pointed to the tall plumed reeds that grow in profusion around the pond. One sees phragmites, or giant reeds, everywhere on wasteland, crowding out cattails and other marsh plants after the bulldozers and drainage crews have left the scene.

"Phragmites used to grow all the way up here to the path, so that you couldn't even see the pond from here," Johnson said. "Then we began to control them with the mowing machine. I know it doesn't have any food value, but we keep some of it around because it grows very thickly and the ducks like to nest in it. Every plant has some value."

Herb Johnson is not a professional wildlife manager. He is a horticulturist who grew up on Long Island, where his father worked as the superintendent of a large estate. Johnson learned horticulture from his father, then joined what is now New York City's Parks, Recreation, and Cultural Affairs Administration. For a while he worked on routine projects, such as testing grasses to be used on golf courses. ("We were trying to keep something on the tees that the people couldn't chop off.") Then, with what Rikki Harrison has called "that tremendous stroke of luck," the Parks Department assigned Johnson in 1953 to the apparently hopeless task of developing a wildlife refuge at Jamaica Bay which would be attractive to both birds and people.

Johnson, who knew little about birds, threw himself into the study of ornithology. He asked ornithologists what books he should read, and what sort of binoculars and scopes he should buy. Today he has become, in the words of one, "a very reliable observer."

But something even deeper lies behind his creation of the physical refuge. Though he read and asked questions and visited other wildlife refuges around the country, he was simply adding to his own innate gifts.

"It seems to me a little old farm boy could do this job as well as a highly trained biologist," Johnson said. "If he was observant, that is. Many times I've noticed a certain kind of bush, and a certain kind of bird seems to enjoy feeding on its seeds or berries. So I put in a few more of that kind of bush. I figure that the birds like it. But you've got to have a feel for this kind of thing."

No one, of course, is able to tell the history of Jamaica Bay Wildlife Refuge as well as Herb Johnson. As I asked questions, the story unfolded.

"When I arrived here they'd just completed pumping the sand out of the bay to build the dikes and make the two freshwater ponds. East Pond is over on the other side of the boulevard. The dikes are pure sand, so it was hard to get any plants started there. We were afraid we'd get some blowouts, you know, because it's so windy here and that sand is fluffy stuff.

"So we got to work right away planting beach grass to tie the sand down, and that was a big job. There was a lot of beach grass growing in the area. We dug it up and processed it and adapted a cabbage planter to get it in the dikes. Just to give you an idea, if we put all the rows we planted end to end, we'd have a single row from here to Boston. But we got finished and we didn't lose a grain of sand."

"How did you attract all these birds to the ponds?"

"Well, the impoundments filled up with freshwater from the

rain and snow pretty quickly. Then we put in aquatic plants, like widgeon grass, and sago pondweed. The East Pond is a little brackish, and we have muskgrass growing in there. That attracts an awful lot of birds. The scaup — they love it. Now a lot of freshwater plants volunteer too. And in the middle of the winter we put out some corn and seed for the few ducks that are left, and we saw out some of the ice, too, to keep part of the pond open."

"What about the trees and shrubs?"

"Well, in a way that was the most important part, because there've always been water birds around here — even the pollution and the jets don't seem to bother them too much. So I had to make this place attractive to land birds, too. You know, it's the hardest thing in the world trying to achieve a natural effect — trying to make everything look wild, especially when you've been trained as a horticulturist."

"Rikki Harrison told me you had to go and collect your own pine cones."

"Yeah," Johnson said, his face breaking into a broad grin. "You know, we're really limited out here as to what we can plant. It's all sand, and the weather is hot and dry in the summer, and very cold and windy in the winter. So we had to settle on about a dozen different plants. I went and got the Japanese pine cones, because those pines do well over at Jacob Riis Park. We grew them all from seed — started them in a frame here in our nursery, and then planted them when they got to be about a foot high."

"What do the birds like the best?"

"Well, there are a great many things I'd like to plant, but they just wouldn't do well out here. It's a lucky thing we've got that autumn olive. That seems to be able to stand all extremes of the climate, and it provides an awful lot of food. *Tremendous!*"

"Who told you about autumn olive?"

"I'd seen it growing on the parkways, where they'd planted a few. It seemed to be doing so well I thought I'd try it here. It hadn't been used much before that for wildlife. It produces nice big pink berries in the fall, and we've got about forty species of birds that feed on them now. In severe winters, we've seen *muskrats* three and four feet up in those bushes eating the berries."

"I've noticed a lot of wild rose."

"Yeah, that's rugosa rose. We've planted a lot of that, and chokeberry and bayberry. Down at the back of the pond over there we mowed a lot of the phragmites a number of times, and finally we got other plants growing in there, and now people have a wonderful time with the warblers. You know, the robin was a rare bird here until the last few years. Now they nest with us. Grass has volunteered in there, so there's lots of worms for them."

"What else nests out here?"

"We've seen three hundred and four species," Johnson said, "and fifty-five of them have nested with us. It's going up every year. Over there is where the terns and skimmers nest. The egrets — they nest in tremendous numbers. In fact, we have nearly all the herons nesting except the great blue. The glossy ibis has become a nester, too."

"Is there much predation?"

"Well, we have both night herons nesting here, and the black-crowned has become a little bit of a menace. That's our worst predator. They eat a lot of ducklings. Oh, once in a while somebody throws out a cat that we have to trap and turn over to the SPCA. But that darned black-crown is the real menace."

"I remember coming out here some years ago to see the white pelican," I said. "Do you get many strays showing up here?"

Johnson leaned back on the bench and grinned again. "That

pelican got a lot of publicity for us, and people came from all over the area to see him. We've had some other good rarities, too. We had that redwing thrush from northern Europe, and last year we had a spur-winged plover. But that was an escape from the Stamford Nature Center — and then to top off the story, the bird had been born in the Bronx Zoo! So we don't claim much credit for that one."

As we talked, groups of men and women carrying spotting scopes and binoculars (and sometimes small children) strolled past us on their way around the pond. Johnson knew many of them, and he had a greeting for all. They asked him the name of a plant, or what birds happened to be around that morning.

These people were part of the more than 50,000 visitors to the refuge each year. Some arrive by subway, others by car; to accommodate the drivers, the city has enlarged the parking lot near the headquarters building. A permit, obtained by writing to the Parks Department, is required for entry to the refuge. Johnson hopes eventually to get the money to build rest rooms (a deficiency which limits the number of visiting school groups), but he has been able to provide a drinking fountain. He also provides a small notebook near the headquarters building, in which birders can list the species they have seen on any particular day. Though an occasional wag adds an ostrich or a cassowary to the refuge's list of strays, the book is generally helpful to visitors.

"Do vandals come in here?" I asked Johnson.

"Oh, we don't have much trouble, mostly because there isn't much here that anybody wants to break or steal. About the only trouble comes at Christmastime, when people get the idea that the Japanese pines would make good Christmas trees. A year or two ago they chopped down about a dozen of them one night, but then they just left them where they fell. Those trees look good in a clump, but once you take one out and get a good look at it, a Japanese pine doesn't make much of a Christmas tree."

"Nobody comes in to steal a duck or a goose?"

"No." Johnson laughed. "Once in a while there's some poachers out in the bay. Part of the bay is in Nassau County and hunting is allowed in season. Usually by the second day of the season all the birds are over here. So you'll get a poacher coming over in a speedboat to take a fast shot at a duck, but he usually clears out in a hurry.

"I'd say the cars are more of a menace to the ducks than the poachers are. That's mainly in the spring when they're nesting. I don't know why, but when the hen hatches ducklings on one side of the boulevard she feels she's got to take them on the other side. You'll hear brakes screeching out there, and then the little ones can't jump the curb, and there's an awful lot of excitement."

"Does this place puzzle a lot of people?"

"Oh, we get some funny ones. People will drive in here and they just don't understand. They'll say, 'Where are the cages?' "

Herb Johnson and his family, almost alone among eight million New Yorkers, live a life that is attuned to wild things. Having grown up on a large estate, Johnson likes it that way, and his wife accepts their singular life. Their daughter Christine, who is now a student at Manhattan Community College, sometimes grumbles at the isolation from her peers, but she carries into life an experience denied to most city children.

But the roar of the jets overhead constantly reminds Johnson that the refuge is not immune to the pressures of a sick city.

"Somebody always has an eye on this place," he said. "A couple of years ago the sanitation commissioner wanted to fill us in. After all, this is very handy, and it's only a swamp. But they beat him down. Then the U.S. Bureau of Outdoor Recreation came along with a study that the city had invested two hundred thousand dollars in. They wanted to fill in the whole center of the bay, with just a narrow channel all around it, and put in ballfields and merry-go-rounds and restaurants and golf courses. The words wildlife and natural areas weren't even mentioned in the report.

"Now our big worry is the airport, and that's the most serious threat. They want to extend the runways all the way over here to the other side of the boulevard. They'd even reroute the subway. Of course, in a couple of years it would all be obsolete, because they can't even handle all the air traffic now, and once they get the people on the ground they can't get them into the city."

If industry and federal officials have their way, all of Jamaica Bay will be converted into a giant gridwork of runways; noise and pollution will settle over the bay like a blanket. A report issued by the Parks Council in 1968 makes plain the nightmare result:

"The airport extension will also contribute directly to both air and water pollution. Additional landfill in the bay would impede water circulation; additional dredging in the bay bottom would cause excavated depressions soon filled with pollutant materials . . . Taking into consideration the added noise, pollution, and the possible need to eliminate the hazard of bird interference with flight operation [now discounted by airline officials], continued use of the bay by migrating birds may be impossible. This, coupled with the disappearance of other wetlands in the metropolitan area, could affect the Atlantic Flyway — the route taken by migrating birds in this part of the hemisphere — and in turn affect the ecology of the northeast United States."

Any discussion of an American body of water would be

incomplete without a reference to the fiendish schemes plotted by the U.S. Army Corps of Engineers for its demise. Jamaica Bay is no exception. The Corps has concocted a plan to control, at great cost ($59 million), local hurricane damage by erecting a barrier across Rockaway Inlet, closing off all but a small part of the opening to the sea. This plan promises to reduce sharply the flushing action which is the bay's sole method of cleansing itself of the domestic and industrial sewage poured into it every day. The barrier would also alter the bay's temperature and salinity, thus changing its ecology as well.

Beleaguered in prospect as well as in actuality, the refuge nevertheless has its enthusiastic supporters. Because of the Board of Education's new interest, the refuge has a prestigious (if not always powerful) friend in the chaotic court of city government. The Parks Council, another invaluable friend, suggests that Jamaica Bay would be a great enrichment to the natural science curriculum of the New York City school system.

No one in an official position, of course, is likely to proclaim that the bay serves a vital urban function simply because it *is*. But an excellent case may be made for the bay that it also serves by only standing and providing a large open space which does not in itself spew pollutants into the atmosphere. Indeed, over its polluted waters hangs a reservoir of reasonably clean air.

There is, however, widespread recognition of the bay's recreation potential. The U.S. Department of the Interior has recommended the creation of a Gateway National Recreation Area at the mouth of New York Harbor, an area into which Jamaica Bay and its refuge would fit along with other sites proposed as bathing beaches and parkland. "We have got to bring the natural world back to the people," former Secretary of the Interior Walter J. Hickel said, "rather than have them live in an environment where everything is paved over with concrete and loaded with frustration and violence."

Again, money and conflicting pressures are formidable obstacles. Not many people are able to discern the human needs that are satisfied by an area designed primarily for wild birds, rather than wrapped in a straitjacket of jetport runways.

"Not long ago I was leading a class of schoolchildren around West Pond," Herb Johnson said. "I found myself walking next to a young boy, and I asked him how he liked the refuge. He said he enjoyed it — and sure enough he was out here again on his own. That morning, just before he left, his father was kidding him about going all the way out to Jamaica Bay to watch the birds.

"Well, the following weekend he brought his father out here with him. Since then, they've bought binoculars and a Peterson field guide, and they're among the regulars."

Johnson and I returned to the headquarters building, where he had an appointment to meet another class of grammar school children. The children, having made their own checklists and visited the birdhouse at the Bronx Zoo a few days before, had been well-prepared by their teacher for this tour of the refuge.

"There goes a gashawk!" Herb Johnson called, pointing at the sky.

His appreciative audience giggled and then, strung out behind him, set off on a new experience.

Migrating snow geese, bound for the
coastal marshes of Louisiana

GEORGE LAYCOCK

Where the Big River Ends

ONE HAZY WARM DAY in early December my mission led me
westward out of New Orleans toward Louisiana's fabled marsh
country. That flat grassy refuge of muskrats, alligators, snow
geese, and Acadian boatmen stretches across four million acres
of southern Louisiana to touch the blue sky over the Gulf of
Mexico. Here, as in nearly every remaining corner of this broad
land, there are impending changes that might alter for all time
the face of the marsh. The age-old balance between land and
water, salt- and freshwater, wild things and tamed, may be at
stake.

Wandering environmental journalists, unfortunately, can become jaded from overexposure to impending disasters. One can
lose touch with the beautiful, find his senses dulled by the
continuous sacrifice of original landscape to concrete and neon,
big dams, and hungry machines. The threats to the marsh country
of Louisiana, I told myself, are no doubt there. But here was
an opportunity to savor a new part of the continent still rich
in wildlife and lonely vistas. And we would begin with the
National Audubon Society's Rainey Wildlife Sanctuary, the wondrous marshy domain of Lonnie Lege.

Lonnie was waiting beside the dock. We quickly transferred
from car to boat, for he was impatient to be off again, back

into the marsh, and delays along the narrow roads had made
me hours late. Full darkness had descended on the delta country.
"If we wait until morning," Lonnie said, "there's sure to be fog,
and we may not get out to the refuge before noon." We slipped
out of the boat channel into the Intracoastal Waterway that leads
through the heart of the marsh.

Lonnie relaxed as we left the mainland. The open marsh is
his home, a broad flat world, half water, half land. He is
superintendent of Rainey and has tramped, trapped, boated, and
fished in the marsh country since he was a small boy struggling
to keep up with his father, Pierre, who had learned the ways
of the marsh from his father.

A muscular, broad-shouldered man in his early thirties, Lonnie
Lege fits quietly into the marsh ecosystem, as much a part of
the delta scene as the wild creatures. This is one of the easiest
places in the world for a stranger to get lost in, especially in
the blackness of night. But Lonnie maneuvered his boat through
the narrow channels without the aid of head lamps.

For miles the only light on the marsh came from the star-
spangled sky. Minute reflections danced on the black waters
of the canal. Then, in the distance, we picked up the yellow
lights of the refuge headquarters, and after a 45-minute run
Lonnie eased his boat against the dock at Rainey Sanctuary.

Lonnie's two staff people, his younger brother Berton and Lloyd
Choate, helped us dock. "We gave you up," Berton said; "figured
you would be out in the morning." "Be foggy in the morning,"
Lonnie volunteered. Berton and Lloyd agreed.

And all three were correct. When I came out the next morning,
Lonnie was standing by the kitchen window, a cup of thick,
black Cajun coffee in his hand. Dense gray fog blanketed the
marsh, blotting out the whole world beyond the yard. "We have
things we can do around here until it lifts, plenty of them,"

said Lonnie, turning away from the window. From somewhere above us came the voices of a flock of blue geese passing over the refuge buildings.

In this place land and sea are in a restless equilibrium. The mouth of the Mississippi River has moved eastward over the ages, leaving behind vast areas built up by sediment carried in the river. Today the older delta region to the west grows prairie grasses. In the central part of the Louisiana coast lie the subdelta marshes, wetter and lower, stretching off to the horizons. Eastward, around the river's modern mouth, are the delta marshes.

Each region has its own pattern of vegetation, which varies so subtly from the others that only those who know the marshes intimately can detect the differences. All lie close to sea level — varying from two feet below to two feet above. Those who tramp the marshes, or pole along in thin-shelled pirogues through spider webs of narrow twisting channels, find water that varies from salt to sweet that is clean enough to drink.

In some areas mineral soils of solid clay lie near the surface, while in other places soils are 80 percent organic matter — a layer of rich, black materials many feet thick. Long growing seasons, ample water, and fertile soil combine to make the marsh country of southern Louisiana some of the most productive land on the North American continent.

This is also the year-round home for the white-tailed deer, bobcat, muskrat, alligator, and in recent times the nutria, an alien from South America. To this list of resident wildlife, autumn adds a long roster of winter occupants. To this terminus of the Mississippi Flyway come flocks of Canada geese, blue and snow geese, white-fronted geese, ducks in wide variety, rails, herons, coots, gallinules, swans, and smaller birds, too — all taking refuge in the open marshes until spring returns.

Toward noon the sun began to burn away the fog. Patch by

patch the marsh emerged from its ragged grayness, until finally it lay flat and brown beneath the warming sun. Until recently Lonnie and his crew had to make their way around the marsh by boat and on foot. But now they have a marsh buggy designed just for getting around in this soggy country. Lonnie backed the massive, tracked vehicle — supported on two big pontoons — out of its shed, and we rumbled across the yard and tilted down the steep bank of the canal. The machine splashed and growled across the water, then crawled up the opposite bank and headed across the marsh.

We had gone only a short distance when a dark, humpbacked nutria waddled out of our way. This cocker spaniel-sized rodent struggles along on ridiculously short legs with its belly fur dragging in the water, a fact that doesn't seem to worry the nutria at all. For it is as much an aquatic creature as the muskrat, with which it now shares the marshland.

The nutria was imported for its fur. During heavy storms and floods, some of the animals escaped from their pens in Iberia Parish. Later another 50 nutria were brought in purposely to seed the marshes. Today, with muskrat populations far below their former level, the southern fur industry has turned to the nutria. As many as 100,000 nutria inhabit Rainey. "Young born in early spring will have young of their own by fall," Lonnie said, "and after that they bear at least two litters a year."

Some old-timers have no love for these newcomers. "I wish I'd never seen the first one," Lonnie's father told me. Pierre Lege grew up trapping muskrats and recalls the old days nostalgically.

But the muskrat is also a recent occupant of the marsh country. The "rats" moved in because men were interested in the hide of another native, the alligator. In his book *The Muskrat in the Louisiana Coastal Marshes*, Ted O'Neil, chief of the Louisiana Division of Fur, tells of the sequence of events that changed wild communities throughout the wetlands. First, coastal people living off the land shipped alligator hides to northern cities at high prices. Usually they routed alligators from their dens by prodding them with long poles. But the tall, thick-growing grasses were a barrier to travel when a man went from one 'gator hole to the next.

This led alligator hunters, plus others who wanted something amusing to do, to set fire to the marsh grasses during winter months. Dark columns of smoke rose to the Southern skies. Then, on foot or in his pirogue, the marsh traveler could move around with greater freedom. Fire, set by lightning, then by Indians, and later by white settlers, had always been a part of the marsh environment. But now this regular winter burning caused new plant successions. Wiregrass, *Spartina patens*, the dominant climax species, was cleared away, leaving the stage set for the subdominant three-cornered grass, *Scirpus olneyi*, whose seeds, after lying dormant in the mud for years, now sprouted.

Marsh managers like to see *Scirpus* flourish. It is a choice food for the 400,000 blue and snow geese that winter in the Louisiana marshes. But it also furnishes 80 to 90 percent of the food of the muskrat. When large-scale burning began, muskrats were scarce. Now the muskrat population exploded — and created a new industry. Through the 1940s, the fur business provided work for 20,000 people in and around the marshes, brought $15 million into Louisiana, and made the state one of the world's major fur suppliers.

But wildlife populations tend to level off after such a peak, and the muskrats were no exception. Their numbers were cut back by natural population controls, and possibly by heavy trapping and the coming of the oil industry.

The idea of firing the marshes survived, however. During winter months, when there are no nestling birds to be killed, Lonnie and neighboring marsh managers burn the brown grass to keep the marsh attractive to blue and snow geese, which pull up the three-cornered grass to feed on the succulent roots. "Sometimes they come in even before the fields have stopped smoking," Lonnie commented.

This planned firing serves to preserve the now dwindling habitat available for waterfowl — and it pulls them into the sanctuary and away from the pasturelands on nearby farms, where their presence would bring howls of complaint from the cattle ranchers. So fire has become a useful tool. Moreover, the sanctuary staff can burn the grass when and where they want to. If they didn't, lightning would burn it when and where they *didn't* want.

During my visit, Lonnie decided to test a new flamethrower, attached to a tank of propane. We drove to the far side of the marsh, where the wind was right, and with Lloyd and Berton taking turns handling the flamethrower, we rumbled across the marsh — touching a row of flames to the brown grass without stopping. "The old way, on foot, that much work would have taken us a week," Lonnie said.

Overhead small flocks of blue and snow geese passed back and forth, talking as they flew. King rails, clapper rails, and tiny sora rails moved out of the way. Deer bounded across the marsh far ahead of the clattering marsh buggy. Muskrats and nutria took refuge in the water while the flames passed. The fire helps make the refuge produce more wildlife food than it otherwise would. And Lonnie measures his success by the wildlife using the wetlands. "A sanctuary is a mother," he said; "she has her family."

Across southern Louisiana more than 600,000 acres lie within wildlife preserves. There are eight refuges along the Gulf Coast. In addition to Rainey Sanctuary and privately owned Avery Island, there are three state and three federal refuges.

Rainey Wildlife Sanctuary — 26,000 acres of marshland —came under the care of the National Audubon Society in 1924, when Grace Rainey Rogers deeded the property to the society to "use the said land in perpetuity as a sanctuary for wildlife."

State-owned wildlife areas in the marsh country protect 400,000 acres; this includes waterfowl management areas as well as wildlife refuges. The refuges are: Rockefeller (82,000 acres), Ward, or the State Wildlife Refuge (15,000 acres), and Marsh Island (78,000 acres).

National wildlife refuges are Sabine, Lacassine, and Delta, which together encompass more than 220,000 acres of prime wildlife habitat.

One afternoon Lonnie took me by boat along the Rainey canals. There were two things in particular he hoped to show me. First there were the alligators. Despite the midwinter season, the warming sun had brought them out to bask on the black mud-banks, and as our boat eased along the canal, the big reptiles slid into the water from both banks. Sometimes there were a dozen in view at once, and before we had gone a mile, Lonnie had enthusiastically counted half a hundred alligators, and he felt good about this. To Lonnie the 'gators are kings of the swamp, and the deep holes they maintain are dry-weather salvation for numerous creatures, large and small, that must have water to survive. In Louisiana, state biologists had assured me that recent protective legislation had put the alligators on the return trail.

Lonnie also wanted me to see a new impoundment. Low dikes held a layer of shallow water on 400 acres. Weeds and sedges stood in the water, and the surface was thick with widgeon, mallards, pintails, coots, and geese. Occasionally a startled flock of ducks sprang noisily from the water, and the drumming of wings filled the air.

Do such impoundments improve the marsh for wintering

waterfowl? On Ward Refuge, managed by the state of
Louisiana, impoundments increased the wintering flocks of ducks
from 75,000 to more than 400,000.

From the Rainey headquarters, Lonnie pointed across Belle
Isle Lake to a miniature island about 50 feet wide and 200 feet
long. The island has a story. Early in 1966, Lonnie and John
Anderson, director of the National Audubon Society's sanctuary
program, wanted to help out the terns and gulls. "Even though
Louisiana has millions of acres of coastland," Lonnie later wrote
in his report, "very little of it is suitable for gull and tern nesting."
Dredges have torn away the offshore shell mounds on which the
birds once nested, and violent hurricanes have destroyed other
suitable areas.

In two long sessions of dredging that summer and fall, the
refuge staff saw their island grow and eventually rise above the
water. Then they barged in reef shell to carpet the island.

Mottled ducks were the first to claim the island as a rendezvous
place. These ducks, as Lonnie explained, "are very peculiar in
some ways. The hen builds the nests and sets the eggs and rears
the young. The drake seldom sees the nest site. The hen meets
the drake at a certain time and place every day." The island
was used by fifteen nesting pairs of mottled ducks that first
summer.

Soon the gulls came. There were laughing gulls, ring-billed
gulls, and herring gulls, as well as blue geese in winter and a
variety of shorebirds. But the gulls came only to loaf. Then
the following spring, when the island was not yet a year old,
the first colony of least terns settled there, and by June 5 they
had begun nesting. Lonnie's records tell of 75 nests, 152 eggs,
and 144 young.

Rainey is a rich, wet ecosystem lying flat beneath the winter
sun, set aside as a haven for wildlife. But will it remain safe

for long? This may be too much to expect in a region wealthy with oil and productive farmland — a region looking for ways to develop its economy.

One of the long-cherished dreams of Louisiana promoters is a plan for digging a giant shipping canal across the southern marshlands. Other visionaries in nearby states covet the mighty waters of the Mississippi. Their scheme is to take as much as one-third of the flow of the river and divert it to irrigate the dry plains of western Texas and eastern New Mexico and turn them into croplands.

The proposed shipping canal, or Intracoastal Seaway, would be created from a section of the existing Intracoastal Waterway that now makes it possible to move barge traffic across southern Louisiana. The present waterway would be dredged out to make a canal 40 feet deep and 400 feet wide, big enough to float oceangoing ships from distant ports.

The state legislature has created a Louisiana Intracoastal Seaway Commission, and there also is a private organization promoting its construction, the Louisiana Intracoastal Seaway Association. Its backers predict that the new shipping lane would bring $5 billion worth of new industry, more than 200,000 new jobs, and make the region one of the country's busiest, most profitable centers of industry, agriculture, and forestry. They speak, too, of the great social benefits. Giant industrial plants, a great population influx? It all depends on how one defines "social benefits."

Prospects for the seaway brightened in 1967 when the U.S. Army Corps of Engineers entered the picture with a Congressional appropriation of $25,000 for preliminary planning studies. Then in 1969 the Corps received $70,000 to enlarge the scope of its work and make a complete water plan for southern Louisiana.

Meanwhile, in nearby states, other promoters have been pushing their idea of diverting the Mississippi 1000 miles west and
4000 feet uphill. This scheme would enlarge the present 6.3
million acres of irrigated lands in Texas and New Mexico to
11 million acres by the year 2020. But it would require using
as much as one-third of the low-flow volume of the Mississippi
near its mouth.

The U.S. Bureau of Reclamation received an initial appropriation of $200,000 to study this plan in 1966, and the idea also
is a part of the now notorious Texas Water Plan, a giant network
of diversion canals and more than 30 storage reservoirs that would
drastically rearrange the water distribution of the entire state.

While Texas has not been able to make much progress in
implementing the plan — voters so far have not been persuaded
to authorize the initial $3.5 billion in bonds needed to finance
it — Congress has taken some steps. Former Texas Senator Ralph
Yarborough, with a last-minute amendment to a public works
bill, obtained authorization for federal construction of three of
the proposed reservoirs and 5¼ miles of a navigation channel
in the Sabine River Valley of eastern Texas. It remains to be
seen whether the large-scale diversion of the Mississippi will ever
become a real threat.

Either scheme, seaway or diversion, is rich in imponderables
and is bound to have disastrous effects on the biology of the
marshlands. Both are viewed with wariness or outright hostility
by conservationists who understand the relationship of water to
the stability of the marsh ecosystem.

Deepening the canal for a seaway would, of course, alter water
level and flow in the marshes. And some think it could increase
the threat of floods to the lowlands to the north during storms
or hurricanes.

As to the possible diversion of the Mississippi, any move to whisk off a third of the river's water at its low stage could turn the marshlands and deltas into areas that suffer seasonal droughts or saltwater intrusions. This could have drastic effects on the wildlife akin to the problems man has created in the Everglades of South Florida.

Recently two more ideas have been advanced to threaten the marsh country, especially the vitally important Sabine National Wildlife Refuge. One of these is the Soil Conservation Service's Cameron-Creole Project. This drainage scheme would "manage" water on 113,000 acres, including 14,926 acres of estuarine refuge. The plan would alter the free exchange of fresh- and saltwater, which is characteristic of an estuary in its natural state, and essential to marine organisms. Biologists who are studying the project feel that the proposed construction would destroy ecological values on much of the national wildlife refuge.

The other threat arises from a laudatory aim to speed evacuation of citizens from lower Cameron Parish in times of hurricane threat. For this, Louisiana State Representative Conway LeBleu has insisted that a new highway be constructed right through Sabine National Wildlife Refuge. One certain result, aside from placing a new highway close to Representative LeBleu's property, would be extensive ecological damage and loss of wildlife. In view of the unstable nature of the substratum, some observers believe the road might simply sink into the marsh. The alternative advanced by conservation workers has obvious advantages. They suggest enlarging State Highway 27 from two to four lanes, a logical suggestion in view of the fact that this existing north-south road lies only a few miles east of the refuge boundary.

Despite a vow not to worry about impending disasters, I could not help but ponder these various threats as Lonnie's boat took us back to the mainland, or, as Lonnie calls it, "the high country." Above the marsh the sky was cloudy, and against the winter gray moved small flocks of blue and snow geese. The pattern was timeless, and I had the feeling that this marsh country stretching over southern Louisiana had not changed much since the arrival of man. I could only wish it would remain forever unaltered.

WESLEY MARX

Island Wilderness
Up for Grabs

I WAS DRIVING AT NIGHT along California's coast on U.S. 101.
A college student, I was on a spring pilgrimage to the beaches
of Southern California. Around dawn the highway sliced through
a silent Santa Barbara, then along the Pacific shore. I glanced
away from the endless macadam and saw what appeared to be
a mountain range moored at sea. This was my first sight of the
northern Channel Islands.

Since then, I have come much closer — to walk on pebbly
shores and to sleep in the protection of rock-walled harbor coves.
I have seen a procession of natural life I could not hope to see
anywhere else.

At the same time I have seen no fluorescent traffic signs or
plastic begonias or sewage outfalls, and but one "billboard" — a
grounded freighter with "For Sale" painted on its rusting hull.
Yet one look to the east and there, trailing on the horizon like
a smudged pencil line, lies Earth's outstanding example of a
man-altered environment. Within a century the hills of Southern
California have been scalped, valleys fast-tracted, rivers rerouted
and dammed, shorelines bulkheaded, beaches eroded, estuaries
buried, skies sullied, and the natural world all but exterminated.
Between this deformed environment and the island wilderness
lies an oceanic moat that could become a thousand-lane bridge —

or a sloppy field steeped in high DDT counts and punctuated
with leaking oil rigs.

On a map the northern Channel Islands resemble geological
debris that litters the near shore. Santa Cruz, the largest island,
stretches 21 miles, has an average width of 5 miles, and reaches
2400 feet at its highest point. Santa Rosa and San Miguel follow
in order of size. Anacapa, the smallest, is but five miles long
and a half-mile wide. Yet Anacapa, with its steep bluffs and
rocky headlands that smash into the Pacific like a fist, exudes
the same rugged personality as its largest neighbor, Santa Cruz.
"The shore is perpendicular," noted one early Anacapa visitor.
This vertical landscape bakes under a "Mediterranean" sun that
leaves a residue of prickly-pear cactus and desolate oaks over
many of the steep hills. When winter rains come, trillions of
drops trace their courses down the gravelly slopes, through
fast-dropping canyons, and over bluffs into the ocean. In a heavy
rain the coastal bluffs become great, wide waterfalls.

Yet within this bold landscape lie inviting retreats. Coves
honeycomb the bluffs. The edge of the cove may be a sand
beach, and the beach may merge into the folds of a canyon that
shelters a waterfall to bathe boaters. Stands of ramrod bishop
pine and rare, wind-bent Torrey pine look down on Robinson
Jeffers's "elfin forest" of thick chaparral. Sociable island foxes,
along with skunks, deer, and feral sheep and hogs, dart in and
out of canyon springs and scamper across grasslands tucked in
narrow, elongated valleys.

In the spring this landscape comes alive. Raindrops that
manage to seep beneath the crust moisten dry seeds, and soon
blue lupine and orange poppies appear. Wildflower perfumes
mingle with sea breezes. Reddish foxes with ears that dwarf
their faces stand chest deep in poppy fields. A treelike plant
with a stubby grayish trunk suddenly sprouts bright green leaves

and yellow blossoms the size of sunflowers. These giant coreopsis may blend into a yellow canopy that can be seen miles out at sea, like a stick of butter wavering on the horizon. Spring is no more than a quickening blush, but of the deepest intensity.

It is on the shoreline that the vitality of the Channel Islands really asserts itself. Ocean currents swirl about these islands, slamming into each other and tossing up surf 40 feet high. The currents bathe the rocky shore with micronutrients, and these nutrients succor thriving communities of mussels, abalone, starfish, urchins, flowerlike anemones, and barnacles. The island shoreline is encrusted with life in hues of purple, orange, green, and bright red. This tidal life — compact, sedentary, seemingly without limbs or senses — flourishes in niches alternately drenched by surf and sun rays. The islands offer a million such niches.

Offshore, the surface of the sea may be blanketed with a rippling canopy of long brown leaves. These filter out nutrients from the rich sea solution and pass them down long, ivylike stems that sustain the giant bladder kelp plant, *Macrocystis pyrifera.* One of the fastest-growing plants in the world, giant kelp can reach a length of 200 feet. Unfurled from a rootlike "holdfast" that grips the rocky seabed, the plant's enormous length sprawls over the sunlit surface of the ocean. The two-foot-long leaves or "blades" hang like streamers from the stem. A colony of kelp plants can form a submarine forest eight square miles in size.

In the Northern Hemisphere giant bladder kelp exists only off the coast of California (both Baja and Alta). The largest forests flourish in the currents off the Channel Islands. A first descent into a sea forest can be somewhat unsettling. The silent, swaying kelp vines seem ready to reach out and ensnare the intruder. The multiarms of an octopus immediately come to mind. But then you see fish of every size and color nonchalantly gliding

The seabird-inhabited islets off Anacapa in
California's Channel Islands

through openings in the foliage, and soon you do the same.
Whereas life within a land forest scampers and hides at the first
man-made crack of a twig, life within a sea forest seems unimpressed by our presence. One looks perch in the eye, only to
be outstared. Schools of smelt pass like rain showers. What
appears to be a flame in search of a fire is a garibaldi, the goldfish
of the ocean.

On the forest rim, bonito, barricuda, and swordfish may circle,
patiently waiting for stray smelt and other forage. Occasionally
an object will crash into the forest from above in a bubbling

cascade and just as quickly rocket skyward. It is a cormorant diving for fish. Above the kelp forests and the shore fly gulls, petrels, pelicans, guillemots, auklets, and black oystercatchers. These seabirds nest in the shore bluffs and on the sea stacks, secure from egg-loving foxes. The Channel Islands rank as a superlative seabird habitat.

The islands serve as a fine habitat for another fascinating spectrum of life. One day the National Park Service power cruiser *Cougar* anchored off San Miguel. I left its solid deck for a bobbing dinghy. From ashore a roar like that from a football stadium carried over the thunder of the surf. Ranger Vern Betts, at the oars of the dinghy, rode the incoming swells as cautiously as a bronc rider. The *Cougar* and the island intermittently disappeared from view as we slid into troughs. Suddenly a beach cove appeared ahead, while a swell began cresting underneath us. We rocketed toward the cove, the hull scraping the rough beach.

I hopped out as the wave receded in a rattle of stones and found myself staring at one of the contributors to the stadiumlike roar, an elephant seal. This one was "small," a ponderous cow, beige-colored, with liquid brown eyes and a sweet doglike face that now bared teeth. The assurance that elephant seals are generally harmless becomes ephemeral when you confront one. Only when she began retreating did I feel assured. It wasn't so much the act of retreat as the manner — clumsily, with great effort, her marine prowess reduced to snail-like sluggishness on land. She kept retreating until she was against the cove walls, along with four other timid giants. My initial anxiousness was replaced by a certain repulsion at how my presence could reduce this magnificent creature to childlike cowering.

Her ancestors were slaughtered by my ancestors as effortlessly as cows in a stockyard to furnish oil for the lamps of the western frontier and sex charms for Chinese mandarins. A last-minute prohibition saved the northern elephant seal. As a result, San Miguel Island, not far from smog alerts and twelve-car freeway collisions, has become a principal stage for one of the most remarkable comebacks in wildlife annals. In 1892, fewer than 100 northern elephant seals clustered on Guadalupe Island, off Baja California. This remnant herd began spreading out to reclaim ancestral rookeries hundreds of miles away. By 1950 there were perhaps 50 elephant seals on San Miguel; by 1959, 412; and today, more than 3000. Amid the elephant seals are other returnees from the brink, the Guadalupe fur seal and the Alaska fur seal. Another ghost from the past, the cublike sea otter, has been seen floating on his back in the kelp canopy, his body gently anchored by an entwining vine.

No aquarium on the mainland can match the magnificence of this sanctuary for the nearly exterminated. Indeed, the kin of the seal you see balancing a colored ball on his nose are probably gliding through a Channel Island kelp forest. Here the California sea lion, favorite of seal trainers, puts on a much more spectacular show, as if confident of not being upstaged by a precocious dolphin. He may leap clear of the surf to land on a rock shelf, later returning to the water by diving off a ten-foot-high ledge. No other animal is so continually loud-mouthed. The islands pulsate with the squeal of seabirds, the snort of feral hogs, and the cadence of the surf, but it is the vibrant roar of the rookery that remains in the ear of the visitor. Sea lion bulls like to collect cows, and the collecting process contributes to the decibels.

The sun-loving elephant seal prefers sandspits to rock coves or sea grottoes. At sea this grandly obese form (up to 8000 pounds and 20 feet long) chases down squid, rays, sharks, and ratfish. Some of the bulls display remarkable agility and stamina on the land as well. On one island rookery, investigators Dr. Burney J. LeBoeuf and the late Dr. Richard Peterson of the University of California at Santa Cruz estimated that 4 percent of the bulls inseminated 85 percent of the females. Given this reservoir of sexual potency, the comeback of the elephant seals is better understood. One bull can go a long way.

Around December the gray whale passes by, en route from feeding grounds in the Arctic Ocean to calving grounds in the lagoons of Baja California. Sometimes the gray whales will go into a pinwheel formation, the heads at the hub, the flukes as thrashing spokes. The flukes are meant for the smaller but swifter killer whale. If the killer whale can avoid the flaying flukes, he will tear out the tongue of the gray, for his mouth is rimmed with teeth instead of baleen.

The display of life on the islands is a magnet for scientists and naturalists. By 1943 there were more than a thousand references to the northern Channel Islands in the scientific literature. For bat devotees alone, there are eight species awaiting observation. Many biologists study the dramatic and sometimes subtle differences between mainland and island life. The island fox, for instance, is generally smaller than its mainland relatives, while the island scrub jay appears to be larger and a deeper blue than its mainland kin. Some scientists contend these differences stem from evolutionary divergence, while others argue that species development has been arrested by isolation from the mainland. The islands thus are fostering a searching and sometimes caustic debate over the basic mechanics of evolution.

These islands, ringed by life as dense and varied as life in relatively unaltered continental habitats, have sustained a rather special human history. In 1947 an archeologist with the Santa Barbara Museum of Natural History, Dr. Phil C. Orr, was rummaging about some bluffs on Santa Rosa when he came across charred bones in a pit burned to brick red. The bones belonged to a dwarf mammoth that flourished at a time when the Santa Monica Mountains of Southern California extended out into the Pacific to include the Channel Islands. To the excited Orr, the location and condition of the bones suggested that one of our ancestors may have been barbecuing dwarf mammoth in an open-air hearth. A carbon 14 test at Columbia University's Lamont-Doherty Geological Observatory determined the bones to be 29,650 years old. If Orr's supposition, which has not received unqualified scientific acceptance, is ever confirmed, the islands would be known as one of the earliest sites to support man's habitation in North America.

With time the ocean rose, the dwarf mammoth disappeared, and the sea forests and the tidal zones ushered in a new environment. A branch of the coastal Chumash Indians came to dwell here. They harvested abalone and mussels for food. Seals provided bladder gourds and soft winter capes. Whalebone supported dome-shaped houses thatched with sea grass. Ground-up cactus was used as chum to attract and trap smelt in fish baskets. Asphaltum from submarine oil seeps served to caulk plank canoes and weight down the sea-grass skirts of maidens. This marine environment supported one of the most dense Indian settlements in North America. San Miguel Island is nine miles long and no wider than four miles. Yet this island alone was inhabited by an estimated 2000 Chumash, according to archeologist Charles Rozaire of the Los Angeles County Museum. These were Indians who never had to learn how to sow seed, propitiate the rain god, or beware of the rattlesnake or the mountain lion.

The Chumash found beauty as well as a bountiful subsistence in their marine surroundings. Clamshells were chipped and rounded into necklaces. Shallow pockets were hewn out of the shoulder bones of whales and filled with hot asphaltum. Pressed into these pockets was abalone shell, whose interior possesses a mother-of-pearl sheen. The shoulder bone with the abalone inlay became a funeral bier. Cave walls were decorated with red, white, and black representations of fish and seals. (This artistic accomplishment of the Chumash is explored in the beautifully illustrated *The Rock Paintings of the Chumash,* by Campbell Grant.) Soapstone was shaped into fish and whales. Soapstone killer whales occasionally smiled with an upturned mouth. The generous bounty of the islands gave the Chumash the time and the inspiration to be cheerful artists. They were, as described by early Spanish explorers, a happy, handsome, and hospitable people.

Today fewer than a hundred people inhabit the northern Channel Islands, and yet the island environment undergoes stresses and strains that the Chumash never exerted. Plundering of the islands' bounty started with the fur and seal hunters of the nineteenth century. George Nidever, Black Steward, and sharpshooters from Russia provided Chinese mandarins with otter pelts to warm their shoulders, seal sex organs to offset impotence, and seal whiskers to clean opium pipes.

At the same time, these entrepreneurs nearly exterminated the sea otter, the elephant seal, the fur seal, and the Chumash. Indian fur hunters imported from the Aleutians terrorized the easygoing natives. The cave painters and soapstone carvers were finally evacuated from their sea-grass homes and converted into Christian "braceros" on the mainland. The Chumash must have brought some beautiful myths, customs, and dances from their island homes, but we will never be able to read about them. While the elephant seals have made it back, the island Chumash died off or were absorbed on the mainland before anthropologists and historians could learn from them.

One island has suffered a fate nearly as complete as that of the Chumash. After putting himself out of business by purging seals and otters, George Nidever decided to import sheep, hogs, and burros to San Miguel. The hunting grounds became a sheep pasture. And the island soil began blowing into the ocean as the sheep consumed the grass cover. Undaunted, Nidever shipped in grain to sustain his destructive flock. Stowed away in the grain were thistles, and these took hold to help choke off the grasses and the shrubs that kept the Indians in berries and the island in spring blossoms.

By the 1930s San Miguel had acquired a new caretaker that didn't mind blowing sand and thistles. "The island itself is unique and made to order for our firings," declared an official of the Department of the Navy. By 1960 another Navy official could describe this punching bag for naval salvos as being "heavily entombed with ammunition."

Another nine years saw environmental violence affecting all the islands escalated to a new zenith. The submarine oil seeps that caulked Chumash canoes had quickened the ambitions of the petroleum industry. And in January 1969 the Santa Barbara Channel offshore oil blowout, a result of inadequate well casing and geological knowledge, smeared the waters and the shore. The Union Oil Company and the federal government, which granted the offshore leases, had minimized the dangerous fact that the seeps, besides indicating the presence of oil, also suggested a weak and fractured channel stratum. Oil slicks washed up on the San Miguel shore and fostered reports of seal pup kills. Investigations verified that seals were indeed coated with oil and that some pups were dead, but no conclusive link was found.

Sea lion pups can succumb to a number of natural causes — malnutrition, lungworm infestation, premature birth or abortion, trauma, and being washed out to sea. A mortality rate of at least 15 percent during pupping season is normal, according to Dr. LeBoeuf and Robert Brownell of the Department of Pathobiology at Johns Hopkins University. However, if the spill had occurred earlier in the pupping season, when females were nursing and their teats were exposed to oil, the pups might have ingested mother's milk liberally laced with Santa Barbara crude. This sort of additive could be deadly. More than likely, seals will be put to this test.

The oil industry's presence collides uniquely with another devastating interest in the Channel Islands area. For the islands lie between the Navy's Point Mugu missile range and the Air Force's Vandenberg missile range. Here, in the Santa Barbara Channel, the Navy tries out heat-seeking rockets and missiles. One oil executive told a Los Angeles *Times* reporter, "One of the things that bothers us is that those things were designed to sink the very sort of vessel we're drilling from." Indeed, three years ago, a Navy pilot fresh from Vietnam cut loose a Bullpup missile that sank a Navy patrol vessel. Another stray missile ignited a brush fire on San Miguel, an island that doesn't have that much grass cover to spare.

Even the U.S. government has become edgy about the possibility of a missile–oil rig mishap, and the federal oil leases in the Santa Barbara Channel stipulate that oil companies hold the U.S. government blameless for damage from stray or aborted missiles. There are also stipulations to suspend and evacuate oil operations when the crossfire becomes particularly intense. While oil personnel can easily be evacuated, oil drilling platforms and seal rookeries cannot.

Nor are seals immune from more mundane firepower. LeBoeuf and other investigators have come across seal corpses riddled with buckshot and bullets. There are people, unbelievable though it may seem, who enjoy shooting at seal rookeries from the decks of their powercraft. Just shooting at tin ducks at penny arcades will not do.

Commercial fishermen may legally shoot sea lions interfering with fishing operations, and some fishermen interpret interference rather broadly because they consider the sea lion a competitor. Yet no correlation has been shown between tonnage of sea lions executed and tonnage of fish caught; indeed, the abundance of fishlife around rookeries suggests that sea lions are more farsighted capitalists than commercial fishermen.

Seals, like pelicans, are at the top of the marine food web. However, scientists had not found the same disturbing uptake of DDT in seals as in pelicans until LeBoeuf and his colleague Michael Bonnell ran tests on the blubber of Channel Island sea lions. They are finding the highest DDT concentrations in seals to date, as much as 2678 parts per million. The Channel Island seals, in their deceptive sanctuary bliss, inhabit waters regularly saturated with chemical pollutants that wash into the channel from the mainland and infiltrate the food chain.

Until recently those waters also got a good dose of DDT from the Montrose Chemical Corporation plant near Los Angeles. Not unexpectedly, it was the Channel Islands where Dr. Robert Risebrough of the University of California at Berkeley came across pelican nesting grounds littered with brittle eggshells and dried-up yolk rather than with young pelicans. Risebrough and other scientists have linked the brittle eggshells to DDT uptake and its impact on the reproductive process. "The effect of organo-chlorine pesticides on sea lion mortality is unknown. California sea lions show the highest DDT residues of any pinniped examined thus far, and investigations of the possibility that pesticides induce premature pupping in this species are just beginning," reports LeBoeuf.

Thus after squeaking by the deadly aim of Black Steward and George Nidever and barely making it into the twentieth century, the seals of the Channel Islands must now face more modern and insidious survival tests.

Today on San Miguel Island, as one looks at a bomb crater, the thistles, and the blowing sands, it is hard to believe that thousands of people who liked to shape soapstone into smiling whales once lived here. Though devoid of a single hardtop road, sewage outfall, or sanitary landfill, San Miguel still smarts from desecration. However, it is these mainland amenities that now threaten to engulf Santa Cruz and Santa Rosa islands, even though the three owners, who use the islands as livestock pastures, are sensitive to more natural island values. They have allowed botanists, archeologists, and ecologists to do fieldwork on these "evolution factories." And the Santa Cruz Island Company has permitted the University of California at Santa Barbara to establish a field station there. In a pioneer exercise in biological control, mealybugs, introduced by entomologists, suck dry the pads of prickly-pear cactus and permit island grasses devastated by sheep grazing to revive. Cattle now munch on this soft green revival.

However, property taxes can make cattle pastures, even at sea, less and less remunerative, and an affluent residential clientele on the mainland makes another land use appealing, so appealing that men's minds undergo wondrous conversions. While formulating a general land-use plan for Santa Barbara County, which includes these islands, planning officials questioned the owners about their property. "These guys almost sounded like they wanted to secede from the Union," recalls one planner. The islands that once supported thousands of Chumash were pictured as a sort of island badlands, dangerous of approach and harassed by incessant winds, low rainfall, and below-freezing temperatures. Agricultural classification was requested and granted.

A few years later a development plan was submitted to the

Santa Barbara County Planning Commission. The plan spoke
of an island graced by a "Mediterranean climate." "Frost is
unknown on the island, and summer heat is tempered by the
sea breezes." The island referred to is Santa Cruz, and the plan's
sponsor is Pier Gherini, an owner of the eastern portion of Santa
Cruz. The plan would accommodate 3000 "financially substantial
immigrants." A 3000-foot airstrip would be surrounded by sand
traps and fairways; the golf course would be surrounded by
fairway residences. Hot asphaltum would once more be in vogue,
but not in the service of maiden modesty. Sixteen miles of
highways would be strapped over the landscape to buckle together two villages. Approximately 100,000 cubic yards of shore
would be shuffled around to accommodate a natural-enough
improvisation in Southern California, an "artificial fjord." A
hunting club would give chase to feral sheep and hogs, while
a reservoir would help lure waterfowl within gun range. It is
a conventional residential plan by Southern California standards.
A hydrocarbon habitat for financially substantial immigrants who
can golf would replace a remarkable habitat for wildlife and
for a growing populace committed to outdoor values.

However, while the Gherini vision was approved for inclusion
in the county's general plan in 1966, the fjord, the sand traps,
and the beauty parlors have not yet materialized. The explanation
for all this intricate maneuvering may lie in the presence of
a prospective property owner who actually views the islands
as islands.

The National Park Service has been interested in the Channel
Islands since at least the early 1930s, but it was not until 1938
that the Department of the Interior succeeded in persuading
President Franklin D. Roosevelt to set aside two islands, Anacapa
and Santa Barbara, which is 40 miles south of the northern
chain, as the Channel Islands National Monument. Some momentum for Park Service protection of the rest of the chain started

building in the late 1950s. A "Pacific Coast Recreation Area Survey" by the National Park Service concluded, "The Channel Islands collectively constitute the greatest single remaining opportunity for the conservation and preservation of representative seashore values, including biology, geology, history, archeology, paleontology, wilderness, and recreation." Although a Channel Island National Park bill introduced in 1963 by the late Senator Clair Engle received strong endorsement by then Secretary of the Interior Stewart Udall, the bill died in committee. In 1970 another report, this one by the Bureau of Outdoor Recreation, entitled "Islands of America" recommended Congressional action to authorize seven national island parks, including the Channel Islands. This time around both California senators, Alan Cranston and John Tunney, have cosponsored park bills.

When the National Park Service enters the picture, property owners are often seized with the need to reclassify their land for higher use and espouse high revenue-producing activity to benefit local tax rolls. If this is indeed the Gherini strategy, a number of factors could militate against it. For the islands manage to raise a number of obstacles to fast-tract development, including the need for transportation from the mainland and extensive investment in water supplies, sewers, and fire-fighting equipment.

Moreover, the islands have unexpected friends. Although local interests are often beguiled by moneymaking visions that promise to thwart National Park Service "takeovers," the Santa Barbara oil spill has awakened an environmental catharsis among residents that tends to counter such hoary visions. The city councils of Santa Barbara and Ventura favor national park status, and even the Chamber of Commerce of Ventura County waxes lyrical on the values of elephant seals, giant coreopsis, and bladder kelp. Even before the blowout, the Santa Barbara County Board of Supervisors approved Gherini's switch in perspective with the admonition that "possible development of the area as a national park would provide, from a planning standpoint, an equally acceptable use of the land without conflict with the county general plan." And the other owners on Santa Cruz and Santa Rosa might be willing to consider mainland grazing property in the public domain in exchange for their island fiefs.

But while the National Park Service may appear to some as the gallant savior in the struggle for the destiny of the islands, some scientists, including Dr. Phil Orr, are not persuaded that conservation and recreation would not mix well on the islands. If the islands were to be developed as intensively as, say, Yosemite, national park status would indeed be a Pyrrhic victory. Park plans, according to National Park Service official Thomas Tucker, would "embrace a pure park concept of management rather than one primarily oriented to recreation."

When and if the time for public visitation comes, Park Service plans for all the islands would ban the automobile and confine all movement to nature trails. Visitors could be brought over on hydrofoil or helicopter ferries, according to Don Robinson, superintendent of the Channel Islands National Monument. Seabird and seal rookeries would enjoy extensive buffer zones. Already the National Park Service has proposed new regulations to ban commercial fishing activities (including sea lion assassinations) off the present two national monument islands, Anacapa and Santa Barbara.

If ever realized, protection for the Channel Islands could hold enormous social potential that transcends traditional preservation concerns. The islands could become a critical ecological and social baseline next door to a region beset by environmental havoc of the most dire sort. These islands have already seen one major wildlife comeback through protective legislation on marine mammals. And marine biologist Nancy Nicholson of the University of Southern California suggests that the Channel Islands may serve as life banks, providing marine fauna to restore and restock beleaguered mainland shores. The intact life-support system of the islands thus becomes a resource in itself, providing the potential knowledge to reverse mainland abuses. Very few urbanized regions are fortunate enough to still retain such a natural reservoir of life. It would be folly to condemn islands that could become such formidable testimonials to our ability to mend our planet.

Amid these perspectives, reports reoccur that Gherini is in negotiations with blue-chip corporations that wield the financial and political clout to water and sewer his property. Associated Press reporter Susan Sward quoted Gherini as saying, when Senator Tunney introduced his bill, that Santa Cruz Island "should be developed for people who can financially afford to live there and pay for the privilege." And in the fall of 1972, the Santa Barbara County Board of Supervisors granted Mobil Oil Company permission to test drill on the shoreline of Santa Rosa Island. Subsequent protests from the state attorney general and a citizens' group called GOO (Get Oil Out) have delayed drilling pending an environmental impact statement. But neither Gherini nor Mobil can be blamed for pursuing the profit motive. The real responsibility for protecting islands of national and international significance lies elsewhere.

"These islands are 'of the sea,' " observes Dr. Stanley A. Cain, former Assistant Secretary of the Interior. "Mighty forces have sculpted them and set them apart, and man must not be allowed to change all this. He *should* be allowed to revel in it." San Miguel and its island sisters can once more provide sustenance for people, but not on the terms of the deformed environment to the east. The soapstone whale in drifting island sands testifies to this. So does Union Oil's signature on the shoe of the beholder.

On a pond along Maine's Allagash River, morning mist surrounds
a lone canoeist and gives the illusion of solitude

AIMÉ GAUVIN

The Allagash
Nonwilderness Waterway

AROOSTOOK COUNTY, state of Maine, is best known for its highly productive potato farms. Less well known is that the world-famous Allagash River is also found there. But the potato lands and the major communities of Aroostook lie in the eastern part of the county, whereas the Allagash is in the west, in the great forest of Maine — millions of acres of dense woodlands crossed only by logging roads.

That forest barrier to a westward line of communication has long troubled eastern Maine's agricultural and economic interests. Canadians in western New Brunswick and southeastern Quebec, separated from each other by the northern protuberance of Maine, also have yearned for a direct road link. In 1955 these combined economic interests pressured the Maine legislature into initiating a feasibility study for a highway from Ashland, Maine, to Daaquam, Province of Quebec. The study indicated that any public benefits of such a highway would be considerably less than the costs, even though the road would be built, for the most part, over existing woods roads.

Highway proponents, however, never give up. The county commissioners have been battling the timberland owners, in and out of court, since 1966 to get control of the land they need. Then, too, agitation for some kind of east-west corridor road has been a constant fact of Maine economic and political life for years. So nobody was surprised when, on November 16, 1971, the commissioners announced they would go ahead with legal work and plans for construction of the highway from Ashland to Daaquam.

What did surprise many, though, was the realization that such a road would cut directly through the heart of the Allagash Wilderness Waterway.

"They can't do that!" cried one outraged conservationist. "We saved the Allagash back in 1966. There's a law against it!" But, like so many who had approved the patchwork of compromise that resulted in state creation of the waterway, he hadn't read the fine print. The fact is, the road is already there — rough, full of potholes and washboards and quagmires, but there nonetheless; owned and used for hauling wood by timber and paper companies. Waterway officials control only the access from the road to the waterway. So, if the county commissioners can take the roadway by eminent domain, they can run a superhighway right across the Allagash Wilderness Waterway, and all waterway officials can do is put up "Keep Off the Wilderness" signs.

People began thinking about saving the Allagash as far back as 1955, when the federally created New England–New York Interagency Committee recommended preservation of scenic and recreational attractions of the St. John River basin, of which the Allagash is a part. At about the same time, a succession of proposals for hydroelectric projects on the St. John, which forms the northern boundary between Maine and New Brunswick, alarmed conservationists the country over. The highway, the proposed dams (the most ambitious of which would have flooded 100,000 acres of timberland and obliterated 97 percent of the Allagash River), a National Park Service plan to create an Allagash National Park of 750,000 acres, and the seemingly endless proliferation of logging roads poking dusty fingers into every corner of the watershed, all combined to rally conservationists to the battle cry "Save The Allagash!"

The Natural Resources Council of Maine deserves special credit for seeing the danger to the Allagash early, and for getting involved promptly in the battle to save the river. It sponsored and raised money for a study of the Allagash and the proposals for development that threatened its existence as a wilderness. That study, by the Conservation Foundation, was released by the Natural Resources Council in February 1962. It was followed in April of that year by the council's "Objectives for the Allagash," and in August by its "Proposals for the Allagash."

In its call for action, the council warned: "The Allagash is not yet lost as a wilderness canoe country. What has been done could be undone, and the region can still be preserved for future generations, as well as for our own. But if signs and past experience mean anything, there is not much time to lose."

Then began a series of skirmishes involving the federal government, the state government, timberland owners, power interests, bankers, and conservationists. The outcome was passage by the state legislature in 1966 of an act to create the Allagash Wilderness Waterway. In November of that year, Maine voters approved the appropriation of $1.5 million of state money to match federal funds, and the Allagash Wilderness Waterway, wholly under state control, came into being. The Allagash had been "saved."

But national publicity resulting from the battle had begun to draw the curious from all over the country. Where hundreds had once paddled and poled their canoes down the Allagash, thousands now swarmed. Long before the official opening of the waterway in 1970, long before the boundaries had been surveyed and marked, long before the small housekeeping staff was ready, the Allagash Wilderness Waterway had become, as Dr. Donaldson Koons, chairman of the Maine Environmental Improvement Commission, put it: "pretty close to being a wilderness slum."

Allagash waters begin in northwestern Maine at Telos Lake and flow northward — except where man has intervened — through some 95 miles of interconnected lakes and streams to join the St. John River, at the village of Allagash. The Allagash River proper begins at the foot of Churchill Lake, where a dam impounds enough water during the spring runoff to keep the river navigable by canoe through the dry months of late summer. Therefore, despite its reputation as the last wild river in the East, the Allagash is in fact artificially controlled, and its waters are rationed according to the needs of canoeists.

The building of a new Churchill Dam to replace rotted remnants of the last of a series of old logging dams was decided upon by waterway officials after two dry summers forced canoeists to walk most of the nine-mile streambed down Chase Rapids, dragging their canoes behind them. State Parks and Recreation Commission Director Lawrence Stuart said of the summer of 1968 that "there was literally not enough water to float a canoe" along the 42-mile stretch between Churchill Dam and Allagash. The dam, completed in the fall of 1968 at a cost of $200,000, has thus far proved adequate in insuring canoeing water for the increasing numbers of visitors to the area.

A look at the map of Allagash country, showing the enormous capacity of its headwater lakes, is bound to arouse wonder at the necessity for such storage facilities. But a bit of logging history quickly explains the problem. The waters of Chamberlain and Telos lakes were diverted from their normal northerly course in 1842 by enterprising lumbermen bent on finding a way to drive Allagash timber south into the profitable sawmills of Bangor rather than north to less rewarding Canadian markets. A mile-long canal from Telos Lake east to Webster Lake siphoned Allagash headwaters into the southerly flowing Penobscot East Branch.

It is ironic that although Allagash, Chamberlain, and Telos lakes are today officially part of the Allagash Wilderness Waterway, their waters (except for a trickle of canoeing water allowed to run between Chamberlain and Eagle lakes at Lock Dam) run into the Penobscot. Effective storage at Telos Dam is about 15 billion cubic feet of stolen Allagash water, which the Bangor Hydro-Electric Company uses today for generating power.

Throughout the legal, economic, and political power struggle that culminated in the creation of the Allagash Wilderness Waterway, only one important voice seems to have raised the issue of restoring those waters to the Allagash. In his book *My Wilderness: East To Katahdin*, William O. Douglas wrote: "Precious water, sorely needed if the Allagash is to be restored as the most wondrous canoe stream in the nation, runs needlessly into the East Fork today . . . We must move fast, if the whole chain of lakes and streams that makes up the Allagash is to be preserved. Relics of old dams must be removed. The natural flow of Allagash waters must be restored. The tributaries of the Allagash must be protected by acquiring a wide corridor on each side of the waterway. This corridor must be free of roads, free of resorts, free of all marks of civilization. The Allagash must become and remain a roadless wilderness waterway. No more cutting of trees. No invasions of any kind."

Unfortunately, no one responsible for working out the final plans for the waterway seems to have shared the views of Supreme Court Justice Douglas on the restoration of Allagash waters. The Department of the Interior, which proposed in succession an Allagash National Park, an Allagash National Recreation Area, and an Allagash National Riverway, apparently accepted the Chamberlain-Telos diversion as irreversible. The members of the state's Allagash River Authority, set up by the legislature in 1963 to formulate a plan for the protection of the waterway, seem to have been afflicted with the same respect for the status quo, and of the seven members of the Allagash Waterway Advisory Committee, two of whom were members of the Natural Resources Council, none is on record in favor of restoration.

In all fairness, however, it must be pointed out that Justice Douglas was not forced to live with the harsh realities of Maine political and economic life, as were the members of the legislature and the committee. The threat of formidable legal obstacles also played a part in the decision against restoring the flow to the Allagash. "There were some very definite statements made that if we ever did it, we could never catch up with the lawsuits that would follow," Larry Stuart recalls. "There would be so many lawsuits that the whole project would be killed."

Most of Chamberlain-Telos narrowly missed being left out of the Allagash Wilderness Waterway entirely. A road had been cut in to Telos Lake by Great Northern Paper Company about 1959, and the two lakes had become playgrounds for the motorized vanguard of today's recreationist invasion. Powerboaters were quick to join with the timberland owners and Bangor Hydro in opposing the inclusion of those lakes. But eventually the legislative committee, under pressure from conservationists, was able to pacify both factions by a compromise that left the watery playground intact for the motorboats, but took control of a strip of land around the lakes so the appearance of wilderness might be maintained along the shores at least.

Those words, "the appearance of wilderness," perhaps best characterize the Allagash Wilderness Waterway as it emerged from the legislature, and as it is today.

Justice Douglas's formula for preserving the Allagash called for a wide corridor on each side of the waterway. The formula adopted established a "restricted zone," varying in width from 400 to 800 feet, within which no logging would be permitted. This was buffered by an outer zone extending for one mile from the high-water mark. Selective cutting is permitted in the outer zone. Existing logging roads were permitted to remain in private ownership, but the State Parks and Recreation Commission has the authority to relocate such roads within the restricted zone — at its own expense. The length of the waterway extends from Telos north to West Twin Brook, a distance of approximately 85 miles.

Before the opening of the Telos road, one began the Allagash canoe trip in pretty much the arduous manner and over the same route described by Thoreau in "The Allegash and East Branch." Today one motors, or flies, to Telos. My first view of Telos, as I arrived by automobile in the summer of 1971, was abrupt and shocking. After traveling many miles I emerged from the woods into a sudden explosion of human activity. There was no sign to warn that the world-famous Allagash Wilderness Waterway was just around the bend, no official presence of any kind; merely a crowded, littered, swampy, lakeshore parking area, swarming with people and vehicles of every description. Powerboats were moored along the shore, and several were racing across the water. Some people were loading canoes for the Allagash trip, but most seemed to be onlookers. I later discovered that many make the journey to Telos just to see the place and look at the wilderness freaks, returning to their homes or motels or campers the same day. Others, however, come to camp.

There is a campground of sorts off to one side, and it was filled with camping vehicles of every size and variety. Picnic tables were covered with paraphernalia: gasoline stoves, refrigerators, lanterns, fishing tackle, and the ubiquitous six-packs of beer.

258 The Assault on Originality

Clotheslines were strung from camper to camper, from tree to camper. Trash cans were overflowing, and there was a waiting line at the outhouse. Children of all ages were doing whatever children do in such situations, parents were lolling in folding chairs, beer cans in hand, listening to ball games on transistor radios.

I had arrived at the Allagash Wilderness Waterway. Had I not been there on assignment, I might well have turned and fled.

Telos and Chamberlain are big waters and can be very rough when whipped up by a good wind. But canoeists with only elementary skills, from children to grimly determined adults, paddle those waters by the thousands every summer. I was astonished at the number of youngsters I saw all over the big lakes, paddling through the choppy waters like so many Abnaki. Most impressive, however, was an ancient, patched, canvas 18-footer with a father and two young daughters aboard. Dad was handling the stern paddle, while a thirteen-year-old was in the bow. The craft was heavily laden and low in the water, and reclining regally on the tarpaulin-covered bulge amidships was a twelve-year-old. They were going the whole distance, the father said, all the way to Allagash. I suggested that he must be an accomplished canoeist to undertake the 95-mile trip. "Never did it before in my life," he said.

It is worth noting here that there have been no drownings from canoe mishaps since the creation of the waterway in 1966. During the many hearings that preceded the birth of the waterway, old Allagash hands had made an impressive case for the dangers of letting greenhorns loose on the Allagash without guides and motors. Other motor proponents joined the chorus, and it was largely on the strength of these arguments that a decision was made to permit the use of motors up to 10 horsepower the whole length of the waterway. I have come to believe that the arguments were self-serving, for it is not uncommon on the Allagash to see a guide with motor towing a string of canoes full of relaxed tourists behind him. At the going rate of about $300 per person, an aggressive, well-advertised guide can do very well for himself in a season.

Motors are barred (as a sop to the purists) in one small sector. Northwest of Chamberlain lies Allagash Lake, which can be reached only by manpower. Voyagers lucky enough to be there when no chain saws are singing in the adjacent timber will get a measure of wilderness experience. One might expect that people willing to pole and paddle the five miles up Allagash Stream would be a special breed of camper, but a Boy Scout party acting as a cleanup squad brought 45 bags of trash out of there last year.

Litter, the universal spoor of the American tourist, is a major problem throughout the waterway. Litter bags are given out with instructions as to their use, but they are usually used as containers for cameras or lunch or dirty laundry. Superintendent Leigh Hoar says, "After five years I have come to the conclusion that the average camper will not pack his trash more than a hundred feet." From mid-May to mid-September, Hoar's rangers spend 75 percent of their time handling trash. During the hunting and fishing seasons 75 percent of the litter consists of liquor and beer containers.

Lock Dam, which controls the stream flow between Chamberlain and Eagle lakes, is an enemy enclave within the waterway. The dam tender, who takes your name as you go through, lives in a neat small house with a lawn. Here, I realized, I was on Bangor Hydro territory. To add to the alien feeling of the place, the dam tender's automobile stood in his driveway mocking the wilderness. The road he travels to get there is on private lands, but is used by many who know the area — one of many leaks in the waterway's controlled access.

The Allagash Wilderness Waterway was used by 4820 persons in 1969. There was an increase of 13 percent in 1970 to 5460, and a 16 percent increase in 1971 to 6345. More and more they come in organized parties of up to twenty canoes, and what one of these parties can do to a campsite has to be experienced to be believed. I had the experience the first night out.

The campsite, designed for four or five small parties well situated among the trees, was located in a grove of mature white pines, probably scorned by early loggers for some "defect" — a crotch perhaps, or a bend in the trunk. Being concerned with aesthetics rather than board feet, I was well pleased with them as I prepared for a restful night. Suddenly a flotilla of canoes descended on me, carrying 24 Boy Scouts, a guide, and a middle-aged scoutmaster. The boys engulfed the campsite in a kind of organized disorder, setting up tents, building fires, gathering wood, cooking, and blowing up air mattresses.

By dusk the troop had managed to get set up for the night, everybody had eaten, and the campground had taken on the disheveled appearance of another Telos landing. The noise level had subsided somewhat, and the scoutmaster wandered over for a chat. He told me they had left the suburbs of Boston at four o'clock that morning, driven all the way to Telos in two pickups, and here they were seventeen hours later in the middle of the Maine woods. He added that the troop went on a similar safari somewhere for two weeks every summer. "It gets them away," said their shepherd. "It gets them off the streets and away from dope."

A worthy objective surely, but I couldn't help feeling, as I tried to ignore the noise and get some sleep, that the city streets had somehow traveled with the boys and dispossessed the wilderness.

Churchill Dam is the site of a collection of old buildings

(remnants of a former logging camp), a new ranger's cabin, an automobile parking lot, a campground, and considerable vehicular traffic. Just below the dam is the start of some nine miles of white water known as Chase Rapids. One registers here, and the ranger decides how much water you need (one gate, two gates) depending on the size of your party. If you decide not to risk the rapids the ranger's wife will, for a fee, truck you and your gear to Umsaskis Lake. I chose to pole the rapids, and the ranger cranked open a gate and a half with the help of a hand-held, motorized gadget not unlike a chain saw in appearance and volume of sound.

While you work your way through the rapids, the illusion of being alone in the wilderness is strong. The river engages your attention to the exclusion of all else, and the roar of the water blots out all other sounds. But the illusion ends at Umsaskis Lake, where sits the Allagash Wilderness Waterway headquarters building, formerly an International Paper Company lodge for VIPs. There, on the crest of a hill, with a lawn sweeping all the way to the boat landing, is the very symbol of luxury vacation living.

Between Umsaskis and Long Lake, the Ashland-Daaquam logging road crosses the waterway. For a description of this area and parts north we cannot do better than repeat an account from Maine's Natural Resources Council bulletin for August 1962. With very minor changes, the area is exactly the same ten years later:

"The road from Ashland is closed to general traffic, but a surprising number of cars from there appear at the thoroughfare bridge. Campers in this vicinity hear, from three directions, the rumble of trucks hauling logs from Maine to Canada, and of trucks, shovels, and bulldozers at work on more roads leading down the west side of the river . . . Continuing down the Allagash, the wilderness is broken again by a bridge below Round Pond, and within a few miles the canoeist is aware of a road on the west bank, a road that already runs from the mouth of the Allagash to a point well above the Allagash Falls and seems to be pushing steadily upstream. Many other roads, on all sides, reach closer and closer to the Allagash waterways."

The most magnificent stretch of water in the Allagash begins below Long Lake Dam. For ten or twelve narrow, winding miles the river passes through what appears to be an untouched evergreen forest unequaled in beauty anywhere in the East. Landowners have managed well here, leaving the riverbanks thick with tall-spired spruce and fir. The result is breathtakingly beautiful — but reality intrudes abruptly as you approach Round Pond, a lovely spot completely surrounded by chain saws.

The saws stop their keening at five in the afternoon, but there then begins a noisy parade of homeward-bound logging vehicles. The roar of the diesels as they take the steep grades, and the *rattlebangclatter* of the trucks over the rough roads, lasts into the evening. Even during the night hours your sleep is disturbed by vehicles traveling on mysterious errands through the forest.

At six in the morning the return caravan can be heard approaching from afar, getting closer and louder, and finally blending into the new day's singing of the chain saws. Round Pond is a beautiful place, but I won't go there again.

After Round Pond the rest is anticlimactic. There is Allagash Falls, to be sure, but then the waterway ends drably at an old trailer in a riverbank meadow. Now one knows what Larry Stuart means when he says, "I never use the word 'wilderness' when talking about the waterway."

In the classic meaning of the term, the Allagash has not been a wilderness for 150 years. Instead, it has been, for the most part, a well-managed commercial woodland, producing a steady flow of fiber to market, while at the same time furnishing a moderate number of hardy folk with excellent recreation in the forms of canoeing, fishing, and hunting. Because of the manner in which it was done, designation of part of the watershed as the Allagash Wilderness Waterway has not changed its essential character. There was a transfer of ownership from private to state hands, and that's about all. One must wonder whether it was worth the time and money spent.

Most of the problems the waterway was expected to eliminate still flourish. Logging roads continue to expand, opening the watershed to more and more motorized public access. The old roads still run through the waterway, and most are heavily used. A new all-weather logging highway has been opened from Millinocket up the west shore of Telos, and a similar road is being bulldozed southward to join with it and start a flow of western Allagash wood down to the Great Northern mills in Millinocket. So, the sights and sounds of a working woodland will continue to intrude on the senses of seekers of wilderness values.

Distrust of federal intervention in state affairs is deeply ingrained in the Maine character, and it probably was this factor more than any other that determined state control for the waterway. As a result there is little money available for the operation of the waterway. It is undermanned and ill equipped to cope with the growing tourist invasion. Federal ownership might have made a difference.

The Allagash National Riverway proposal, for example, planned for the expenditure of more than $7 million for acquisition and physical improvements, plus an additional $300,000 for management, and $100,000 for annual operation. Under the compromise plan finally adopted, only $3 million (federal and state) was allocated for acquisition, planning, and development.

The state must pay its own operation and maintenance costs. So the waterway is run by a superintendent and three full-time rangers, plus two seasonal employees.

The national riverway proposal would have banned the use of motors and the landing of planes on Allagash waters. It would have blocked and obliterated all roads not needed for administrative access. I believe it was the better plan although it would not, any more than the present system, have created or preserved a true wilderness area.

A true wilderness preserve in the Allagash would have required bold planning and bold action, backed by the support of the people. The people of Maine and their representatives were unwilling to take that action. So they created a quasiwilderness recreation area. And now even that is in danger of being overwhelmed by recreational pressures. The State Parks and Recreation Commission is aware of the threat and is reacting with a gradual tightening of controls. The danger is that we may have already passed the point of no return. It has been said that we don't generally know the carrying capacity of a given natural area until it has been destroyed. There is a strong possibility that this may be the ultimate fate of the Allagash.

Meanwhile, more and more people make the Allagash trip and return home to write waterway officials glowing letters of thanks for having provided them with an unforgettable wilderness experience.

When I told Larry Stuart of my personal objection to the availability of a motorized transport service around Chase Rapids he said, "Why that's one of the things we get the most praise for."

PAUL BROOKS

Baja California —
Emergency and Opportunity

ROMAN GLADIATORS considered the net an even deadlier weapon
than the sword. So the highways that enmesh our countryside
may ultimately prove more destructive than the gun or the ax.
In how many parts of the United States can one drive for more
than a few hours out of sight or sound of a paved road? Mexico
is more fortunate, as speed-weary North Americans have discovered. But will this discovery itself be fatal? Nowhere is the
answer more crucial than in that uniquely beautiful and still
largely roadless peninsula on our border, Baja (or lower) California.

Lying in approximately the same latitude as Florida, and of
nearly equal area, Baja is longer, skinnier, and a good deal
rougher. From Tijuana on the border to the tip of the peninsula
is about 800 miles as the crow flies, but the distance on the
ground is more than a thousand. Transplanted to the East Coast,
Baja would extend from Columbia, South Carolina, to Havana,
Cuba. At its narrowest point, it is only 30 miles wide. And
whereas the greatest elevation in Florida is a few hundred feet
above sea level, the highest peak in Baja is over ten thousand.

Up to very recent times, Baja has been a sort of wild paradise,
saved from the blight of progress by its inaccessibility. Discovered
by Hernán Cortés more than four centuries ago, this rugged desert

country has defied exploitation. Mining operations — copper, silver, gold — flourished briefly and failed. The Spanish missionaries, men of incredible hardihood and zeal, were the first to gain a foothold. Their achievements were extraordinary, but eventually they too failed, as the Indian population whose souls they sought to save died off from the European diseases they inadvertently brought with them. Such of the great mission churches as still stand today tower above villages too small to supply their congregations; the mines have left only ghost towns. In large parts of the peninsula the primitive quality of the land remains, looking much as it must have looked to the first explorers.

"To the biologist the peninsula is a treasure chest, barely opened, which remains to be explored," remarked Dr. George Lindsay, director of the California Academy of Sciences and an authority on Baja California. "There are mountains as yet unvisited by scientists. There are plants and animals still unknown to naturalists. And it is possible that the peninsula holds keys to discoveries of broad principles which can explain the riddles of the specialized life of the desert."

Owing to the wide range of altitude as well as latitude, Baja contains an extraordinary variety of climate and habitat; from coniferous forests on the high plateau of the north central region, to true desert at lower elevations, to tropical beaches at the southern tip, which extends below the Tropic of Cancer. Mountain ranges, continuous with those in Southern California, run the length of the peninsula; like the Sierra Nevada, they rise gradually from the west and drop off sharply to the east. In the northern section, and again below La Paz, the exposed rock is largely granite; the midpeninsula mountains are volcanic.

Separated from the mainland of Mexico by the Gulf of California, Baja is politically divided into two parts: the north is now a state of Mexico, the south remains a territory — Territorio de

Baja California Sur. The dividing line is the 28th Parallel. Needless to say, the farther you get from the United States border, or from the coastal resorts, the less Americanized, the more purely Mexican, the land becomes.

As Baja aficionados point out, the country's charm has been preserved quite simply by bad roads. Now, however, the highway is creeping down from the north, up from the south; only a third of the old road is left, and the president of Mexico has promised completion of the pavement in three years. Soon the heart of Baja will be only a day's drive from the most mobile, gasoline-powered population on Earth. Here — to use an overworked term — is a true conservation crisis. The Chinese character for "crisis," I am told, is a combination of "emergency" and "opportunity."

To assess the extent of the emergency, and to get some idea of the opportunities still open for protecting this national treasure, my wife, our son, and I recently spent a fortnight traveling through Baja, first in the mountains of the north, and then on a ten-day trip down the full length of the peninsula in a four-wheel-drive truck. Though this was my third visit to Baja, I realize that I have barely shaken hands with a country that is an old friend of countless scientists, photographers, and wilderness lovers. Yet to know it only superficially is to recognize its place in the world conservation picture, and passionately to share the hope that its character may endure.

Only a decade ago, a trip down Baja was a thousand-mile adventure, as the late Joseph Wood Krutch demonstrates in his charming book, *The Forgotten Peninsula.* The adventurous part — the unpaved road — has now shrunk to less than half that distance. And long before Krutch wrote, the airplane had made La Paz an easy trip from Los Angeles, and several towns on the Gulf and Cabo de San Lucas accessible to sport fishermen.

Yet hundreds of miles of coastline, containing deep bays and sheltered lagoons of untold beauty, remain unspoiled, and the rugged interior desert has held its own. "Not until that possibly still rather distant time when a real road is built," wrote Krutch, "will its [Baja's] now unmarred beauty be successfully exploited and the coast turned into that string of beach resorts that may be its ultimate fate."

On the first leg of our journey, along the coastal expressway south from San Diego, we recalled Krutch's prophecy. Only his timing was off. As one speeds down a nearly empty toll road designed for Americans weekending in Ensenada, one sees miles of beach cluttered with dilapidated motels, trailer parks, and dead automobiles; the come-on signs are all in English. An occasional monarch butterfly on migration seems curiously out of place. Then as the road winds among the foothills, it enters agricultural country: olive groves, vineyards, fields of chili beans and bright splashes of red where the beans are drying on the hillsides. When it drops back to the seacoast, civilization has at last been left behind. Mountain ranges, layer upon layer on the eastern horizon, are silhouetted in deepening shades of gray. As darkness fell, we followed a track through a cactus-covered plain to the sand dunes, and spread our sleeping bags within sound of the surf. The night wind reminded us that the Pacific currents here are cold.

Work on the highway is proceeding apace. All the following day we jolted along the churned-up right of way, detouring on the old road when we could. We were traveling through farmland and cattle country — a country of windmills and cactus fences, of sparrow hawks and bluebirds on telephone wires and killdeers and avocets in irrigation ditches. At last we reached Rosario, where the road turns eastward, becoming no longer a road but a track. Here begins the great central desert, comprising some six thousand square miles, from Rosario to La Paz. For the next five days we would be on our own.

Our first desert camp was made at nightfall, which comes early in November. When you are surrounded by cacti, hunting for firewood after dark is hazardous; fortunately there was light enough to collect a supply of dead cholla without getting prickled in the process. Woody, perforated with holes where the spines have fallen out, cholla cactus makes a quick, self-ventilated fire. It was a moonless night, and the stars were incredibly bright in the clear dry air; there was rime on our sleeping bags when we rose before dawn. The desert was still in shadow as the first shafts of sunlight lit golden torches in the treetops. Yes, treetops — though perhaps the strangest trees in the world. These were the famous boojum trees (*Idria columnaris*), known locally as *cirio*, from the resemblance of the straight unbranched specimens to wax candles used in church. Actually they grow in every conceivable and inconceivable shape, from the "upside-down carrot" effect of the younger trees to loops and swirls and curling tentacles that — like cloud forms — suggest unlikely creatures to the imagination. I recall, for example, an almost perfect sea horse against the sky. The leaves of the boojum are a fuzz of green on the tapering trunk; the flowers (which we were lucky to see in such profusion) burst from its tip in a bouquet of yellowish blooms.

Boojum trees, which are related to the ocotillo but in a genus by themselves, grow in only two places in the world: a restricted area of Baja California and one spot on the Mexican mainland. Their presence is one factor in making this central desert botanically unique, worthy of preservation for all time as a wilderness area. In the Old Testament "wilderness" generally meant "desert," and the words were sometimes used interchangeably in Colonial times. The country we now entered was a true desert, complete with ravens (as ubiquitous here as they were on the islands of southeast Alaska, where we had camped the previous summer). I think that it would also qualify as a wilderness by most standards, since the works of man are not obtrusive and are confined to a few threadlike tracks winding through an immensity of space.

The street pattern of downtown Boston, it is quite clear, was determined by cows; roads across the Appalachians follow old buffalo trails. The desert roads of Baja lack such planning. They bear testimony to man's durable optimism: a new route must always be better than the old one, since it could not possibly be worse. "There are many branches through deep dust," states the guidebook, describing one characteristic stretch; "it is usually best to keep right." Or again: "Described here is the most westerly of the possible combinations." Since a single heavy rain can change the combinations completely, the advice is not reassuring. One seeks comfort in the thought that the most imaginative diversions generally find their way back to the main track. Yet with a little inattention it is easy to get lost.

Worming its way down the narrow peninsula — with an occasional sidetrack to an abandoned mission, an isolated "ranch," or an onyx quarry such as that at El Mármol — this track varies in quality with the nature of the terrain. Over much of it, ten miles an hour is a reasonable speed; on the steepest, rockiest slopes we could outwalk the truck. Sandy stretches were generally easier driving, and when we reached the smooth surface of a "dry lake," we could really open up. But traveling mostly at the speed of a bicycle, and equally in contact with the earth, we felt a part of the passing scene as never from a highway. There was no problem (in fact considerable relief) in stopping to watch a ground squirrel or listen for the note of a quail, to examine the bloom of a cactus, a delicate hairstreak butterfly poised on a desert flower, or the infinitely subtle gradation of colors of the lichens on the rocks, ranging from orange through lemon-yellow to blue-green, tinting whole hillsides.

There were long dull stretches, such as the broad Pacific plain, where the land seemed utterly dead; then suddenly we had the rare and beautiful sight of a century plant in flower. When the terrain looked least hospitable, a charming spot to camp seemed always to turn up, such as the canyon with blue palms and great granite boulders where we spent our second night. The floor of coarse sand was bright with flowers, including in the very center a dense round mat of sky-blue lupine. In the shrubbery was a blue-gray gnatcatcher. One had a sense of intimate, enclosed space that contrasted with the broad sweep of the desert across which we had been traveling. To me the greatest beauty of desert country lies in the distant views or intimate close-ups rather than in the often forbidding middle ground: in the warm colors of the mesas and the changing light on distant peaks or — at short focus — in the detail of a boojum blossom or the red fishhook spines of the barrel cactus. These cacti gave the only spots of color in some of the starker areas through which we passed, as — in other such areas — did the yellow-green of the prickly-pear.

Except when one is lucky enough to strike a flowering period after a rain, desert colors tend to be subdued; it is the fantastic shapes that catch the eye. Almost as weird as the boojum — though botanically unrelated — is the elephant tree: a child's drawing of a tree, with thick trunk and heavy branches tapering toward the tip. Then there is the tree yucca, close relative of the Joshua tree, so named for its supposed resemblance to a man raising his arms to heaven in supplication. During the course of our trip we encountered it at various stages; we admired the pineapple-shaped clusters of white flowers and sampled the ripe fruit, which tasted rather like dates.

Towering above all were the great cardóns, the Mexican relative of the saguaros that dominate so much of our Southwestern desert. We met them first when we turned inland from Rosario, and we followed them southward. In that classic story of Baja in mission days, *The Journey of the Flame*, the narrator, Juan Colorado — who is traveling up the peninsula from the south — salutes the cardón. "The Mission of Rosario marked for me the final break with my own land. To the pitahaya and many southern cacti I had already said good-bye, and now the last cardón moved me almost to tears . . . It was over forty feet high, erect, gaunt and forbidding, like a great giant barring the north to those of the south. Forbidding equally the south to those ignorant water-guzzlers who exist in the north, but who lack foresight, strength and endurance for my own delightful country."

The pitahaya, to which Juan Colorado had already said good-bye, is the organ-pipe cactus; its fruit was so prized by the aboriginal Indians that they calculated time by its fruiting season. Earlier in the narrative he recalls " 'The Time of Pitahayas' — those three months during which life was one continuous pleasure. Then there was no hunger and little work. Young and old thronged our thorny forests, eating juicy, ripe, red pitahayas as large as a horse's hoof; eating and drinking continually; sleeping when tired of dancing, and eating again as the languor of sleep passed.

"This was the mating season when young men, seeing for the first time the charm of some slim girl, would select for her the ripest and best pitahaya, and at night would sing for her. If two followed the same *enamorada*, and she, not loath to be fought over, encouraged both, older men intervened between drawn knives, exclaiming: 'While the pitahaya ripens, eat, dance, and

Organ-pipe cactus in bloom on the shore of a calm *bahia* along the coast of Baja California

be mirthful. He insults "The Time of Pitahaya" who does aught else.' Thereafter, both suitors followed her laughing and singing."

We were to see plenty of organ-pipe cactus during our journey, but none alas in fruit. And though we were ignorant water-guzzlers from the north (we carried four five-gallon containers), we were sorry to reach the end of the stretch through the central desert, which is now also the end of the old road. We had been almost five days on the rough track when we began climbing slowly up the mesas toward the mission town of San Ignacio, along the worst stretch of road of the whole trip. Birds seemed somewhat more abundant: Gila woodpeckers, mockingbirds, red-tailed hawks. Butterflies too: the queen (the southern relative of our monarch), yellow sulphurs that I did not identify, and what appeared to be a pale version of our painted lady. Bare ground gave way to a thin cover of grass, on which fed a few range cattle; a windmill with a huge, many-bladed fan marked the location of a ranch.

One of the great moments in any trip down the Baja peninsula is the first sight of San Ignacio after days of dry camping on the desert. Creeping in low gear down into the arroyo where the mission lies, we had a sudden glimpse of a broad, deep-blue river; then we were among the date palms (originally planted by the Jesuit missionaries) and a moment later in the town square, shaded by ancient laurel trees. Looming above the thatch-roofed adobe buildings is one of the most beautiful and well-preserved of all the mission churches. Begun by the Jesuits in the early eighteenth century — when San Ignacio was the northernmost outpost — and finished by the Dominicans, who succeeded them, it is built of lava rock. That Indian labor could have produced the stonework of the great arched ceiling is almost beyond belief.

Most of the mission churches are now in ruins. The early adobe structures had already vanished by the early eighteenth century. "Now all is gone," we read in *The Journey of the Flame*. "These Southern California Missions, built of adobe, when once unroofed melt away in the rains as quickly as Christianized Indians also disappear." But the great stone churches that still stand as originally built (unspoiled by later restoration), such as

San Ignacio and San Javier, give one a sense of the past that adds immensely to the charm of this rugged country. Here California history began; indeed the name "California" — derived from a fictional island of the Amazons — originally applied only to the peninsula, which was settled first; the land to the north was known as Alta California. That the Mexicans retained Baja after the war with the United States, thus saving it from the pressures of progress, is one of the happy accidents of history.

Beyond San Ignacio, however, we faced the future that we left behind five days before at Ensenada. Bulldozers were cutting and filling a broad, straight path for the highway (which is already hard-topped from the southern tip of the peninsula north to Santa Rosalía on the Gulf). The precipitous switchback road down to the desert floor that Krutch termed "almost as steep and very little wider than the mule trail down Grand Canyon" is still the only route, but the level line of the new road has now been cut through the hills and the old way will soon be obsolete.

Almost as breathtaking as the first sight of an oasis like San Ignacio is the approach to Santa Rosalía from the west: the sudden transition from the interior desert to the Gulf of California, more picturesquely known as the Sea of Cortés. This is still desert country, where more than a year may go by without a drop of rain. But now there are frigatebirds overhead, pelicans diving offshore, a curlew and a night heron among the mangroves; willets and snowy and reddish egrets on the gleaming, sickle-shaped beach. We stripped and swam in the warm waters of Concepción Bay, which stretches for 25 miles south from the old town of Mulegé, and is considered by all who have seen it one of the loveliest bodies of water on the continent.

This was familiar territory. Seven years ago, in April, my wife and I had explored the bay and several of the offshore islands

as guests of Kenneth and Nancy Bechtel on one of many expedi-
tions sponsored by the Belvedere Scientific Fund — the object
of which has been to make scientific studies of some of the choicest
areas of Baja California with a view to their preservation. Scenes
from that previous trip were still vivid in my memory: the ravens,
jet-black against the pinkish rock, feeding on shrimp; the frigatebirds soaring on thermals above the headlands (all males; the
females were on the nests); the porpoises, cutting the surface
of the bay in a series of arcs; the osprey perched on a cardón;
the ocotillos bright with their "desert candles," and the palo-
verdes covered with yellow flowers.

At that time the Gulf coast was still a roadless area; the old
El Camino Real skirting the bay was merely a rough track. Now
it is a broad highway, along which the cars whiz at seventy
miles an hour. Nowhere is the inevitable conflict between
progress and nature more sharply defined. Will easy accessibility
for all mean eventual value to none? Haphazardly "developed"
like some of Baja's other beaches, the charm and beauty of Bahía
Concepción could be lost forever. Here, if anywhere, is an
opportunity for wise land planning, for setting aside at least part
of this unique bay as a national reserve dedicated to public
enjoyment rather than private profit.

The new road south to La Paz is fast, sometimes scenic, and
wholly without adventure. Yet inland from Loreto — the first
permanent settlement in California and for more than a century
its capital — lies another national treasure: San Javier, the finest
Jesuit church in Baja. The mission is reached by a narrow
mountain road as varied and enchanting as any we encountered
on the peninsula. Winding among towering cliffs, it plunges into
canyons shaded by giant fig trees and great fan palms that rustle
in the wind. Brown-and-purple butterflies hover over the flowering shrubs; a rock wren is singing a few feet from a pair of

cardinals; a snipe (which I never thought to meet in the desert) darts along the stream that flows down the center of the arroyo. Here we made the acquaintance of the whisker cactus, one of the organ-pipe family known as *Senita* (old man) from the long gray spines that cover the upper stems. As we reluctantly drove up out of the canyon, we felt that this was a spot where one could camp for weeks without exhausting its wonders. "Bad roads" will not save it, since it is a short drive from the highway, and the road is negotiable by private car or taxi from Loreto. "The most beautiful church in my country and having eight bells" (as the author of *The Journey of the Flame* described it when it was already two centuries old) is bound to attract more and more tourists from the north. We can only hope that the rugged approach through the canyons will remain as unspoiled as the ancient church itself.

La Paz, capital of the Territory of Baja California, once famous for its pearl fisheries and now a busy seaport, has long been accessible by air, but as recently as a decade ago the road south to the tip of the peninsula was, according to Krutch, rugged and primitive. Of one stretch he warns: "The traveler had better be aware of the road southward which runs down an arroyo so deep in sand that even a vehicle with a four-wheel drive may dig itself hopelessly in." Today an afternoon's easy driving will take you to the Cape. Elegant hotels have risen on the rugged shoreline; already it is hard to find access to the beach. The first track we followed led only to a barbed-wire fence and a private property sign, the second came to a dead end in the brush. We managed at last to reach the ocean by following bits of the old road. Here was a perfect campsite on yellow sand, almost like fine gravel, interrupted by masses of sculptured volcanic rock, ranging in hue from near black to pale ocher. The profusion of flowers a few yards inland, the soft air, the butterflies and hummingbirds reminded us that we were indeed in the tropics. Encamped in a nearby cove was a group of underwater enthusiasts from a diving club in San Francisco. The southern end of Baja is a superb area for snorkeling, as we had discovered on a previous visit to the island of Espíritu Santo off La Paz. As the region becomes more accessible, there will be need to protect these offshore reefs and islands as well as the mainland itself.

The highway ends abruptly at Cabo de San Lucas. Next day, circling back to La Paz by the old road through Todos Santos, we camped again on the shore of the Pacific, as we had on our first night out from San Diego. But here we were truly remote — the only human beings on a crescent of fine white sand that stretched for miles between two rocky headlands. Well out to sea beyond the line of breakers we spotted a plume of vapor and a dark form surfacing for an instant — then another, and another. Too far south for gray whales, I thought, having in mind their famous breeding ground in Laguna Scammon farther up the coast. But I have since learned that they also migrate into the Gulf. Grays are one of the few species of whales that have been successfully protected — which provides yet another reason why the future development of Baja California is of world concern.

So long as Baja remained essentially roadless, its future as a unique natural area seemed reasonably secure, despite the airplane and the four-wheel-drive vehicle, and the increase in population through immigration from the mainland of Mexico. Now quite suddenly all is about to change. As soon as the highway is finished, the floodgates will be open for tourists fleeing the smog and congestion of Southern California. Nor will the flood consist only of holiday visitors. For the first time, the Mexican government is encouraging American investment in the very areas from which it has hitherto been excluded.

The Mexican constitution prohibits direct ownership by foreigners of land located within 100 kilometers (62 miles) of its borders and — even more important in Baja — within 50 kilometers (30 miles) of its coastline. Since the average width of the peninsula is only 75 miles, the restriction applied to a large proportion of the land area. But on May 1, 1971, President Luis Echeverria Alvarez issued a decree that gets around this provision by setting up an official trust system whereby a foreign individual or corporation may obtain all the rights of ownership. Hitherto, outside interests have operated illegally, using Mexican nationals as a front in their business deals. Now the authorities are cracking down on these fraudulent schemes. Simultaneously, however, Mexico is inviting legal American capital on a grand scale.

The object of the presidential decree (in the words of a spokesman for the foreign minister) "is to foment tourism and industrial development in these previously closed areas . . . Through the trust system, foreign citizens can legally acquire rights in Mexican real estate along our borders and shores for a permanent home, a vacation cabin, or to derive an income from the rent of such properties." The director of the Baja California Department of Tourism foresees development in three stages: first on the road south from Tijuana, second on the shores of the Sea of Cortés, third in "the mountain range that runs the length of the Baja peninsula and remains mostly untouched." In some areas land prices have already soared upward more than 200 percent. A tourism school in Tijuana is offering a bachelor's degree for training in "hotel management, restaurant operation, and other aspects of the tourist industry."

Farewell, wilderness? Not necessarily. Granted that Baja will never be the same, there is still room for enlightened land planning rather than idle nostalgia. It is not for Americans to try to tell the Mexican government how to administer its land; one look north across the border would vitiate such advice even if it were wanted. Moreover the economic pressure for development is real. "Our very survival depends on tourism and foreign investment," stated the vice-president of the Banco Nacional de México.

The government has already demonstrated its interest in preserving the scenic and recreational values of the Baja coastline, and in eliminating the ugliness that has pervaded so much of it in recent years. Mexico's laws for controlling its beaches are in fact better than ours. For 20 meters back from high-tide line there can be no permanent structures, and no interference with public access. Up to now the law has been widely ignored; but last September, as part of the new program, the federal authorities suddenly cracked down. They began with the notorious trailer-home, beach-cottage sprawl that we had seen from the highway to Ensenada at the very beginning of our trip — a product of the uncontrolled real estate boom that hit this border area some years ago. "The Roman holiday of free-swinging real estate deals and fraudulent land leases along Baja California's coastline is coming to an end," announced the San Diego papers. One of the first to go was "Uncle Sam's Trailer Court," south of Rosarito Beach. Buildings below the 20-meter line have been confiscated; they will be destroyed and the owners — who rented them to gullible tenants — will be prosecuted. This is just "the beginning of an enormous crackdown," as the federal agent put it, "which will involve hundreds of structures . . . The Americans are welcome. But we are going to insist that the investment is done legally and within the framework of Mexican law."

In these public announcements little has been said about the preservation of wildlife and natural areas. There is reason to believe, however, that the Mexican government is becoming increasingly aware of what is at stake. At present, Baja has two national parks in the northern forested plateau, and a bird sanctuary on the tiny island of Raza in the Sea of Cortés — established following the Belvedere Fund trip. That's it. No federal protection for the Gulf shore, for the Gulf islands (except Raza), for the Cape, or for the Pacific Coast. The most casual visitor can see the need to set up natural reserves in such areas as Concepción Bay, the unique interior desert, and the still largely unspoiled Cape region — all of which are, or soon will be, reached by the new highway.

Scientifically, the thirty-odd islands in the Sea of Cortés are of prime importance. "Many of them," writes Dr. Lindsay, "have plants and animals found nowhere else. The isolation of populations has speeded the process of evolutionary change, and now the islands are natural laboratories for the study of speciation and evolutionary development." The California Academy of Sciences and the Sea of Cortés Institute of Biological Research have both drawn up lists of areas proposed for protection. Leading American scientists and concerned laymen are in personal contact with officials in Mexico City. A marine reserve is planned for protection of the gray whales in Scammon's Lagoon, and the Dirección General de la Fauna Silvestre proposes a game refuge in the adjacent desert. Other sanctuaries are being considered, and one hopes they will be acted on quickly, for time is running out. As was said when our Congress passed the Wilderness Act, what we save now is all we will ever save.

The world owes a debt of gratitude to Mexico for refusing to cede Baja California to the United States in the settlement following the Mexican War. With a few dismal exceptions — which should serve as warnings — Baja has been spared the worst horrors of the automobile age. Progress, Hollywood style, has been largely kept out. The ambitious plan of a group of California businessmen to "buy Baja California and develop it similar to Southern California's magnificent coastline" has happily not yet been realized. It is an emergency, all right, but the opportunity is still there — the opportunity to assure to future travelers the rare rewards of remoteness, wildness, and peace.

III. The Assault
on Sensibility

The 2075-megawatt Four Corners power plant in New Mexico spews its pollution into the desert dusk

ALVIN M. JOSEPHY, JR.

The Murder of the Southwest

ON FEBRUARY 14, 1971, a dramatic confrontation occurred around
a kitchen table in the home of a Hopi Indian in the little village
of Oraibi, Arizona. Present — some barely restraining their anger,
one with tears of frustration running from her eyes — were four
Hopi traditionalists — Indian men and women who remain deeply
loyal to the beliefs and life values of their ancestors and who
carry on their fathers' resistance to the pressures of the white
man that corrode and destroy that legacy. Across from them,
sympathetic but immobile, sat a non-Indian businessman from
St. Louis, a vice-president of the giant Peabody Coal Company,
a wholly owned subsidiary of Kennecott Copper Corporation.
His firm, under a lease encouraged and approved by the Department of the Interior — the trustee and supposed protector of
American Indian lands and resources — is engaged in strip-mining
coal in a massive earth- and water-ravaging project on sacred
reservation land in Arizona used jointly by the Hopi and Navajo
tribes.

Although neither side may have thought in such terms, the
Hopi Indians represented the past, and the coal company executive the present. But both represented a future — two futures
that were completely different and in the most profound conflict
with each other.

From the past, through the present, to the future, the Indians believe in harmony with nature and in life, in the sacredness of all things — people, animals, plants, earth, stones, and water — and their properties. A person guards an inheritance of natural resources and passes it on to the next generation, undiminished and uncorrupted. The coal company man represented the old non-Indian American dream, to exploit and use natural resources for gain, to employ them for economic growth, development, and "progress." To the Indians, this was a tradition of death, of conquering and destroying what lives, of making life foul, barren, and eventually unendurable.

The meeting was one of irreconcilables. The Hopis were adamant in wanting Peabody to halt the strip-mining and go away. To the industrialist from St. Louis, who had come to acquaint himself with the traditionalist Indian opponents of the mine and to hear their point of view, the idea was unthinkable. He heard them; he may or may not have understood them; but there was nothing he could do.

The Indian girl with tears on her cheeks almost screamed at him: "You are taking our water. You are destroying our land. You are threatening our cornfields. How can we live? Our villages will dry up. It will be the end of our way of life, the end of the Hopi people." Her silent, white-haired grandfather, his hands folded on the top of the cane on which he was leaning, nodded.

The man from the coal company, embarrassed, could say nothing and, in time, left. He was of a different present and a different future. He had to think about signed leases and contracts, multimillion-dollar investments, heavy equipment already at work, customers taking the coal, profits in hundreds of millions to be made for the parent company, and the power needs of today and tomorrow for the vast, mushrooming, non-

Indian urban growth of the entire Southwest, from the Pacific to the Rockies, from Salt Lake to the Mexican border.

One of Peabody's customers had earlier put it into words. Utilities, said L. M. Alexander of Arizona's Salt River Project, a purchaser of coal that would come from the strip mine on the Indians' land, have to "make certain there is enough electricity to operate every air conditioner, heater, and other type of electrical appliance our customers may want to use. They dictate — it is up to us to respond."

"Progress," growth, and development would not be stopped in the United States by a handful of Indians trying to keep life as it had always been.

But would it be stopped? There was an uneasiness in the mind of the Peabody vice-president as he drove away, past the ancient mesa-top villages of the Hopis, one of which, Old Oraibi, had been continuously occupied by the Indians for a thousand years. A corporation did not tangle lightly with Indians. Their present-day appeal to the general public could be great and emotional. They had treaties and special Congressional enactments and laws, many of them complex and tricky to lawyers unfamiliar with the Indian legal field. Moreover, ecologists, environmentalists, anthropologists, conservationists of all stripes — even garden club ladies and birdwatchers from as far away as Alabama and New England — were giving support to the Hopis, writing letters to newspapers and Congressmen and to Peabody and its parent company, Kennecott, demanding that the strip-mining be stopped. Peabody, indeed, was already a well-marked target of such groups because of its ruinous strip-mining in the coal areas of the East. There was reason to pause — but, of course, the mining on the Indians' land had to continue. The coal company executive drove on to Gallup, New Mexico, and eventually flew back to St. Louis.

The issue of the Indians' coal — far from being settled that day — is a momentous one, not alone to the Hopis and Navajos, but to people throughout the country who are growing increasingly alarmed at its use, for it is playing a key role in what is coming to be seen as the most enormous and hideous case of pollution and environmental damage confronting the nation.

The facts of the case are monumental and, in many respects, appalling. In a vast, coordinated plan to meet power needs (a deceptive term that obscures such things as the wasteful and unnecessary use of power; chamber of commerce lures to industry to come and use power; advertising by utilities urging consumers to buy and use more and more electrical appliances; and the hungry greed of cities and regions to attract more population and capital and grow bigger and bigger), 23 major investor-owned and state, municipal, and federal power companies and agencies united in a consortium known as W.E.S.T. (Western Energy Supply and Transmission Associates). The consortium is in the process of operating, constructing, or planning six of the country's largest coal-fueled power plants, together with a satellite system of smaller ones, in various parts of the previously unspoiled desert and red-rock canyon land of the Southwest to supply electricity to such diverse metropolitan areas as Southern California, the Las Vegas region of Nevada, and the Phoenix-Tucson urban and agricultural centers of Arizona.

All of these areas are among the fastest-growing in the United States. From 1960 to 1970, for instance, Los Angeles County's population increased by 931,962, and Orange and Ventura counties in Southern California grew by 100.2 and 88 percent, respectively. Maricopa County, Arizona, now the twenty-fourth largest in population in the nation, grew by 45.2 percent, while Mohave County, Arizona — America's fastest-growing county — and Clark County, Nevada, which contains Las Vegas, sprang ahead by 224.6 percent and 112.6 percent, respectively.

Two plants in the far-flung W.E.S.T. complex are already in operation. One of them — known as the Four Corners plant because of its location at Fruitland, New Mexico, in the area where Colorado, Arizona, Utah, and New Mexico meet — is a 2075-megawatt abomination, probably the most shocking single polluter of the atmosphere anywhere in the United States. In the past this area of the San Juan Valley was one of the most beautiful in the Southwest. But today a small plane trying to fly across the region to view such scenic splendors as famous Ship Rock Peak must rise above a sea of dirty brown smoke that obscures a large part of the Earth. From the stacks of the plant's five units is spewed out more particulate matter — 300 tons or more per day — than is let loose by all stationary sources of air pollution in New York and Los Angeles combined. At times the pollution hangs over an area of 10,000 square miles, creating a smoky haze in the Rio Grande Valley and reaching as far away as Santa Fe and Albuquerque. At other times a thick, filthy plume extends like a wall across the polychrome desert for more than 150 miles. In one celebrated space photograph, this was the only man-made object visible on the Earth and was seen stretching from New Mexico into Arizona and Colorado.

By a network of transmission lines that do their share in disfiguring the land, the Four Corners plant supplies power to six members of the W.E.S.T. consortium: Arizona Public Service, which also operates the plant, Southern California Edison, Public Service of New Mexico, the Salt River Project of Arizona, Tucson Gas & Electric, and El Paso Electric. The source of its energy further scours nature, for it is fueled by coal, strip-mined nearby, without sign of reclamation or conscience, by the Utah Mining & Construction Company. The plant stands upon land leased from the Navajos, and the coal is being stripped from Navajo land.

The devastating sight of the pollution erupting from the plant's stacks does not please the industrialist members of the consortium, who are becoming increasingly defensive about such public displays of their handiwork. The plant's operators say they will soon be able to do something to cut down the pollution, which includes heavy doses of sulfur dioxide and oxides of nitrogen as well as highly visible fly ash — none of which is good for men, animals, or the Earth. (A number of recent studies, including one by the federal Air Pollution Control Office, provide evidence that a dangerous health situation and damage to vegetation are already facts of life in the area.) The plant, belatedly, was told by New Mexico to clean up or shut down, but it is questionable whether the state has the means or power to carry out the ultimatum. The utility's intentions, moreover, are viewed only as promises, and the record of promises, which runs like a theme through every part of W.E.S.T.'s great coordinated grid, provides more reason for skepticism than hope.

Example: The Four Corners operators installed less than one-third of the pollution-control equipment specified in their contract (i.e., promise) with the Navajos and approved by the Department of the Interior on July 6, 1966. The violation is well known to the Department of the Interior, as well as the Department of Health, Education and Welfare, which made a special study of the situation, but the pollution still goes on, making the Four Corners area what to many persons has now become a highly unfit and unhealthy place in which to live. In addition, the 1966 lease called for periodic tests and measurements of the pollution and reports on those studies by the plant's operators at least annually to the Department of the Interior. The studies have never been made, and thus far the Department of the Interior has taken no action to enforce their being made. As a result, the health, the property, and the welfare of people in the vicinity — Indians and non-Indians — are jeopardized. In the case of the Indians, both the Department of the Interior and the Department of Health, Education and Welfare, which are charged by law with protection of the Indians, can be accused of having abdicated their responsibilities.

It may be questioned why the plant is not shut down until state-of-the-art pollution-control equipment is installed and tested to satisfaction. It may also be asked why the plant was permitted to start operating in the first place. The answer to both questions may possibly be that the Department of the Interior, and particularly its Bureau of Reclamation, as a principal member itself of the consortium, has become so enmeshed in the secrecy and skullduggery of the huge power complex that it would be wringing its own neck if it made a move to bring the Four Corners plant to heel.

Bad as that plant is, however, it is only the beginning of the mess that threatens the Southwest. Late in 1970 a second unit in the desert-spoiling complex, the 1580-megawatt Mohave plant, went into operation in Clark County, Nevada, near Bullhead City, Arizona, where the Colorado River, having passed Hoover Dam, runs southward between Arizona and the southern tip of Nevada. This plant is operated by Southern California Edison, which takes 56 percent of its power output. The rest is shared by the Los Angeles Department of Water and Power, the Nevada Power Company, and the Salt River Project of Arizona.

The Mohave plant brings us back to the Hopis, for its source of fuel is the coal Peabody is strip-mining from land that tribe shares at present with the Navajos. The mine is 273.6 miles east of Bullhead City on the northern part of Black Mesa, a magnificent 3300-square mile "island in the sky" in northeastern

Arizona. In the north the mesa is 8000 feet above sea level, rising in a spectacular escarpment 1500 feet above the surrounding Navajo Indian countryside. Along the mesa's southern border, canyons cut into the island, forming fingers of the mesa, now only 2000 feet above sea level, on which the Hopis have lived for centuries in a string of independently governed villages.

Like all the region, the mesa is arid, and water is a precious commodity. It comes suddenly in storms, pouring southward down the washes to nurture the Hopis' small, carefully tended corn and bean fields. Springs and wells scattered on the mesa top provide a steadier water supply, especially for the Navajos who graze cattle and sheep and raise small gardens in the north. The central basin of the mesa is a silent land of sage, sparse grass — much of it overgrazed by sheep — and forest. The rims are black with juniper and piñon. To the Hopis and Navajos it is a sacred land of shrines and spirits, where man comes close to unity with nature and the supernatural. To the Navajos, Black Mesa is the Female Mountain whose eternal and natural balance with neighboring Lukachukai, the Male Mountain, provides harmony, which with beauty is the Navajo Way of Life. "If these mountains are damaged," Navajo traditionalist leaders warn, "the Navajo Way will be destroyed." Even the unbelieving white man visiting the mesa can feel the truth of the warning, for it is an awesome and timeless region of solitude, wonder, and beauty not experienced in urban man's usual haunts.

Peabody's present leases (the coal company was considering the lease of another 10,240 acres on the mesa to get at 84 million more tons of coal) cover 24,858 acres on the mesa top that lie within the borders of the Navajo reservation and 40,000 acres that lie in an area that is now jointly used by the Navajos and Hopis, pending settlement of its ownership between them. Of this total of approximately 100 square miles, some 22 square

miles are known to contain 337 million tons of bituminous coal
lying in seams up to 8 feet thick near the surface and perhaps
up to 65 feet thick a little lower down.

With dragline and huge 14- and 36-cubic-foot (and eventually
90-cubic-foot) buckets that scoop up overburden (piled in towering ridges of dirt and rocks beside the gaping trenches) and then
the coal itself, Peabody provides the fuel for the Mohave plant,
ten tons of coal a minute, five million tons a year. In addition,
the coal for Mohave requires staggering amounts of Navajo and
Hopi water, 2000 to 4500 gallons per minute, drawn from wells
more than 2000 feet deep in the mesa, for the coal is pulverized
at the mine, mixed with an equal amount of water, and pumped
as slurry through an 18-inch, underground steel pipeline across
Black Mesa and northern Arizona the entire 273.6 miles to
Bullhead City. It was a marvelously ingenious and economical
idea, a testament to modern technology and engineering, but
in a dry country where water is scarce, somebody — and in this
case, the Indian — is quickly losing a vital resource that required
ages upon ages to store up and that will require further ages
upon ages to replenish.

At Bullhead City, the Mohave plant removes the water from
the coal and may use it at the plant — about 3200 acre-feet a
year — for cooling the condensers. In addition, since the cooling
requires more water than that, the plant has received permission
to use 30,000 acre-feet a year of Nevada's limited right to water
from the Colorado River, a river whose waters are already in
short supply among its many users.

Unlike the Four Corners plant, Mohave has installed electrostatic precipitators (pollutant cleaners) claiming a 97 percent
efficiency. Because of their use, together with the construction
of a 500-foot-high (but not aesthetically attractive) stack and an
assurance from Peabody that the Black Mesa coal has only an

8 percent ash and a .5 percent sulfur content (which puts it in the ranks of low sulfur content coal but not low enough, for example, to meet the legal standards of the state of New Jersey), the plant's operators promised that "the amount of air pollution at any given point in the area will be negligible." The problem is that it was another promise. In February 1971, the mined product arriving from Black Mesa had an ash content considerably higher than 8 percent, possibly caused by the huge buckets' scooping up overburden along with the coal, and Mohave had to suspend operations. More serious is what is meant by "negligible." A study made by biochemist Mike Williams of the John Muir Institute in Albuquerque reported that each day, even with 97 percent-efficient electrostatic precipitators in use, the Mohave plant emits 30 tons of fly ash, 157 tons of sulfur oxides, and 91 to 140 tons of oxides of nitrogen. This is excessive pollution and perhaps not such good news for the Lake Mead National Recreation Area, which is immediately north of Bullhead City; the various Indian reservations as well as the new Havasu City development, lying along the Colorado River not far to the south; and visitors to Grand Canyon slightly to the northeast.

The power, one is told once more, is needed for the growth of Southwest urban areas, although it should not be overlooked that the beneficiaries of the Indians' coal and water, of Black Mesa's ravishment, and of the new pollution in the desert include such questionable users as the operators of searchlights at shopping center openings, the owners of Las Vegas casinos, whose banks of light bulbs blink on and off round the clock on garish sidewalk marquees, and so forth. Again, a question might be asked: If this plant was so necessary to consumers, why was it not located among them? The answer: Its pollution is so great that no city would tolerate it in the neighborhood. So, like the other plants in the complex, it was put where only a few people could complain — out in the desert, and the hell with what it did there.

Even more atrocious is the case of the third great plant in the complex, the so-called Navajo plant (called un-Navajo by some of the Indians), whose three units, generating 2310 megawatts, have been under construction since early 1970 at Page, Arizona, hard by Glen Canyon Dam, which, one remembers, just had to be built to produce electric power and which obliterated Glen Canyon, one of the gem stretches of the Colorado River, with Lake Powell. The incongruity of the fate now facing Lake Powell and the entire surrounding canyonland recreation area can only be grasped (and gasped at) by understanding also that a fourth plant, the supermonster of all of them — Kaiparowits, with an ultimate output of at least 5000 megawatts — is planned for construction beginning in 1973 *on the opposite side of Lake Powell from the Navajo plant.* In effect, the two power plants will bracket the recreation area and make sure that no acre of lake surface or surrounding canyonland escapes a film of soot and no blue sky remains for vacationers in this former wonderland of the Southwest.

Follies upon folly? Not to the Bureau of Reclamation, which even while it was cajoling the American public into acceptance of Glen Canyon Dam was deep — and secretly — in negotiations with the private utilities for the coal-fueled plants. The bureau had the usual self-serving reasons for busying itself with these added projects, for, as everyone knows, without projects there is no need for the bureau. But there were other motivations. The bureau is also interested in the industrial growth of the entire region, possibly because development and growth have been the bureau's traditional aim, and the region, undeveloped and sparsely populated, is one of the last sections of the United States in that unhappy condition. Never mind that the Navajo and

Kaiparowits plants will pollute and seriously affect the beauty of such majestic creations of nature as Grand Canyon, Rainbow Bridge, Monument Valley, Canyon de Chelly, and the wonders of Bryce, Zion, and Canyonlands national parks. The region "cries" for the bureau's prescription for industrial development.

As another reason of the same stripe, the Navajo plant at Page will bring added industrial development and income to the Navajo Indians, who leased the site and provided the water for the plant and who will receive revenue from the coal required by the plant and jobs and additional income from the economic growth the plant is expected to inspire. Many of the Navajos, like the traditionalist Hopis, are vehemently opposed to this kind of development, with its accompanying threats to their values and life-styles, destruction of the beauty and harmony of their universe, and assault on their health and well-being. But the Department of the Interior's policy is to encourage the industrialization of the reservations, and little attention has been paid to the opposition of the traditionalists.

Finally (although the bureau's rationalizations for the plants that will bracket Lake Powell go on and on), there is the broken-record strain of the urgent need for more power. Glen Canyon Dam was built only a few years ago to meet Southwest power needs. But the new plants that will dwarf it and make it look silly and obsolete raise again the inevitable question of why the dam was built in the first place.

Navajo's three units will go into operation in 1974, 1975, and 1976. The plant, with three smokestacks 70 stories tall, will be operated by the Salt River Project of Arizona, and its power will go also, via more cross-country transmission lines, to Arizona Public Service, the Nevada Power Company, the Los Angeles Department of Water and Power, and Tucson Gas & Electric. In addition, Southern California Edison will receive 24.3 percent of the power output on a temporary basis until the Bureau of Reclamation is ready to use it for its own need — to pump water from the Colorado River to the Central Arizona Project. Hence the bureau's intimate interest in this plant.

The Navajo plant takes us back again to the Hopis, for like the Mohave plant, its fuel will come from Peabody's strip mine on Black Mesa. This time the coal — eight million tons a year, three million more than will go to Mohave — will be shipped over a new 78-mile railroad that will be built across Indian land between the mesa and the plant site at Page. Chalk up another scar for the presently undefiled landscape.

All the planning, testing, negotiations, and lease and contract signings associated with the different elements of the huge power complex were carried out so quietly that they provide a classroom example of how serious has become the lack of accountability by government agencies working hand-in-glove with industry in the United States today. Many federal, state, and local agencies, many public and private bodies, many communities, many groups of people, and individuals with many different interests will be seriously affected by the plants and their impact on the environment. But none of them knew what was going on until it was too late. There were no announcements prior to signed contracts, no public hearings, no Congressional hearings, no chance for anyone to ask questions or receive answers, no opportunity for independent, disinterested studies on the impact on air, water, or the quality of the environment, no public reports to the Federal Power Commission and no statements of the kind required by the National Environmental Policy Act of 1969. The atmosphere and environment, fundamental to the quality and future of life of a huge part of the Southwest, encompassing thousands of square miles in many states, was literally appropriated by the members of the power consortium.

The confusion, wonder, frustration, and anger that resulted when word did get out — after everything was firmly signed and in the works — underscores how grave has become the government's failure to protect — or even to inform — the public. An incident regarding the Navajo plant is typical. On March 11, 1969, a member of the Arizona Game and Fish Commission wrote a somewhat nervous letter to the superintendent of Glen Canyon National Recreation Area, relaying some information he had just received from a person connected with the Salt River Project (the operator of the Navajo plant, which had not yet begun building) concerning a "proposed steam electricity plant on Lake Powell." He had heard "some spectacular statistics revolving around the burning of 23,000 tons of coal per day and the diversion of over 39,000 acre-feet of water annually." It was clear from the tone of his letter that he did not wish to be thought of as butting into something that was not his business, but "we, of course," he gingerly explained, "are interested directly in possible water pollution aspects of this plant" and also "have a general interest in how the aesthetic impact of this plant will affect the quality of the experience of fishing on Lake Powell."

His innocent query let the cat out of the bag. The superintendent of Glen Canyon National Recreation Area, almost equally uninformed about a power plant near the lake, forwarded the letter to the Southwest regional director of the National Park Service, who might know better what was going on and could answer it. The regional director, in turn, wrote for information to the director of the National Park Service in Washington but got no reply — possibly because the director was also in the dark (though both the National Park Service and the Bureau of Reclamation are in the Department of the Interior). Later in the summer of 1969 the Southwest regional director turned elsewhere and sought information from the regional office of the

Bureau of Reclamation in Salt Lake City, and on September 5 he received, as sole explanation, a copy of the contract signed by the Salt River Project and Secretary of the Interior Stewart Udall *on January 17, 1969*, for water service from Lake Powell for the plant to be erected at Page!

On October 20 the regional director of the National Park Service again wrote to the director in Washington, telling him how little his office knew about what was going to happen to Lake Powell and the recreation area, which the Park Service was supposed to administer, and complaining that all the planning and negotiations for the Navajo plant were "obviously" conducted "with the greatest possible secrecy." Indeed, they were! Officials of the Salt River Project were reportedly furious when they learned that one of their people had "leaked" information to the Arizona Game and Fish man, occasioning that first hesitant letter of inquiry in March 1969 — two months after the contract with the Department of the Interior had been signed.

Indeed, it was months later before any other interested agency in the Department of the Interior, much less a state agency, the newspapers, or the affected citizenry, could pry loose enough information from any source to know what was being planned — in fact, what was already agreed upon and signed.

Despite the publicity that has since come to the power complex as a whole and to the elements that are already in operation or under construction, little is yet known about those plants that are still to be built. Kaiparowits, to be constructed in Utah at one of two sites still under consideration about 12 miles north of Page, is officially "under study," and interested persons who are anxious about its pollution effects are told little more than that Southern California Edison is spending a great amount of money (some $4 million already) on the studies. If Kaiparowits is built, it is known that its coal will come from an underground mine 10 to 15 miles north of the plant on the Kaiparowits Plateau.

Some nine miles north of the Four Corners plant, work on a fifth power producer, the San Juan plant, was commenced late in 1970. It will be fueled by coal strip-mined at the plant, and will ultimately have three units of 330 megawatts each. If Four Corners does not already produce enough pollution by itself to make the point with everyone in the vicinity, the addition of the fly ash, sulfur dioxide, and oxides of nitrogen from San Juan should go far toward making the area notorious as one of the most dangerously polluted spots on Earth.

The sixth giant plant in the complex, Huntington Canyon, is scheduled to go into operation in June 1974 some 29 miles southwest of Price, Utah. It will have an initial output of 430 megawatts but may ultimately quadruple that figure. It will be operated by Utah Power and Light and will be supplied with coal by Peabody from an underground mine two miles from the plant. In addition, five smaller coal-fueled plants are already in operation in a number of states as part of the grid, two more are projected, and three more units are being considered. The last three would be erected at Four Corners, which should just about finish for good whatever beauty remains in that area.

Altogether, the six plants, with a projected total output of nearly 14,000 megawatts, will bring profound environmental change for the worse to more than 100,000 square miles of the most beautiful land in the Southwest — what is advertised by the tourist bureaus as the Enchanted Wilderness of the Colorado Plateau. The air, water, and landscape will all be affected, as will the environmental quality of six national parks, 28 national monuments, two national recreation areas,* scores of national historic landmarks and state parks, and 39 Indian reservations.

* The national parks are Grand Canyon and Petrified Forest in Arizona; Zion, Bryce Canyon, and Canyonlands in Utah; and Mesa Verde in Colorado. The national monuments affected are Grand Canyon, Marble Canyon, Canyon de Chelly, Navajo, Wupatki, Pipe

Even if regulations are enforced and each plant equips itself with the pollution-control equipment called for by its contract, the daily pollutants streaming out to blow as plumes in different directions with the wind, or to disperse and blanket huge areas with smoky haze, will include about 240 tons of fly ash, some 2160 tons of sulfur dioxide, and 850 to 1300 tons of oxides of nitrogen. But even this is not all, for the utilities that comprise W.E.S.T. have only begun; by 1985 the big complex plans to be producing a total of 36,000, rather than 14,000, megawatts, three times the power of the Tennessee Valley Authority and seventeen times as much as the High Aswan Dam in Egypt. In effect, the utilities' plan has the character of turning the least populated part of the Southwest into a colonial region, producing the power for the great megalopolises that will surround it.

It was said that a corporation does not tangle lightly with Indians. From the beginning the use of Indian resources — traditional source of big money and easy money to white looters, aggrandizers, exploiters, and their lawyers — has been a cornerstone of the W.E.S.T. complex. With the help of the Department of the Interior — and some very questionable deals reminiscent of land steals from Indians in the past — Hopi and Navajo possessions were fitted nicely into the consortium's grandiose plan. But when one deals with Indian tribes today, it should be obligatory to know and respect the history and culture of those distinct and unique American peoples. None of the corporate members of W.E.S.T. seems to have informed himself

---

Spring, Sunset Crater, Walnut Canyon, Tuzigoot, and Montezuma Castle, all in Arizona; Aztec Ruins, Chaco Canyon, El Morro, Bandelier, and Pecos, all in New Mexico; Rainbow Bridge, Arches, Natural Bridges, Capitol Reef, Cedar Breaks, and Timpanogos Cave, all in Utah; Hovenweep, in Utah and Colorado; Black Canyon of the Gunnison, Great Sand Dunes, Colorado, and Yucca House, all in Colorado; Joshua Tree in California; and Lehman Caves in Nevada. The national recreation areas are Lake Mead in Arizona and Nevada, and Glen Canyon in Utah.

adequately about the backgrounds of the Hopis and Navajos. And if the Department of the Interior, through its Bureau of Indian Affairs, did not protect the tribes, neither did it protect the utilities by providing them with the knowledge they should have had about the tribes. As a result, the first of a series of costly surprises is now threatening the great grid.

Both the Navajos and Hopis have a long history of conflict within the tribes between their traditionalists and those who have come to be known as "progressives" — the people who want to abandon old ways that appear to stand in the way of the economic development of the reservations and the rise of their standards of living. Through the years, the conflict has been fostered and encouraged, directly and indirectly, by the federal government and the pressures of white men. The progressives, responding to those pressures — urging the people to discard their traditional Indian beliefs, systems, and habits and adopt the ways of the white men so that they can prosper like white men as part of the mainstream of the white men's world — have come to be regarded by the traditionalists as something close to traitors to their people.

The conflict, which dates back to the nineteenth century, came to a head in 1934 with the passage of the Indian Reorganization Act, which called for each tribe to write a constitution for itself conforming with the provisions of the act, and under that constitution elect by democratic method a tribal council and tribal officers who would represent the tribe in dealings with the federal government and with others. Although the act intended that Indians would set up their organs of limited self-government (the federal government retained ultimate veto power over important matters) in the image of the way white men, rather than the Indians, were used to conducting their affairs, the act was generally beneficial to many tribes that had

had no semblance of self-government since the times in the nineteenth century when the United States had destroyed their traditional tribal organizations. Thus tribal councils came into existence on numerous reservations.

On the Navajo reservation traditionalists were opposed to the act, but although the Navajos to this day do not have a written constitution, the progressives did bring into existence a tribal council and a large apparatus of tribal government that has worked consistently for the economic development of the people. With the advice and guidance of non-Indian tribal lawyers, who must be approved (and, indeed, are often appointed) by the Department of the Interior, the tribe has entered into many contracts with corporations for the exploitation of natural resources on the reservation, receiving rents and royalties and providing modest employment for some of the Indians. Thus, in 1957 the tribe leased to Utah Mining & Construction the coal lands near Fruitland, New Mexico, that are now being strip-mined to provide fuel for the Four Corners plant; in 1960, pressured by Arizona Public Service ("delay" in waiting for the next scheduled meeting of the tribal council "would be fatal"), the tribe leased the land for the building of the Four Corners plant; in 1964 it leased to Peabody Coal Company some of its land on Black Mesa; and in 1966 it joined with the Hopi Tribal Council in leasing to Peabody acreage on Black Mesa that the two tribes jointly used. The Black Mesa coal was earmarked for the Mohave and Navajo plants.

In the case of all the leases, the corporations followed the advice of the Department of the Interior and conducted negotiations and the signing of agreements in what seemed to be a legally sound manner — dealing with the lawyers for the tribes and the tribal councils and tribal chairmen. They were all from the same nest. The Department of the Interior was encouraging anything,

including unrestrained industrialization, that would bring income
to the reservations; the tribal lawyers, with fees to earn and
the approval of the department and the tribal chairmen to retain,
guided the tribe along the route to new income; and the tribal
chairmen and most of the tribal council members, being progressives, listened to the promises, asked their lawyers if it was all
right, and gave their approval.

Thus, in 1960, when Utah Mining & Construction sought
approval from the Department of the Interior to sell the Navajo
coal at Fruitland to Arizona Public Service for the Four Corners
plant that would be built on Navajo land, it wrote Secretary
of the Interior Fred Seaton that the plan of development would
have "the greatest resulting benefit to the Navajo Tribe in terms
of revenue, employment, and *the desired* industrialization of
adjacent areas of the Reservation." (The emphasis is mine.)
Again, in 1965, when Secretary of the Interior Udall announced
his approval of Peabody's plan to supply coal to the Mohave
plant from a strip mine on Black Mesa, he stated that the
agreement would mean "new jobs, large tax benefits, and tremendous economic advantages not only in royalties and jobs for the
two Indian tribes, but also for the entire Southwest," and added
a commendation to "all parties involved in this agreement and
for taking a giant step forward in development of a formula for
joint public and private resource development in the Colorado
Basin that will become a model for the Nation."

Udall's action, in light of his known opposition to strip-mining
anywhere, and his feelings about the pollution of the environment
and the deterioration of the quality of life — as expressed in his
book *The Quiet Crisis* and in many of his other writings, then
and since — reflects how enormous was the political pressure from
a complex of public and private forces. The interests of the
kilowatt-hungry urban areas, the self-serving public utilities, the

industrialization of the reservations, the growth of the Four Corners area — all coincided to provide what Udall termed a "model" development for the nation.

Uppermost among his concerns, as time went on, was also the dilemma of the Bureau of Reclamation, which was committed to finding the power necessary to pump Colorado River water to the Central Arizona Project. When opposition developed to building dams for that purpose near the Grand Canyon, Udall finally sealed the fate of the dams by proposing the construction, instead, of a large coal-fueled plant. The Salt River Project, which would build and operate the plant — selling the necessary power to the Bureau of Reclamation — had to locate the plant in Arizona and near water and coal. It chose Navajo land at Page, near Glen Canyon Dam and Lake Powell. Again, many interests seemed to coincide, for the Navajo progressives were eager for the new income and job opportunities that the Salt River Project negotiators promised them. But the Navajo eagerness did them in. Somehow, in a classic repeat of business dealings between Indians and whites, they failed to realize that they held very good cards in their hand, and neither the Department of the Interior — which should have protected them, but instead participated in the poker game against them — nor their tribal attorneys guided them in playing their chips to their own best advantage.

What happened does not make pleasant reading. Back in 1948, the upper basin states of the Colorado River Basin reached agreement on the apportionment among themselves of their share of that river's water. Arizona received 50,000 acre-feet a year from that agreement. Although a court might one day rule that the Navajos, possessing very early rights to the river's water, were entitled to a large share of it, they were not taken into account, and it was assumed that the tribe would have to get whatever water it required by applying to Arizona for part of that state's 50,000 acre-feet. Nevertheless the prospect of a Navajo court claim upsetting everything made the upper basin states uneasy. Therefore, before giving his approval to the Central Arizona Project (the recipient of power from the Navajo plant), Congressman Wayne Aspinall of Colorado, the powerful chairman of the House Committee on Interior and Insular Affairs, persuaded the Bureau of Reclamation and the Salt River Project to end the Navajos' threat by getting the tribe to sign away its rights to any more of the apportionment than Arizona's 50,000 acre-feet.

The Navajos seem to have been kept uninformed about the behind-the-scenes power play to get their water rights away from them. They were told, instead, that the plant — which they were eager to have — could only be located on their land if they agreed to waive their rights to any more than Arizona's 50,000 acre-feet, and if, in addition, they *gave* 34,100 acre-feet of that allocation to the Salt River Project for cooling water for the plant. Although this left the tribe with less than 16,000 acre-feet of Colorado River water for their future needs, the tribal council on December 11, 1968, passed a resolution — which had apparently been written in Washington and brought to the reservation by a Department of the Interior official — waiving their untested water rights and donating the 34,100 acre-feet to Salt River. In return, they were reassured that the plant would be put on their land, that it would use coal from the Peabody mine on their land at Black Mesa, that a small number of Navajos would receive preferential employment at the plant and the mine, and that $25,000 would be paid each year for five years by Salt River to the Navajo Community College.

The entire deal, which has been characterized as a bilking of the Indians, was furthered by the Bureau of Reclamation and

Secretary of the Interior Udall, who was persuaded that a storm would erupt in Congress and among the Indians if he overruled the "expressed desires" of the Navajos. In addition, a conflict of interests seems to have been overlooked in the rush to get the deal settled. As trustee for the tribe's resources, the Department of the Interior was leasing the land at Page, giving away the Navajos' water, and selling the coal at Black Mesa; but, through the Bureau of Reclamation's role as a purchaser of power at Page, it was also on the receiving end. It had a vested interest in the acquisition of the site and water at Page and the coal from Black Mesa. In a sense, it was both buyer and seller.

So much for those on the side of Navajo "development." But it is not the whole story. On the reservation the traditionalists still oppose what happened, and is happening, to their land. There is resentment over the threats and the rush that caused the Navajos to give away, or lease for less than their proper value, their land and water resources not only at Page and Black Mesa, but at Fruitland, where Navajo water interests also suffered. Kent Smith, a member of the tribal council when the Black Mesa lease with Peabody was being negotiated, said, "We were asked, in effect, to say yes or no to the proposal" without being given the chance for enough deliberation or discussion. Members of chapters, the local organizations on the Navajo reservation, did not even know the negotiations were going on. The Black Mesa lease was signed without many of the people knowing anything about it.

Opposition to the strip mine on Black Mesa has been boiling up among Navajo traditionalists in recent months, particularly among those who live nearest to the area. Meetings have been held by "Save Black Mesa Committees," organized at Kayenta and Chinle, at which all sorts of complaints have been made against Peabody's operations. One sore point concerns the fate of about 600 Navajos (more than 75 families, many of them grazing flocks of sheep), who will have to be relocated, family by family, as the strip mine intrudes on their homes and grazing lands. Such lands are scarce on the reservation, and other families already hold allocations to what is available. Anger also fills the traditionalists' homes over the new roads, the company's cars and trucks, the use of precious water that is mixed with the coal, the defacing of the land, and the hiring of "progressive" Navajos, held in contempt by the traditionalists, as intermediaries between the coal company and the people of the mesa.

It is unlikely, however, that the Navajo traditionalists will have the power within their own tribe to force a halt to the mining operations. The new tribal chairman, Peter MacDonald, who has called for "Navajo control of Navajo resources," has indicated a desire to renegotiate some of the leases with Peabody and the utilities to secure better terms for the tribe. He may also support moves to force the utilities to reduce pollution and treat the land, water, and air with more concern than they are now showing. But he has given no sign that he endorses the traditionalists, who wish to bring the strip-mining operation to an end.

In the case of the lease for the land used jointly by the Navajos and Hopis on Black Mesa, Peabody entered an arena of another long-standing conflict among Indians — and the one that contains a potential threat to the future of the Mohave and Navajo power plants.

The Hopis are among the oldest peoples in the Southwest. They lived where they now live long before the arrival of the Navajos, whose ancestors originally dwelt in the far northwestern part of North America and migrated to the present-day Southwest, reaching there probably less than 500 years ago. From the start, the intruding Navajos treated the Hopis aggressively. Even after the United States brought intertribal peace to the area and established reservations for the two groups in the late nineteenth century, the Navajos, with their greatly expanding population (Navajos today, about 130,000; Hopis, about 5000) and land needs, continued to press in around the Hopis, simply appropriating Hopi land as they felt they needed it. The original Hopi reservation, a block of land entirely surrounded by the Navajo reservation in Arizona, was created in 1882. By 1910 four-fifths of the Hopi land was overrun by Navajos. In 1943 the federal government infuriated the Hopis by designating one-fourth of their original reservation as theirs and tacitly leaving open the rest of it to the Navajos. A suit, instituted by the Hopi Tribal Council (and opposed by the Hopi traditionalists, who said that their deity had given them the contested land and they did not want a white man's court to decide whether or not it belonged to them), ended by temporarily giving the Navajos and Hopis equal rights and interests in the use of the contested three-fourths of the original Hopi reservation. Although the Bureau of Indian Affairs has tended to favor the Navajos' use of the area for sheep grazing, the matter is not ended; a bill now in Congress may eventually partition the area into separate Navajo and Hopi sections. The effect of the legislation, if passed, would be to remove Navajos from large sections of the jointly owned land.

Meanwhile, Peabody's lease with both tribes for the strip mine on that joint-use portion of Black Mesa has aroused opposition among traditionalist Hopis to an extent even greater than among the Navajos. The 35-year lease, made on June 6, 1966, calls for a sliding scale of royalty payments for the coal — based on whether it is sold on or off the reservation and on current market prices, but averaging generally about 25 cents a ton. This will bring the Hopis a total of about $14.5 million over the course of the lease. The Navajos, with the additional lease on their own land, expect to receive a total of $58.5 million. Peabody, the lessee, will receive $750 million, or 98.4 percent of the total gross income received from purchasers of the coal.

In addition, Peabody will pay the Hopis $1.67 per acre-foot for the water it pumps from Black Mesa. The Navajos did better; they will receive $5 an acre-foot. But neither price is very good in water-scarce country, even though Peabody says it will cost $65 to pump and accumulate each acre-foot of water. Finally, Peabody has guaranteed to hire Indians for at least 75 percent of an employment roster at the mine that will eventually reach 375, and to pay them prevailing wages, which now average about $10,000 a year. About 80 Indians, almost all of them Navajos, have received jobs.

The desecration of their sacred land — including widespread bulldozing; the cutting of roads that lead in all directions across the mesa; the blocked drainages and black pools of water; the main access road that sends shivers up the spines of conservationists; the ridges of overburden, the piles of coal, and the long, deep trenches in the earth — has angered the Hopi traditionalists. Peabody promised to return the property to the Indians on termination of the lease "in as good condition as received, except for the ordinary wear, tear, and depletion incident to mining operations." It also promised to reseed "areas where strip-mining activities have been completed and to bear the full expense of such reseeding program."

But the meaning of those promises is far from clear, as is evident enough from their loose wording. Peabody will push overburden back into the trenches, smooth it out, and seed it. But not all the overburden will go back into the trenches; the earth will not repack as tight as it was originally, and a series of huge parallel ridges will remain. Moreover, the company has made no guarantee about the results of the seeding and has made public no detailed reclamation plan that commits the company to a final result. It does not intend, at present anyway, to introduce new topsoil, and with little available rainfall and only the overburden as topsoil, hopes for satisfactory results from the seeding are precarious. In sum, Peabody promises to make an effort to heal the land but provides no guarantee of satisfaction. Furthermore, the last trench in each series of cuts would have to be left unfilled, or overburden from the first cut would have to be trucked around to fill it. Peabody's intention is to let water accumulate in the last trench as a pond; the Indians view that as wrong — very little water would accumulate from the sparse rainfall, and it would be dangerous to man and animal, as well as a miserable eyesore on the land.

In addition to anger, deep and legitimate fears disturb the Hopis, and not the traditionalists alone. At the height of its operations Peabody will be pumping approximately 3 million gallons of water a day from its wells on Black Mesa — almost 37 billion gallons during the 35 years of its lease. This is an astronomical depletion of water reserves on Indian reservations, where water is a precious commodity for the future. In accordance with its contract, Peabody has sunk its wells to a deep aquifer, more than 2000 feet down, and lined them with casing to avoid draining the higher reserves of water that supply the springs and shallower wells used by the Indians. But many dangers of seepage, the collapse, cracking, or shifting of strata, and the gradual draining of the higher-level water into Peabody's aquifer remain, holding up for the Hopis the specter that sometime during the course of the 35-year lease desiccation will increase, and their own springs, wells, and groundwater supply will no longer provide them and their farms with adequate water. If that occurs, all that is presently Hopi would cease, for without their present villages and corn and bean fields, the spiritual base of their existence would disappear. For a thousand years or more an annual cycle of religious ceremonies has surrounded the cultivation of the two crops; Peabody's threat to the Hopis can be likened to a force threatening the end of Christianity — and all meaning of life itself to a body of devout Christians.

Many studies have been made of Black Mesa's hydrology, but none of them has agreed concerning what might or might not happen to the water supply of both the Hopis and Navajos (whose wells in the nearby Kayenta area may decline 100 feet during the lease). Peabody recognizes that the danger exists. Its lease states that if the Secretary of the Interior finds that the Indians' water supply is being endangered, he has the option (but not the obligation) to require Peabody to deepen the Indians' wells so that they again receive water in the quantity and of the quality formerly available to them. Or he may require Peabody to obtain its own water from another source "that will not significantly affect the supply of underground water in the vicinity."

Again, it is loose wording that offers precious little protection for the Indians. The Secretary of the Interior will have to know immediately when the Indians' water supply is endangered; he will have to take steps immediately to restore the water. But how will he know before it has actually happened? And will he then act — and how? No one, including Peabody, will guarantee that the Indians have no reason for fear. Peabody, for example, has no idea where it will get substitute water for its own operations — or for the Indians — if it has to stop pumping on Black Mesa. And if it finds another source, who judges whether its use "significantly" affects the supply of underground water "in the vicinity"? The promise is another one in the great web of promises. The environmentalist views it with skepticism; the Indians look on it with the deep gnawing of a life-and-death fear.

For the same reason, the Hopis are fearful of the effects on their growing season of an atmosphere occluded by air pollution. An even greater threat is the possibility that the runoff from spoil banks at the mine (the ridges of overburden left from stripping) and eroded shale from the mine's 15-mile-long access road, which cuts across all the drainage washes in that part of the mesa, will come down the washes to cake their fields. Some of the runoff, they fear, will bring with it dangerous sulfur concentrates from the mine. If that happens, the Hopis' cornfields will be ruined. No one, including Peabody's officials, can guarantee that it will *not* happen — though, again, they promise to take all precautions to prevent such a tragedy.

The Peabody lease with the Hopis was negotiated with the predominantly "progressive" Hopi Tribal Council, which was advised by its Interior-approved lawyer, John Boyden of Salt Lake City. And there may lie the difficulty for the Mohave and Navajo plants. The tribal council was the instrument created by the Indian Reorganization Act of 1934. At that time the act's provisions for the creation of a single governing body for the people so affronted the Hopis, each of whose villages had been autonomous and had been led by a Kikmongwi (Father of the People, the hereditary village chief), that a constitution and bylaws, drawn up for the Hopis by two whites, received the support of only 651 Indians in a referendum. Nevertheless, it was a majority of those who voted, and the constitution was declared valid by the federal government.

An important provision of the Indian Reorganization Act and of a federal statute relating to the act required tribal constitutions to vest in the tribes or their tribal councils the right "to prevent the sale, disposition, lease, or encumbrance of tribal lands, interests in lands, or other tribal assets without the consent of the tribe." In drawing up the Hopi constitution, its framers evidenced an intention, supported by the solicitor of the Department of the Interior, to maintain the Hopis' traditional village-based form of government and to vest in the tribal council powers "as close to the legal minimum as possible." The council, for instance, was *not* given the power or authority to lease or sell tribal lands, only to prevent it. Provisions in the Hopi constitution, including the omission of the words "without the consent of the tribe," reflected the government's intention to respect the Hopis' traditional system of government and meant, according to the traditionalists, that the tribal council, created by the constitution, did not have the power or authority to lease the Black Mesa lands.

As one cause for complaint, the Hopi constitution clearly calls for the election of village members who shall be certified by the Kikmongwis to represent their villages as tribal council members. Because of the opposition among most villages to the constitution and the tribal council, only the Kikmongwis of the villages on the Hopis' First Mesa ever certified representatives to the council.

"So far as the traditional hereditary chiefs are concerned, and the majority of the Hopi people," says Thomas Banyacya, Sr., interpreter for the traditionalist chiefs, "the council has been illegally operating since 1936. The real Hopi Chiefs have never recognized the council as it is not the Hopi Way of self-government."

As a result, some of the villages have never been represented on the council, while others have been represented by Hopis who appointed themselves or were selected by progressives on the council.

On May 16, 1966, when the lease with Peabody was approved, there were 18 seats on the council. Seven were vacant, unfilled by villages that did not recognize the council. Of the remaining eleven, four, from First Mesa villages, had been properly certified by their Kikmongwis. Two others had been chosen under provisions of their village constitutions. The other five had not been certified by their Kikmongwis. The constitution provided that a quorum of ten properly certified members were needed for a vote. The vote for the Peabody lease was 10 to 0, but only six members had a right to vote and they were not a quorum. It was apparently a clear violation of both the letter and spirit of the Hopi constitution.

Furthermore, although Peabody Coal Company seems not to have been aware of it, the negotiations and the signing of the lease (carried on by the Sentry Royalty Company, an alter ego for Peabody) were conducted by the council and their lawyer in such secrecy that few other Hopis were aware of what was going on. If one traditionalist had known about it, most if not all of them would have learned of it. Some non-Indians are convinced that there are only a handful of traditionalists left in the Hopi tribe. The obvious error of this opinion is reflected by the continued potent position of the Kikmongwis and the loyalty of the great majority of Hopis to their traditional religious beliefs and clan systems. At any rate, the hereditary village chiefs, the traditionalists, and the entire Hopi people were left out of the decision. Contrary to the intent of the Indian Reorganization Act, no opinion was sought from the people, no referendum was held, and *the consent of the tribe* was not given to the lease of interests in the tribal lands on Black Mesa. It was only in the early spring of 1970, almost four years after the lease was signed, that Peabody's extraordinary activity on the mesa occasioned rumors and questions. And then it was only with great difficulty that the traditionalists were able to piece together what was happening and learn for the first time of the threats that were developing to their lands, their water, their fields, and indeed their very existence as Hopis.

As late as March 2, 1971, Thomas Banyacya stated: "So far

this original contract [the 1966 lease with Peabody] has never been shown or read or explained fully to the Hopi Leaders and the people."

As a result of these violations, the Black Mesa mine and the two plants, Mohave and Navajo, that depend on its coal could be in jeopardy, facing the threat of the sustaining of a legal complaint to set aside the Peabody lease because it was illegally approved by the Secretary of the Interior for the Indians.

There is no doubt that the lease was a deal of white men, playing with the Indians' property. At a meeting at the Bureau of Indian Affairs' Hopi office at Keams Canyon, Arizona, on August 18, 1969, the bureau's land operations officer at the agency stated that even the members of the Hopi Tribal Council "didn't know they were going to pile mountains of dirt and just go off and leave it. If they [the council] had known what they were going to do, you couldn't have got that lease for any amount of money."

When asked why no one in the bureau had warned the council before the lease was signed, the officer shrugged and said he did not know. The lease was really worked out by the Hopis' lawyer, John Boyden, and "Washington" (principally by members of the bureau's Appraisal Division of the Economic Development Branch), he stated. When the lease came down to him, he made some caustic remarks about it and sent it back. But he was told to let "Washington" handle it. His local office was to keep quiet. The tribal council never asked him for advice, and he apparently gave none. Eventually the lease, signed by the Hopi tribal chairman, was approved up the line, through the hierarchy of the Bureau of Indian Affairs, and no one questioned the absence of guarantees to the Hopis on such vital matters as water supply, reclamation, or runoff from the spoil banks, or seemed concerned that the procedures set forth in the Hopi constitution were not adhered to. All that seemed to matter was that the reservation was going to be industrialized and that money would come to the Hopis (though there are charges today that much of the revenue from the coal goes to the administrative expenses and salaries of the tribal council).

There is still a chance that appeals to the courts can save the Southwest, or a large part of what is now threatened. Improved pollution controls could be forced on the plants, and the monster installation, Kaiparowits, might be halted before it is built. In addition, the Senate Committee on Interior and Insular Affairs was awakened to all that has been going on, and from its public hearings on the consortium, requested by New Mexico's Senator Clinton Anderson, may come legislation that will bring about a greater degree of responsibility and accountability by the utilities and their partners in government than now exists.

But more in order, for the long run anyway, will be determined efforts to develop geothermal or other nonpolluting sources of power for the Southwest, to change the habits and demands of power consumers, to halt waste and profligacy, to stop the headlong race for growth, development, and "progress" that is suicidal, and to learn that the traditionalist Hopis' religious view of their relationship to nature — of *stewardship* of the Earth — is the only outlook that matters today. The understanding that all human creatures and everything human must fit into a much larger drama is the only understanding from which to begin and from which, as the Hopi Way tells, all things flow.

GARY SOUCIE

Oil Shale — Pandora's New Box

They tell the story, in places like Rifle, Colorado, and Granger, Wyoming, and Upalco, Utah, of Mike Callahan and his famous fireplace. The tale, apocryphal though it may be, varies from saloon to saloon only in its embellishments.

Mike, it seems, settled in the early days near Rifle, and when he built his ranch house he decided to make the fireplace out of the strikingly beautiful and unusual black rock he had found in the cliffs west of town.

It was a late fall day when he finished, and Mike decided to toast away the High Country chill before his fine new fireplace. But as the kindling caught fire, so too did the fireplace rocks — and the new house.

Mike Callahan had discovered oil shale.

And if there is a moral to this story, it is that black rock can be dangerous, and one should know what he is doing before he tries to use it.

On June 29, 1971, Secretary of the Interior Rogers C. B. Morton announced plans for a prototype leasing program to develop oil shale resources on federal lands in Colorado, Utah, and Wyoming. While this event made banner headlines out where the project would take place — the West Slope of the Rocky Mountains — and caused at least a ripple in the business press and among oil companies and conservation groups, the general public took no note.

Yet a more portentous announcement concerning America's natural resources would be difficult to imagine. These oil shale formations, which could include as much as 25,000 square miles of public lands, contain hundreds of millions — perhaps trillions — of barrels of oil. At the going rate of $3 a barrel, this could mount up to between $5 trillion and $10 trillion. To put it another way, each man, woman, and child in the United States owns upward of $25,000 worth of oil shale in those three mountain states.

But to remove these riches from the land, using present technology, would lay waste some of our finest untouched Western lands — lands that still shelter abundant fish and wildlife populations, to say nothing of magnificent High Country scenery. To get the oil out, the land would literally have to be chewed up and cooked, leaving as waste millions of tons of powdery dirt.

This built-in environmental threat, however, is only one of the complications that have kept the oil shale country untouched, for the situation is complex, confused, fraught with hazards, utterly Byzantine. Despite astronomical estimates, no one really knows how much oil is locked up in the rocks — or even the extent of the oil-bearing formations hidden beneath the Earth's surface. Further, a thicket of legal complications has grown up over several decades, involving the question of who can claim a whole series of other valuable minerals that appear to be abundant in the same rocks.

Before pursuing the labyrinthine tale of oil shale, some basic definitions are needed. For a start, oil shale is a fine-textured, relatively impermeable sedimentary rock that yields oil in substantial amounts when crushed and heated to about 900 degrees. The rock does not necessarily have to be shale; in fact, many of the oil-bearing "shales" actually are marls. But it must yield oil, though how much oil is open to different interpretations. Generally, from 5 to 10 gallons of oil per ton of rock will make the grade. The "rich" oil shales, however, contain from 25 to more than 100 gallons per ton.

The oil-yielding substance in the shale is called "kerogen," from two Greek words meaning "producer of wax." When the shale is "distilled" or "retorted" by applying heat, it yields a heavy oil similar to petroleum, except that it contains more nitrogen and less hydrogen. It also contains a great deal of sulfur.

The existence of oil shale has been known for centuries. Long before the first white settlers reached Colorado, Ute Indians were using "the rock that burns" for campfires. And in 1694 a patent was granted in Shropshire, England, for a process of distilling "oyle from a kind of stone." Deposits have been found around the world, but technological problems and competition from cheaper petroleum crude oil have thwarted oil shale's entry into the world energy budget.

Fairly large-scale oil shale industries were launched in France and Scotland during the 1830s and 1850s, but their development was effectively nipped in the bud by imports of cheap petroleum from the United States, following the discovery in 1859 of the Pennsylvania oilfield. At present, commercial oil shale industries exist only in the USSR (principally Estonia) and mainland China (Manchuria and Kwantung), although another seems on the verge of development in Brazil.

Oil shale processing involves a series of steps — mining, crushing, retorting, and upgrading. Either surface (strip) or underground mining techniques may be used. After crushing, the rock is fed into a retorter and heated to about 900°F. This converts the kerogen into oil vapors and gases — and the rest of the rock into spent shale, which occupies more space than it did before it was mined. Because the high nitrogen content of the crude shale oil makes it unsuitable for conventional refining processes, it must be upgraded before shipment to a refinery. This step converts the nitrogen to ammonia and removes the sulfur as hydrogen sulfide, creating two useful by-products.

Estimates of the amounts of oil in shale deposits around the world are staggering. According to the 1965 U.S. Geological Survey Circular 523, *Organic-Rich Shale of the United States and World Land Areas*, it is estimated that worldwide shale deposits contain up to two *quadrillion* barrels of oil. For the United States alone, the estimate is 170 trillion barrels of oil. At $3 a barrel, the American shale oil alone is worth $510 trillion. (The federal debt is "only" about $350 billion.)

But oil shale figures — whether in tons, barrels, dollars, or

The way to oil-shale — from strip-mined rock to a variety of petroleum products, by-products, and the raw materials for petrochemical plants

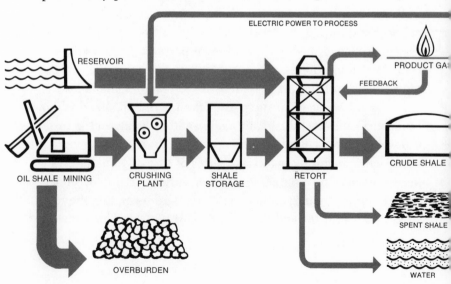

square miles — are so immense they lend themselves to all sorts of statistical legerdemain. And in discussing oil shale, it matters very much whether one is an oilman or bureaucrat, a stock promoter or geologist, a petrochemist or politician, a Coloradan or Texan. Or a concerned conservationist attempting to understand the ramifications of this latest federal attempt to develop *your* oil shale on *your* semiwilderness public lands.

For instance, the 170 trillion barrel figure cited by USGS for oil in organic-rich shales in the United States is the total for five different grades of shales:

First and most important are the known higher-grade and accessible oil shale deposits (generally 10 or more feet thick and containing 25 or more gallons of oil per ton of shale) that are considered recoverable under present conditions. These deposits contain an estimated 80 billion barrels of oil.

Second are known lower-grade (10 to 20 gallons per ton) or

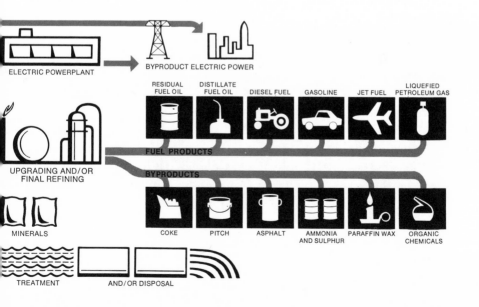

ELECTRIC POWERPLANT

BYPRODUCT ELECTRIC POWER

RESIDUAL FUEL OIL   DISTILLATE FUEL OIL   DIESEL FUEL   GASOLINE   JET FUEL   LIQUEFIED PETROLEUM GAS

FUEL PRODUCTS

UPGRADING AND/OR FINAL REFINING

BYPRODUCTS

MINERALS   COKE   PITCH   ASPHALT   AMMONIA AND SULPHUR   PARAFFIN WAX   ORGANIC CHEMICALS

TREATMENT   AND/OR DISPOSAL

less accessible oil shale deposits, considered marginal or submarginal under present conditions, and containing 2.1 trillion barrels of oil.

Third, the possible extensions of known deposits based on the best scientific conjecture — 10.6 trillion barrels.

Fourth and *fifth,* those deposits of organic-rich shales about which available information is so sketchy that they are classified as "undiscovered and unappraised." The distinction between "oil shale" and "organic-rich shale" is based on the difficulty of extracting the oil. These "undiscovered" shales in the U.S. containing more than 10 gallons of oil per ton of rock are estimated to contain 23 trillion barrels of oil; organic-rich shales rated at 5 to 10 gallons per ton may contain 140 trillion barrels.

So there are 2.2 trillion barrels of oil in *known* oil shale deposits, both recoverable and marginal to submarginal. But don't bother to memorize that figure.

Back in the 1920s, when the first oil shale fever was upon the land, known deposits of oil shale in the U.S. were estimated to contain only 140 billion barrels of oil. By 1963 the estimate had leaped to 2 trillion barrels. No one can safely predict where it will all end, but it is an odds-on bet where it will all begin: in the Piceance Creek Basin of Colorado.

Oil shale deposits have been discovered or "inferred" (a petrological connecting of the dots between sites of actual mineralogical information) in at least 30 states. Regionally, only the Pacific Northwest, New England, and Hawaii have been spared. In the Atlantic coastal states, oil shale discoveries have been limited to the westernmost Appalachian tips of Maryland, Virginia, North Carolina, and Georgia. Of the other blank spots on the map, North Dakota and perhaps Arizona look safe, but Wisconsin, New Mexico, and Louisiana appear ripe for future discovery or inference of oil shale.

Far and away the richest and ripest oil shale deposits are those of the Green River Formation in Colorado, Utah, and Wyoming. These are the target of Interior's proposed prototype leasing program. This is not to say there isn't a lot of shale oil in other states. Based on scanty samples taken in the northwestern foothills of the Brooks Range in Alaska, the deposit there is inferred to contain 50 billion barrels of oil in high-grade shale, while the possible extensions of that deposit are estimated at 250 billion barrels in high-grade shale and more than 200 billion barrels in marginal or submarginal grades. However, with 10 to 20 billion barrels of liquid petroleum — more easily and cheaply developed — in the Prudhoe Bay oilfield just to the east, the oil companies simply aren't interested in Alaskan oil shale.

The oil shale deposits of the Green River Formation cover 25,000 square miles (16 million acres) of land in those three states, of which 17,000 square miles (11 million acres) "are believed to contain oil shale of potential value for commercial development in the foreseeable future," according to Interior's statement. The deposits are situated in the Green River, Fossil, and Washakie basins of Wyoming; the Uinta Basin of Utah, and the Piceance Creek and Sand Wash basins and Battlement Mesa and Grand Mesa in Colorado.

The Green River Formation oil shales constitute the world's largest known hydrocarbon deposit. The total oil content is 1.8 trillion barrels, of which 600 billion barrels are contained in high-grade deposits. The federal public lands contain 72 percent of the oil shale lands by area, 80 percent of the total oil, and 81 percent of the higher-grade deposits. The rest is owned by the oil industry, land speculators, West Slope landowners, and the states.

Taken alone, these figures have little meaning. But compare them with known petroleum reserves. As mentioned, the huge

Prudhoe Bay–North Slope oilfield in Alaska (largest in the United States) may contain as much as 20 billion barrels of oil. The East Texas oilfield, on which much of the nation has been polluting merrily along since 1930, contains 6 billion barrels.

As noted in a 1968 Interior Department report, *Prospects for Oil Shale Development*, "the 1.8 trillion barrels that could be classed as 'known reserves' . . . is more than 60 times the present U.S. 'proved reserve' of crude petroleum . . . and represents the potential equivalent of enough oil to meet U.S. needs for hundreds of years." And the USGS Circular 523 says, "The possible extensions and possible upward revisions of the oil shale resources of the Green River Formation are estimated to be about equal to the known resources."

The Green River oil shale is not equally distributed, either in area or in richness, throughout the three states. Wyoming has the largest area (9200 square miles), followed by Utah (4700 square miles) and Colorado (2600 square miles). Colorado, however, has more than 80 percent of the oil in high-grade deposits and half of the oil in lower-grade deposits.

Nearly all of Colorado's high-grade oil shale, containing 500 billion barrels of oil, is in the 1350-square-mile Piceance Creek Basin. In the center of the basin, where the shale is richest, the beds are 1500 to 2000 feet thick. Thus the Piceance Creek Basin has been, and will continue to be, the center stage for the oil shale drama. So far it has been mostly melodrama and comedy, but tragedy is waiting in the wings.

On early maps, the creek's name was spelled (and pronounced) Pissants. But apparently some prude in the Geological Survey changed the spelling to Piceance, and the pronunciation was bowdlerized to *Pee'-ahnts*. You will be hearing this name a lot in the future.

The shale-bearing Green River Formation is a series of lake

deposits of Eocene age laid down at the rate of about one one-hundredth of an inch per year. The richest oil shale deposits vary in thickness from a few feet to several hundred feet, while leaner shale beds may extend to depths of 10,000 to 20,000 feet.

The Wyoming deposits are not nearly so rich as those in Colorado or even Utah, but they occur more widely. In all three states, the overburden of non-oil-bearing rock varies from none, where there are outcroppings of shale, to 1500 feet or more. If strip-mining were to be employed, all of this overburden would have to be removed — and piled elsewhere — before a shovelful of oil shale could be mined.

Then there are the complications caused by the presence of other minerals. The Green River Formation in Wyoming contains large deposits of trona, a glassy sodium bicarbonate mineral from which industrial soda ash is extracted. Three trona mines are in operation, and a fourth is under construction. Coal-mining and petroleum and natural gas extraction are growing industries here, too.

In the Utah oil shale region, Gilsonite mining and processing constitute the largest industry. Gilsonite (or uintahite) is a solid, black hydrocarbon from which gasoline, metallurgical-grade coke, acids, alkali, and waterproof coatings are produced. Oil and natural gas also occur here in significant amounts, though generally outside the best oil shale areas. And tar sands — oil-impregnated sandstones — are generally situated beneath the Utah oil shale beds. Though the tar sands are largely undeveloped, most of the deposit is under lease and is estimated to contain 4 billion barrels of oil — at least one-fourth of this within the optimum oil shale area.

The oil in tar sands can be recovered by forcing hot water through the porous rock, as is being done on a small scale in Alberta, Canada.

Colorado has the thorniest problems stemming from deposits
of other minerals, especially in the Piceance Creek Basin. A
large saline zone contains huge quantities of mineral salts,
particularly halite (common salt), nahcolite (sodium bicarbonate
or baking soda), and dawsonite (potentially a major source of
aluminum). Common salt is mixed with some of the trona beds
in Wyoming, but in the Piceance Creek Basin it is a pure deposit.
Nahcolite deposits — like trona a source of soda ash — amount
to at least 30 billion tons. Most problematic of all is dawsonite,
which contains an element that is the "active ingredient" in
Rolaids.

All of these sodium minerals may treble the total value of
the varied deposits in the Piceance Basin. In *The Elusive
Bonanza*, a highly readable distillation of the oil shale story, Chris
Welles cites studies showing that a single square mile in the
center of the Piceance Creek Basin "might contain, in addition
to nearly a billion barrels of shale oil, 126 million tons of soda
ash from nahcolite, 100 million tons of sodium chloride [common
salt], and 42 million tons of alumina, from which aluminum is
easily extracted, which would equal more than one and one-half
times the United States' entire supply of bauxite, the present
source of commercial aluminum."

Dawsonite, which would yield the alumina, was discovered
in 1874, but until great amounts of it were found in the Piceance
Basin between 1957 and 1964 it was thought to occur in nature
in very small amounts. The identical ingredient used in the
stomach remedy is manufactured artificially by a patented
process.

The entanglements arise from the fact that a substantial portion
of these valuable sodium mineral deposits are under lease — leases
that may conflict with future oil shale leases on the same land.
How do you mine and process nahcolite or dawsonite or halite

without mucking up somebody else's oil shale — or vice versa? On the other hand, where separate sodium leases or claims do not exist, the extra minerals will be a bonus to the oil shale leaseholder.

But multiple mineral development could, in some cases, result in very little oil production. A plant designed to extract as many of the minerals as possible, and convert them into commercially useful products, could conceivably use most of the oil shale on the spot to produce the electricity. Staggering amounts of power are needed just to process aluminum.

From the exploiter's point of view, the chief value of these associated minerals may be their usefulness in gaining access to the oil shale lands. From the conservationist's point of view, their chief value may be in delaying exploitation of oil shale indefinitely.

Indeed, the untangling of land claims could go on for years. The present Mineral Leasing Act was passed in 1920, reserving nonmetalliferous minerals — oil shale, oil, coal, natural gas, phosphate, sodium — on the public lands for leasing, with royalties paid to the federal and state governments. But before that, oil shale claims were staked like other mining claims under the General Mining Law of 1872 (which is still the nation's basic mining law) and the Petroleum Placer Act of 1897. Pre-1920 oil shale claims numbered 36,000 in Colorado and 120,000 in Utah and Wyoming, covering millions of acres. Exact figures are impossible to determine because of the insane provision in the mining law for filing claims in county offices, with no central record at either state or federal levels, and because so many claims were staked on top of each other.

These old claims entitle the claimant to a patent, or fee simple title, to the land as well as the minerals if certain loose requirements are met. Suspecting that these requirements — especially the stipulation that $100 of development or assessment work be performed annually — had not been met, the Department of the Interior set about nullifying many of the earlier claims. But an adverse Supreme Court decision in 1935 halted the cancellations. And appeals were filed by some whose claims had been declared void. But later court decisions, which seem in part to reverse the 1935 ruling, have encouraged Interior to mount a new series of challenges against the outstanding pre-1920 claims.

Meanwhile, adverse publicity in the late 1920s over a controversial Interior decision, involving conflicting claims for a piece of Colorado oil shale land, led President Herbert Hoover to "temporarily" withdraw all public oil shale lands "from lease or other disposal." This executive order, which has never been rescinded, was made under authority of the Pickett Act of 1910, which specifically exempted metalliferous minerals. The importance of this limitation on executive authority will soon become apparent.

When uranium was discovered in the early 1950s on public coal lands — which, like oil shale lands, are reserved for leasing — Congress passed the Multiple Mineral Development Act of 1954, which stated that public lands reserved for leasable nonmetalliferous minerals could be staked for locatable metalliferous minerals occurring separately. The leasable minerals would remain in public ownership. Curiously enough, and perhaps only coincidentally, the Multiple Mineral Development Act was authored by Senator Eugene D. Millikin of Colorado, who had personal oil shale interests.

Once dawsonite, the aluminum-bearing sodium mineral, was discovered on the oil shale lands in the early 1960s, the West Slope prospectors and speculators lit out for the hills once again with boundary stakes, claim markers, and resurgent hopes. By the time Secretary of the Interior Stewart L. Udall withdrew the oil shale lands from all claiming (a withdrawal made under no specific statutory authorization), 97 percent of the Piceance Creek Basin had been claimed for dawsonite. One prospector, a colorful ex-convict named Merle Zweifel, filed 20,000 claims covering 4 million acres.

The dawsonite claims raise interesting legal questions. Is it a leasable sodium mineral or a locatable aluminum mineral? (The Interior Department in 1968 declared it to be a sodium mineral, thus nullifying the claims, but this may have to be resolved in the courts.) Did President Hoover's executive withdrawal of the oil shale lands from leasing "or other disposal" prevent metalliferous claims? Can a mineral commingled with the oil shale be removed without damaging or destroying the publicly owned oil shale resources? For which mineral, oil or aluminun, are the lands in question "chiefly valuable"?

Until these questions are answered, the pre-1920 oil shale claims, dawsonite claims, and other metalliferous mineral claims (gold and silver, for example) cloud the title of 6.7 million of the 7.9 million acres of prime federal oil shale lands — 1.1 million acres in Colorado, 3 million acres in Utah, and 2.6 million acres in Wyoming.

Interior's prototype oil shale leasing program does not deal directly with these problems, as there are enough public lands where no claims exist to provide for a pilot program the size of the one proposed. As with prototype development in any field, its purpose is to toss something into the air to see if it can fly in an economical manner. Through sealed bidding, Interior will grant a maximum of two 20-year leases, of up to 5120 acres each, in each of the three states. Rents and royalties will be paid to the government, with bonding and performance requirements to assure restoration of the areas.

The potential bidders, having conducted core drilling, already have nominated the areas in which they are interested. Interior, in consultation with the governors' oil shale advisory panels in Colorado, Utah, and Wyoming, will examine the nominated sites — considering land uses, plant and animal life, aquatic resources, and historical, archeological, and scenic values. The mining waste disposal system most likely to be employed also will be weighed against these values. Any site found to pose insurmountable environmental problems or an unacceptable impact on existing resources will be rejected.

Interior's draft environmental impact statement (required under the National Environmental Policy Act of 1969) lists 14 criteria to be used in judging a site's acceptability, including the effects of air and water pollution; disturbance of natural vegetation so it cannot be re-created; creation of areas subject to wind erosion; loss of critical fish or wildlife habitat; adverse effects on wildlife refuges or fish hatcheries; blocking access of wildlife to essential range areas or of hunters and outdoor recreationists to wildlife; destruction of historic, archeological, or outstanding scenic sites; and residential development without necessary services.

During the prototype program the actual environmental impact would be compared with the predicted impact through monitoring by site operators and federal and state governments. In the event of unforeseen environmental effects, "operating procedures will be changed consistent with the terms of the lease to control such effects to the maximum extent possible."

What are the anticipated environmental effects? Very few, if one is to believe Interior's environmental impact statement. Pollution standards for air and water will be set and enforced. Restoration of disturbed land will make the area over as good as new. In some cases, we are informed, the oil shale operations might even enhance the area, for "mines often become major points of interest in themselves." Apparently the author of that phrase envisions an oil-shale strip mine becoming the twenty-first century's Baths of Diocletian. One ought to find solace in learning that our faceless bureaucracy contains such men of vision, but instead one is haunted by images of southern Appalachia.

The entire area to be affected by all phases of the six 5120-acre leases — mines, overburden storage, crushing and retorting plants, waste disposal, parking, roads, gas transmission lines, power plants, water lines, electric lines, shops, offices, housing, schools — totals 30,000 acres for the oil shale operations themselves, and 20,000 more acres for off-site land requirements, including urbanization. But as the environmental impact statement reminds us over and over again, those 50,000 acres are only "0.5 percent of the total area believed to be commercially valuable for development."

Some of the nonnumerical aspects of the project also are worth considering, however. The oil shale area is a semiarid, sparsely populated, semiwilderness region of rough terrain. Water is serious business in the Colorado Basin, and a hard line is likely to be taken regarding water conservation and water quality protection. Wildlife resources, meanwhile, include about 300 species. The Interior statement goes into detail about the potential impact on fish and wildlife and the measures that might or will be taken to prevent, reduce, or alleviate those effects. Because hunters and fishermen usually come first when political decisions concerning wildlife are being made, at least the game species ought to be accorded pretty fair protection. Some intolerant species — mountain lions, bear, elk, mule deer, antelope, sage grouse, blue grouse, and some migratory birds — are not likely to fare well under the increased noise and human disturbance, but Interior does not expect "dramatic" population declines.

Lands already dedicated to other purposes have been declared
off limits. Included are all national forests, Flaming Gorge
National Recreation Area, Seedskadee National Wildlife Refuge,
Sand Wash Historical Landmark, Desolation Canyon, various
critical wildlife ranges, experimental and management areas,
historic sites and trails, known archeological sites, three naval
oil shale reserves, and reclamation projects. But at least one
important area is left vulnerable — a portion of the Green River
that may qualify under the Wild and Scenic Rivers Act of 1968.

Increased population and urbanization may have the greatest
impact. The 17,000-square-mile oil shale area covers seven rural
counties in the three states with a total present population of
117,000. Employment in the oil shale industry by the end of
the six-year construction period would be 18,000, with a total
population increase of 47,000, or 40 percent.

The region's fish and wildlife are likely to bear the brunt of
the impact from noise and other disturbance, increased hunting
and fishing, and traffic, particularly off-road vehicles. Certainly
the semiwilderness character will succumb.

As for the social impact of urbanization, the Interior statement
notes that the "prototype program would significantly alter
existing social structures and institutions" and that it would be
impossible to measure the degree to which this would be detri-
mental "since the benefits and costs of urbanized life versus rural
life are a matter of personal value judgment." The anonymous
author then concludes that "the net social changes could be
considered beneficial."

Taking a long view that falls short of the view of the Interior
bureaucrat who sees mines as scenic wonders, one can conclude
that it isn't the prototype program per se conservationists should
be concerned about. There are, to be sure, some risks — to
groundwater, to intolerant wildlife species, and from oil pipeline

breaks. But the environmental consequences of the prototype program probably can be held to a minimum if the federal government accepts a recommendation made by the Colorado governor's Oil Shale Advisory Committee: "A critical review of the tentative [environmental] standards by conservation groups representing the public interest should be solicited promptly to insure that plans for implementation of the leasing program can benefit from the expertise of these groups prior to the commencement of industrial activity."

But prototype programs, like the supersonic transport and the "training airstrip" in the Everglades, do not exist in a vacuum. Once established, they gain a momentum that is almost impossible to stop. Consider the regional economic implications. West Slope developers and politicians have been waiting for half a century, their hopes constantly being raised by government reports predicting oil shale development within the decade, then dashed by each new petroleum discovery, each oil company decision to close down its oil shale experiment. Now, at last, the bonanza is within reach.

Or consider the political implications of these figures: between 1973 and 1983, $3 billion will be spent on plant and urban construction; local property taxes would total $328 million; state income taxes on oil shale profits and the state's share of the production royalties would amount to $393 million; the cumulative payroll would top $2 billion.

Nothing steamrollers politicians like jobs, and at the end of the six-year construction period some 11,000 men would suddenly find themselves out of work in a region that employed only 44,000 people in 1970. Interior's statement simply suggests that "as long as the prototype program and any resulting industry would continue to develop, shifting of construction personnel would probably take place between the different plant sites." There is no contingency plan in case the prototype program doesn't continue to become a full-fledged industry by 1980.

Care is taken by Interior to point out that water for oil shale development is available even in the semiarid Upper Colorado Basin. Water for the prototype program would come from existing reservoirs, but for a full-scale oil shale industry new dams and reservoirs would have to be built. And the beauty of the scheme is the royalty distribution under the Mineral Leasing Act: 37.5 percent to the state in which the oil shale is situated, 10 percent to the federal treasury, and 52.5 percent to the Reclamation Fund used to build — you guessed it — dams.

Extrapolating the impact of mining and waste disposal for six leases covering 48 square miles to a full-scale industry throughout the 17,000 square miles of the prime oil shale regions is an overwhelming task. But as former Interior Secretary Udall said in a recent interview, "Unless you can develop an *in situ* process where you can get at the oil without mining the shale . . . My God, that whole western slope of Colorado is one of the finest outdoor recreation playgrounds in the country. Unless you leave it in the ground, can you do anything but turn it into a wasteland?" The *in situ* (in place) process Udall referred to involves fracturing and retorting the oil shale underground, obviating the need for mining, surface crushing and retorting, and waste disposal. Even the most optimistic oil-shalers admit this process is a "sometime, maybe" proposition. Except for the Atomic Energy Commission, which has this plan to take 500-kiloton nuclear bombs and . . .

How likely is it that a full-scale oil shale industry will develop in the near future? It is difficult to predict, in light of the technology that has yet to be proved, the tight economics of oil shale production compared to the artificially stabilized domestic price of crude oil, and the less than complete enthusiasm of the oil industry. Except for Union Oil Company of California and, more recently, Atlantic Richfield Company, the oil firms have played a wait-and-see game on oil shale, preferring to buy up the private oil shale lands as a hedge bet, rather than committing large sums of capital to developing an oil shale operation. How the site selection and lease-bidding goes will provide part of the answer.

In 1968, in an election-year gambit that Udall called "testing the industry's *bona fides*," the Interior Department offered an oil shale lease sale and there were no oil-industry takers. The Oil Shale Corporation submitted two low bids, and a man from Oregon offered $625. All were rejected.

This is not to say the oil companies wouldn't like to get at all that shale oil; it's just that their perspective is different from Uncle Sam's. In 1962 Shell Oil Company proposed to the Interior Department that it be given a 50,000-acre lease in the Piceance Creek Basin to develop a large-scale commercial oil shale operation. When a quick check revealed there was enough oil under those 50,000 acres to keep Shell in full production for 660 years, Shell was given a polite but firm "no thanks."

Of course, the oil companies can afford to take a posture of vigilant disdain. At present their refineries and pipelines are chock-full of crude oil, prices are high and import quotas low, their ledgers are blacker than the Piceance Creek shale. But when oil shale's time has come they will be ready to move, and quickly. They own two-thirds of the privately owned oil shale lands. They control the piping and marketing of oil, insurance against an outsider muscling in on the market. The oil industry is on standby alert.

The American public, which owns the oil shale and the land it is under, is neither vigilant nor ready; it is a lazy Sunday morning at Pearl Harbor, 1941. This is the most frightening aspect about oil shale. No one seems to know or to care. As Chris Welles put it in the last chapter of *The Elusive Bonanza*, "The oil industry seems happy enough without it. Government officials are scared to touch it. The general public has never heard about it. Except for a couple of members with vested interests, Congress couldn't care less about it."

There are those who urge oil shale development as an alternative to the Alaska pipeline and Machiasport, to oil exploration in the Big Cypress Swamp of Florida and the Great Barrier Reef, to well blowouts in the Santa Barbara Channel and supertanker breakups wherever they may occur, to the proliferation of pumped-storage and atomic power plants. That is like setting off, full steam ahead, through a dense fog toward an unknown Charybdis because you don't like the looks of Scylla.

Oil shale may be the most complex and perplexing environmental and natural resource conservation problem in history, involving as it does the whole chronicle of federal land and resource policy, the Jekyll-and-Hyde role of the Department of the Interior as both protector and dispenser of the nation's land and resources, the economic and political structure of the world's oil industry and market, the hypnotic mating dance of government and industry in our heavily regulated free-enterprise system, our national energy nonpolicy, revenue sharing, the old clash between East and West over conservation and development, and the wrangling over water in the Colorado Basin.

But nothing is quite so informing as information, and it isn't too early to begin informing ourselves about oil shale. It is our land, our shale, our oil. We should make it our decision.

SKIP ROZIN

People of the Ruined Hills

THE WORD IS TERRACIDE. As in homicide, or genocide. Except
it's terra. Land.

It is not committed with guns and knives, but with great,
relentless bulldozers and thundering dump trucks, with giant
shovels like mythological creatures, their girdered necks lifting
massive steel mouths high above the tallest trees. And with
dynamite. They cut and blast and rip apart mountains to reach
the minerals inside, and when they have finished there is nothing
left but naked hills, ugly monuments to waste, stripped of
everything that once held them in place, cut off from the top
and sides and dug out from the inside and then left, restless,
to slide down on houses and wash off into rivers and streams,
rendering the land unlivable and the water for miles downstream
undrinkable.

Terracide. Or, if you prefer, strip-mining.

It has become more and more common in the last fifteen years,
in the South and the Southwest and the Far West, in Pennsylvania
and Ohio and Texas. But the worst is in Appalachia. In West
Virginia, and especially in Kentucky. Eastern Kentucky, in the
mountains.

There is where the people live right on the steep, proud
mountains, on the mountains and all through them, and in the

hills and along streams that form hollows and tiny valleys. They
have lived there for five and six and seven and eight generations.
The same homes in the same mountains.

To the mining companies the mountains are large, green coal
mines, just as they were timber forests to the men who first
bought the rights a hundred years ago in questionable dealings
for forty or fifty cents an acre, then sold those rights when they
were through.

The deeds are the same, infamous broad-form deeds that bought
the rights to everything above and below the soil. Still being
sold from company to company, and still held legal. The prize
is different. Now it is coal, and the cost to the hills is greater
than when they were cutting timber. But the attitudes of the
companies are the same — they take and leave.

And the people, they are much the same.

Mountain people tend to be slow to change. Not that they
are against progress. They are not. They have cars, or trucks,
and television, even some color sets. Few are paid for, of course,
but that is not the point. They accept the decorations of the
1970s.

But inside, deep inside where people decide who they are,
they change very little. Men whose fathers and grandfathers
were coal miners are coal miners, as are their sons. A man born
and reared on Turkey Creek may have moved to Camp Branch
or as far as Dry Fork, but the odds of his having left Letcher
County by the time he dies are slim.

Some do. Especially now, the younger ones are sifting away
to the cities in greater and greater numbers, for school and work
and for no reason other than that they now know another world
exists out there.

But their parents and their grandparents remain, in the same
counties and the same hollows, and even in the same houses.

It's the mountains, they say, they hold a man. And of those who leave for a year or so, to go to Cincinnati to work in the soap factory or to Detroit to the car plants, most return to the mountains.

Bert Caudill spent two years in Detroit back in the fifties, and Bessie Smith twice went north with her husband and children, but they came back. And Joe Begley worked for a while in Connecticut, but he came back. Most of them come back, back to the mountains.

"I believe in this place," Joe Begley told me on the front porch of his general store in Blackey. It was after lunch one day early in the summer. He likes to close for an hour or so just past noon, to work at his desk or just sit on the squeaking front swing and look across Highway 7, past the creek and up into the hills.

"I believe in the mountains and the streams. I think they're Jesus Christ, or God maybe."

Those are not casual words; Joe Begley is not a casual man. He comes by his feelings honestly. His grandmother was a Cherokee Indian, and though his father wanted to raise him as a white man, the old woman taught her grandson to love the trees and the water and the hills as living deities.

The lesson stuck, and has made the destruction he has witnessed in his 53 years in eastern Kentucky a repulsive sight, and it has helped him choose a path.

He is a strange man, tall and lean and dark, with the dark eyes and black straight hair of an Indian. In his little office off the store are books on trees and animals and the land, titles like *Nature and Wildlife, Environment and Cultural Behavior,* and *Yesterday's People,* and a dozen more stacked up on the desk and on the floor and against the door, along with copies of *The New Yorker* and *Audubon.*

His formal education has been sparse, and he dresses in blue jeans, but he is defending his land against the army of machines with the tools of men whose walls are lined with degrees and who wear imported neckties and double knits, fighting with lawsuits and courts.

From his store he has helped organize the people of the area, of Blackey and Elk Creek and Jeremiah and Caudill's Branch, trying to help those who live in the hollows and the mountains fight the broad-form deeds, trying to make those who would sign new agreements aware that ten cents a ton is not worth what will follow, trying to keep the strippers off.

"This strip coal is cheap, dirty coal," he told me on the hard, metal porch swing, "and seventy percent of it's bought by the TVA. The government. The government's scalping our land."

And looking out across the two-lane road, up into the hills: "The game's all gone, the streams is gone, the mountains is gone, all destroyed for just a little bit of money by greedy people."

He says he isn't asking much, only that the people not sell away the rights to their coal. But that is an odd request in these mountains, a foreign idea. If ever there were a one-industry area, that area is eastern Kentucky, and the industry is coal. That is the way it has been since the end of the nineteenth century and the coming of the railroad.

Coal is everywhere. It is everybody's business.

In addition to the deep mines and the strip mines there are thousands of truck mines, little mines by the side of the road and in people's backyards. Coal lies in chunks by the side of every dirt road and highway, having fallen from or bounced out of the trucks that haul it. It lies by the endless miles of railroad track, and dots the streets of downtown Whitesburg and Hazard and Pikeville and a hundred other towns.

It is coal country, plain and simple. Even the little children

A hollow in eastern Kentucky — its once clean-running stream
and its once verdant hills ravished by strip-miners

play with model dump trucks and bulldozers, making believe
they are digging for coal in the yard, strip-mining under the
front porch.

In such an environment it is difficult to convince people that
digging for coal is anything but the most natural of processes.
Coal is a friend. It always has been and always will be. That
is the reality in these mountains. No one entertains the notion
that coal is an exhaustible resource, that mining — deep or

strip — can only continue for so long, and that if the area is going to survive, alternate industries will have to be developed.

That's not smart talk in country where King Coal is everybody's big brother.

Whatever problems might result from an area being stripped, they are viewed as isolated phenomena, totally unrelated to any other area being stripped, and certainly unconnected to the coal found deep in the ground and reached through conventional means.

Bert Caudill certainly has nothing against coal. He has been a miner all his adult life, as was his father and are his sons. It is what he does — *all* he does.

He spent two years working in a Detroit assembly plant and earned more money than in any other two years in his life, but he came back to the mines, back to the mines that took his father's life and his brother-in-law's life, the mines that have given him black lung disease and are slowly taking his life.

"That's the mines," says Caudill. "Some gets killed in airplanes and some in cars."

But there was no philosophy in his voice when, after he sold the rights to his land for stripping, the side of the mountain came sliding down one night in a rainstorm, tore away his barn and fence and covered his spring. That was two years ago, and still the mountain shifts, sending rocks and boulders dangerously close to the house he bought from his two years' work in Detroit, the first house he has ever owned.

"Every time after it rains I climb up to the top of the mountain," said Ruby, Caudill's wife, "just to see what's slid down and what's gonna be comin' next."

Bert and Ruby Caudill are not the only two to sell the rights to their land, then regret it. Hundreds have done the same thing, even recently. Some only after being shown an old deed "Xed" by a long-dead relative and told that the mining would go on regardless, that they might as well sign and get paid. Some without such pressure. But all thinking of bringing in a little extra money to pay the bills.

Columbus Sexton didn't think it was a bad idea to let them strip the coal above his house, and Bill Bates figured his property on Elk Creek might bring in something extra. Now Columbus Sexton has had to abandon his house and build a new one, and Bill Bates swears they'll never get another inch of his land.

Both are intelligent, well-informed men holding responsible business positions, and both had seen what the strippers had done to other men's land throughout the state. But, somehow, until it happened to them it meant nothing.

"You want to know who's to blame," Joe Begley said from his porch swing. "It ain't the government or the strippers. They're crooked and you can't expect no better of them. I blame the people, the good people around here that lets 'em come and take their land."

In his way, Joe Begley has been fighting strip-mining for a long time. Like Tom Gish, editor of the *Whitesburg Mountain Eagle*, and Harry Caudill, lawyer and writer, he has been trying to stop the desecration of the mountains. It has been difficult, and every once in a while he gets impatient with those not so fervently committed as he, those who years ago did not hear the word.

But Joe Begley would be the first to tell you that the mountains are a special place of special people. Things are not the same there as in the cities or even the plains. Thinking is different.

Ever since the days when the Cumberland Plateau was part of America's early frontier, its people have been staunchly independent, exercising a degree of privacy approaching isolation. Today, with pockets of civilization still formed only around select streams and creeks, much of that early attitude has remained.

It is not that mountain people are unfriendly toward their neighbors. Mostly, in any particular hollow, everyone is related through one or a number of genetic channels. There are half a dozen Nieces on Camp Branch, twice that many Days on Cowan Creek, even more Sextons on Sandlick Road, and Caudills in groups and bunches all over.

They exchange pleasantries on the road and will always offer a helping hand. But there is also a great deal of letting alone. Breathing room, some call it. The tendency is for a man to see to his own needs and problems without bothering to step back for a long look at what repercussions might result.

For generations and generations, without interference from the outside, it was a good way. Strip-mining has made it a dangerous luxury. What is happening on Kingdom Come Creek tells it best.

Kingdom Come is a truly beautiful little hollow that runs for ten or twelve miles along the creek from the point where it leaves Route 588, crosses under the red metal bridge, and climbs to the headwaters deep in the mountains. It is green and lush and thick, very cool and very quiet, the only regular sounds the gurgling of the creek and the chirping of birds, the only dissonant sight the old scavenged car bodies so common to Appalachia that line the creek bed and peek out from deep in the brush.

This is the place where, at the turn of the century, John Fox, Jr., came to write his novel about a young mountain man in the Civil War, *The Little Shepherd of Kingdom Come*. Aside from the changing models of abandoned cars, it is hard to believe that the hollow is very different from what Fox saw as he traveled the dirt road that parallels and crosses and occasionally becomes the creek.

Thirty-eight families live in the hollow, a large percentage of them Isons or related to Isons. And for years coal companies have been trying to buy the rights to the mountains at the head of the creek, the rights to strip them for coal, but no one would sell. Not until last year, when a family that once lived near the head but had moved sold the rights. Then a second family, also moved, sold.

Still no stripping began, because the company needed more land. Then, after several months of trying, the company convinced Sally Ison to sell her rights to the coal. A large section of one mountain was left to Sally by her father, who had inherited the same section of mountain from his father.

She became the first person actually living on the creek to sell.

"They were after me for a long time to sell," Sally told me from her wheelchair. A woman in her sixties, she is crippled with arthritis, so severely crippled that she requires the assistance of a wheelchair or walker to get around. "I kept telling 'em no, but last October they said the rest of it was theirs so I let 'em go ahead."

She used her arms to shift position in the chair. Then, again settled, she looked from me to the bare, wooden floor where her five children, all grown now and gone from the hollow, once played.

"I didn't see how it would affect us," she said. "We weren't using the mountain."

Sally Ison is as far from being a villain as one could imagine. A sweet, lovable woman who wheels herself around the house, cleaning and cooking for her husband and two grandchildren spending the summer, she did what seemed logical with land she could see serving no immediate use, land for which no children or grandchildren were waiting.

Then it began. "They said they had to build a dam on the

bottomland," she said. "They hadn't said anything about that bottomland, not till after I signed."

She tried to stop them, but apparently they had a legal right. The bottomland, considered to be among the best for planting in the hollow, immediately became useless. They also changed the course of the creek, and when they began moving in big machinery and blasting the following month, the once clear water of Kingdom Come Creek was ruined.

And all because a mining firm from California convinced Sally she deserved some income from her land.

"I tried to stop her from selling, but it's her land," Sally's husband, Marion, told me as we drove to the head of the creek in his old pickup, bouncing along the creek bed. He and Sally had known each other all their lives, both having grown up in the hollow.

"They put up a pitiful tale about getting that coal," he said, holding tight to the jerking steering wheel. "Just kept on and kept on, telling her what it'd look like after it was over and what she'd get out of it. Said she'd rather have it that way than before. Said they'd fix it back up, sow grass and put in trees."

He spit out the open window, as if to comment on their promises. "Even if they did fix what's ours, the rest of the hollow'll never be the same."

We went as far as we could by truck, then pulled up on a level piece of land and walked up to the head of the creek. We climbed to a wide canyon, recently dug out of the hillside, flat on the bottom and lying at the base of high, straight walls. It was the bottomland, he said, where they were going to make their dam to catch the silt from mining.

"They cut it out and everything," he said, pointing to the scooped-out walls nearly sixty feet high on each side, "then they run into clay and had to tear up some other land above." On three sides the mountains loomed around us, the mountains that had just begun to be strip-mined. Slides had already scarred the face of one, ripping off trees and bushes as they came.

"I told her I didn't figure it would bother me and her," Marion Ison said as he stood where his freshly cultivated field once stood. "We ain't got many more years, but later on, well . . ."

On the way back down toward the red metal bridge, I stopped to talk with Dewey Ison, cousin of Sally and Marion. A former miner nearly seventy, he had lived all his life on Kingdom Come Creek, as had his father and father's father, on back for five generations. He told me about the blasting, every evening about five o'clock, that shakes the windows and knocks jars off the shelf, and about the crystal-clear water that just isn't anymore. But when I asked him about Sally selling the rights to the land he stopped, thought a minute, and pushed the hat back on his head.

"Her land," he said, "but I wished she hadn't done it."

And thinking another minute: "Not her fault. They didn't read her the fine print. And they didn't say nothing about that bottomland. Best bottomland round here."

He pulled his hat back down over his eyes, told me again how it wasn't Sally's fault, but that he doubted the hollow would ever be the same.

Every hollow in eastern Kentucky is not Kingdom Come Creek. Men like Tom Gish and Joe Begley have alerted enough people to the horrors of strip-mining so that many have resisted.

When they came onto John Caudill's land he met them with his thirty-eight and escorted them off, and the exploits of Dan Gibson holding 40 strippers at gunpoint on Hardburly Ridge in Knott County are legend.

And in last year's Kentucky primary, Bessie Smith, a poorly educated mother of nine, challenged incumbent U.S. Representative Carl Perkins for his seat on the issue of strip-mining.

Mrs. Smith, a fiery welfare recipient who in January of 1972 led 21 women onto a strip-mining site and closed it down for fifteen hours, collected nearly 3000 votes, votes she feels will give her some leverage after the November election.

"Welfare and food stamps keeps the people quiet while the strippers take their land," the chunky blond told me in a makeshift office in Hazard. And straightening up in her chair: "I have been asked for my support in the fall campaign, but before I give it I must hear the word on banning strip-mining."

There are others who have tried to stop the devastation, both in the courts and at their own property lines, but not enough, not nearly enough. Mostly, like Sally Ison, they give up.

Each story is more depressing than the last, with a neighbor selling mining rights for a couple of hundred dollars, only to ruin an entire community. It happened in Johnnie Collins Hollow, where half a dozen families besides Bert and Ruby Caudill were affected. And over on Elk Creek, Bill Bates sold the rights to his land at the head of the creek, land behind the house he had been renting to Tiny Walters and her seven children for sixteen years.

"They started working up there in April," said Tiny, a large, blond woman who says she has no idea how she got her name. "I'd already had my garden cleaned up, and I wasn't about to leave." But then they started to blast, and the first boulder came crashing through Tiny's garden, and she packed up her kids and left.

"I never thought Bill'd do me like he did," she said, "but you never really know people till you comes down to a point."

Everybody loves Sally Ison, and except for Tiny Walters and maybe three or four of her kids, nobody really hates Bill Bates. But both sold the rights to their land, and the damage can never be repaired.

Both are sorry now, but it's late for that. The crime has been committed. In California and Texas and Florida, where the land that is being stripped is flatter, reclamation at least is possible. In these mountains it is not; they are simply too steep. They could be helped, certainly: new topsoil brought in, permitted to settle, the entire area seeded, and new trees planted. It would not undo the damage, but it would help. It would also be a monumentally expensive operation, requiring more time and money than any mining company now in Appalachia has suggested spending.

What is left now when the strippers move on? Not much. Vast tracts of land, restless land. Sliding, always sliding. Great mountains stripped of everything living, left barren and naked, once as permanent as time itself, now less steady than a child's sandpile.

And what of the water? Clear, pure wells and streams are now contaminated with mud and minerals, with enough sulfur to alter the taste of the water and cause rashes and infections in the people who drink it, and to chase away the wildlife that used to.

Not just at the source, not just where they are mining, but for miles and miles downstream, far from Letcher and Perry and Knott counties, down the Kentucky River, down Russell Fork and Poor Fork, down into the Ohio and beyond.

And for how long? No one can tell that.

But there is no need to wait to see the effects of a land destroyed. Not here, not in the Cumberlands. The mountains and the people are too closely allied. Already in a severely depressed area, with massive welfare rolls and one of the highest unemployment rates in the nation, the people of eastern Kentucky are in growing trouble.

Walking down the streets of Whitesburg, seat of Letcher

County, I was struck by the absence of vital life signs. A dearth of children playing on the sidewalks, of the sound of young voices. And no music.

Old men stand on the street corner near the post office and in front of the New Daniel Boone Motel, congregate in the coffee shop and on the steps of the courthouse. After dark there is nothing. No cars on the main street, no lights in the shops. No restaurant is open past nine any night, and none past midafternoon on Sunday.

No amusements are planned for the young, no place for roller skating or dancing. Of the town's two theaters, one is now a laundry and the other, only recently reopened, does not seem confident enough to advertise its programs on its own marquee.

It is an area that is losing its youth to the cities. And in those who remain there is an immense lethargy and lack of enthusiasm. Nothing much is happening, and nobody seems to care.

"A lot of us are just wore out," Joe Begley told me. "Wore out worrying about the government and lawsuits, wore out worrying about if the mountain's gonna sweep away our house."

And the stripping goes on. At the current pace over 60,000 acres of Letcher County alone will be "disturbed" by strip-mining by 1990, leaving less than 700 acres of farmland.

Seventeen years from now, in 1990.

But this is the Cumberland Plateau — Daniel Boone country.

These are mountain people, and the mountains hold a man in place. They always have. But what happens when the mountains are gone?

The word is genocide. As in terracide.

FRANK GRAHAM, JR.

The War on
the Dreaded Gypsies

ON MARCH 31, 1971, the citizens of Ridgefield, a pleasant and
wealthy community in southwestern Connecticut, assembled for
a special town meeting. They were there to deal with a matter
of urgent local concern. One faction, determined and well-
organized, pushed through the following piece of business:

"That an appropriation by the board of finance for $12,000
for the purpose of spraying to eradicate and eliminate the gypsy
moth and linden moth within and for the town of Ridgefield
be approved."

The matter apparently was settled. Many of the local residents
had been given a nasty turn the summer before by an outbreak
of caterpillars that had defoliated their shade trees, crawled in
dense masses over their houses and patios, and sometimes piled
up on town roads in such great numbers that their squashed
bodies greased the surface like a winter ice storm.

Supported by the action taken in the town meeting, the
Ridgefield selectmen planned to hire a commercial applicator
to spray town lands and roadsides from a helicopter with the
insecticide Sevin. They would bill property owners who wanted
their lands sprayed at the same time. The town fathers even
appointed a "spraying coordinator" to handle private requests
and gave him a desk in the town office. Then they sat back

and waited for late May, when the caterpillars (including those of the notorious gypsy moth) usually emerge from their eggs.

But this is the Age of Ecology, and town spraying programs no longer slip through automatically as they once did. The gypsy moth has received a bad press, but so has the exclusive reliance on chemical poisons to solve our pest problems, and the town of Ridgefield was soon up to its exurbanite ears in controversy. The Ridgefield Conservation Commission had been caught off-balance and was yet to be heard from. Moreover, a notable absentee from the town meeting had been Daniel M. McKeon, a prominent resident and dairy farmer who has had some experience in past controversies over gypsy moth control programs.

McKeon lives among Ridgefield's rolling hills in a spacious yellow farmhouse that dates back to the Revolutionary War. He is a slender, implike man with a fringe of whitening hair. On the morning I visited him he came downstairs partly dressed in the barest essentials of the riding garb he would wear when he and his wife went fox hunting that afternoon.

He spread the contents of a thick folder, labeled "Gypsy Moth," on the dining room table. As he talked about the local controversy I glanced through the windows at the farm pond below the house and at the cows that stood motionless in front of a well-kept barn.

"I was away when they had the town meeting," McKeon said. "I am absolutely opposed to spraying from the air close to other people's property because the spray cannot be contained. It drifts over onto adjoining land, and so it's an invasion of privacy. When they used to spray for the gypsy moth just over the line in New York state, the DDT drifted onto my property, and my milk was contaminated. I testified about this at the famous DDT trial on Long Island back in the nineteen-fifties.

"Now they've switched to Sevin. But Sevin is lethal to bees, and I keep bees, too. Why should I pay taxes to have my livestock poisoned?"

As soon as McKeon heard about the plans to spray he asked for another town meeting to reconsider the program.

"But the town counsel called my petition 'frivolous,' " he said, grinning broadly at the memory. "So some people on the conservation commission and I hired a lawyer and sued to stop the spraying. The town said they had to spray as a safety measure because the caterpillars made the roads slippery. I said that was silly, why didn't they sand the roads?"

McKeon and his allies got a break when a cold spring retarded the caterpillars' emergence and thus gave their lawyer time to get their case into court. Meanwhile, they kept their foes on the defensive. Someone arranged to have the local school open and close an hour later on the day the spraying was to take place so that the children would not be exposed to the chemical.

"That *really* made a lot of people think." McKeon grinned.

At the same time their lawyer sent a note to Chemapco, the Massachusetts applicator that had been hired to do the spraying, warning that the plaintiffs would "hold responsible" the firm for any damaging side effects.

Early in June, just before the date scheduled for the spraying, the case opened in Superior Court in Bridgeport. McKeon's lawyer had assembled his witnesses and his depositions, ready to prove that Sevin's side effects were harmful and that the applicator could not guarantee all the pesticide would be confined to the target trees. But he needn't have bothered. His letter had already won the case.

"Ridgefield's town counsel produced a letter from the spray company that withdrew their offer to enter into a contract for aerial spraying," McKeon said. "Their reason was that a 'well-meaning but ill-advised bunch of do-gooders' had threatened to sue them. They couldn't guarantee against some spray drifting because of the checkerboard pattern."

The case was closed. Amid some grumbling, Ridgefield used its $12,000 to spray town trees at critical points from the ground, and property owners were free to take protective action on their own initiative or to let nature run its course.

The Ridgefield incident is typical of the confusion and bitterness that has marked the war against the gypsy moth for more than fifteen years. Controversy has split professionals and non-professionals alike. But now the control specialists, who have been asked some hard questions and forced to admit past failures, are trying to devise a set of sophisticated integrated controls that may yet form a model program for solving our pest problems in a truly ecological fashion.

This serious pest is not native to the United States. It was imported to this country a century ago, and in recent years it has intensified its outbreaks in many parts of the Northeast while spreading southward and westward with rapidity. An estimated two million acres were attacked in varying intensity by the gypsy moth in 1971.

"We used to work with a map of the Northeast," says a government forester who is active in the control program. "Now we need a map of the United States."

In 1971, one-third of Connecticut's woodlands were described by foresters as "heavily defoliated." They called it the worst year on record for gypsy moth infestations. The insect's numbers are increasing in Massachusetts. A half-million acres were infested in the Hudson River Valley. Isolated male moths are being found as far away as Ohio, Wisconsin, South Carolina, Florida, and Alabama.

"The whole state of Pennsylvania may be infested in two years," a state forester says. "In areas where the predominant species are oaks, we are going to take a shellacking. There's one area I know in Monroe County along the ridges where *all* the oaks will be dead."

There are about 10,000 species of defoliating caterpillars in the United States, only 20 or 30 of which have been described as serious pests. The great majority of caterpillars are rare because natural controls keep their numbers under the "pest threshold." Why is the gypsy moth among the few forest insects that have escaped from natural controls to become a major pest? How does it spread its range? Why, among the few pests that concern a broad spectrum of the human population, does the gypsy moth arouse such an emotional response? And what are we going to *do* about it?

First, let's examine this awesome creature. The eggs hatch in late spring, when a tiny, brownish-yellow caterpillar, bristling with pale yellow hairs, eats its way to freedom. Spinning a long silken thread, it suspends itself from trees and is often carried long distances by the wind. (In an experiment, one caterpillar that had just hatched spun a thread 69 feet, four inches long!)

The young caterpillar grows rapidly, feeding at night on a great variety of deciduous leaves, especially oak, birch, poplar, and fruit trees, and in times of shortage resorting to pine and hemlock. By day it crawls away to hide in bark crevices or in leaf litter on the ground. This is the gypsy moth's troublesome stage, when it defoliates to one degree or another large tracts of woodlands. (A "heavy defoliation" is generally one in which the insects consume 75 percent or more of the area's leaves. Surprisingly, however, the several states and federal agencies have yet to establish a uniform standard.)

By early July the caterpillar has reached a length of about two inches. To the objective observer (of whom there seems to be a great scarcity) it is a rather handsome beast, large-headed, its back dotted with prominent blue spots toward the head and red ones toward the rear, and with tufts of pale yellow hairs sprouting from its sides. At this point the caterpillar pupates, spinning its cocoon in out-of-the-way places, to emerge in several weeks as a moth.

As adults, these insects are prime examples of sexual dimorphism. The male moth's ruddy brown color was likened to a gypsy's complexion in England and apparently gave the moth its common name. On the European continent it has carried a number of common descriptive names, including the German "Grosskopfspinner" (great-head spinner) and the French "le bombyx disparate" (the dissimilar silkworm, a reference to those striking differences between the male and female moth that also contribute to its scientific name, *Porthetria dispar*).

And the female *is* dissimilar, a much larger moth, white with black zigzag lines on its broad wings. It is, however, flightless, apparently unable to lift its large body packed with hundreds of eggs off the ground. It simply crawls a few inches from its cocoon and attracts a male with its scent.

After mating, the female deposits its eggs in a cluster, usually about 500 or 600, but sometimes 1000 or more if she happens to be on the fringe of a vigorous population that is rapidly extending its range. Each cluster, an inch or more long, is deposited in a protected place, perhaps the underside of a stone, a branch, or a log. The female moth spins a covering of brownish-orange fuzz for the cluster and then dies.

The variation between sexes is carried over into the various strains of this species. For a long time the gypsy moth nearly rivaled the fruit fly as the subject of genetic experiments. It is able to maintain itself in widely different habitats, extending across Europe, North Africa, and Asia to Siberia, China, and Japan.

A head-on portrait of the insatiable gypsy moth larva

"It's hard to make any statement about this beast without qualifying it," says entomologist Robert W. Campbell of the U.S. Forest Service. "The females aren't supposed to fly, but females were captured in a 'flight' of these moths near Moscow. And sometimes you hear that the climate limits their northward spread, but there's a strain of this species in Finland. And we've recently heard reports that some were captured in New Brunswick and Nova Scotia."

There are serious gypsy moth outbreaks from time to time in Europe, with reports of damage in orchards and local forests. On the whole, however, it does not seem ever to have been a menace on the scale that it has become in the United States.

It was in 1869 that a French naturalist named Leopold Trouvelot, who was living in Medford, Massachusetts, imported the eggs

of a number of moths to complete his studies on their potential
as silkworms. Among the eggs were those of the gypsy moth.
Apparently a violent early summer storm hit Medford one
evening. The cage in which M. Trouvelot kept the caterpillars
that had hatched from his eggs opened, and the insects escaped.
For about ten years the gypsy moths fought their lonely battle
with the New World's environment, and little was seen of them.
Then, suddenly, they began to swarm in the neighborhood of
M. Trouvelot's former home. The eyewitness reports, nearly a
century old now, that those long forgotten citizens of Medford
left with the authorities about their private plague would serve
nicely in a newspaper story describing a current outbreak.

"We moved to Medford in 1882," a woman recalled. "The
caterpillars were over everything in our yard and stripped all
our fruit trees, taking the apple trees first and then the pears.
There was a beautiful maple on the street in front of the next
house, and all its leaves were eaten . . . They got from the ground
upon the house and blackened the front of it . . . The caterpillars
get into the house in spite of every precaution, and we would
even find them upon the clothing hanging in the closets. We
destroyed a great many caterpillars by burning, but their numbers
did not seem to be lessened in the least."

By 1889 they were spreading all over town.

"My sister cried out one day, 'They are marching up the
street,' " another woman said. "I went to the front door, and
sure enough, the street was black with them, coming across from
my neighbor's . . . and heading straight for our yard. They had
stripped her trees, but our trees at that time were only partially
eaten."

Homeowners gathered the caterpillars in baskets and burned
them. Pedestrians felt them fall from trees onto their hats or
down their collars; some residents carried umbrellas, even on

fine days. Ladies squealed as they trod dozens underfoot and returned home with their long skirts stained by squashed caterpillars. One man reported the caterpillars "were so thick on the trees that they were stuck together like cold macaroni."

As fruit and shade trees died and property owners complained, the state finally intervened. E. H. Forbush, the noted New England ornithologist, was named "Field Director in Charge of the Work of Destroying the Gypsy Moth." Forbush led a vigorous campaign that, had he been allowed to carry it out, might have finished off the troublesome insect.

Manpower was cheap then, and it was put to work. Crews searched out egg masses and painted them with creosote. They cut and burned small, heavily infested woodlots. They sprayed the caterpillars with arsenate of lead. One of the most effective measures in parks and around homes was to tie a burlap bag, its flap hanging down, around the trunk of a large tree. At daybreak, when the caterpillars moved down the trunk in search of hiding places, they crawled under the burlap bag, where they could be easily collected and burned.

Unfortunately, the state of Massachusetts thought the war had been won and prematurely abandoned its many-pronged attack. This decision has proved to be an expensive mistake. It is estimated today that Americans have spent nearly $100 million in fighting the gypsy moth, and the situation is worse than it ever was before.

This ecological disaster is an example of man's miscalculation and bungling, ever since that night in Medford when M. Trouvelot let his caterpillars escape. The gypsy moth, unchecked by the natural predators and parasites that in the Old World held it in reasonable control, invaded the Northeastern woodlands, where decades of man's abuse had left the trees especially vulnerable to insect attack.

Three-fourths of the forests in Massachusetts and Rhode Island have been burned at least once in the past century. These fires have destroyed the diversity of woodland species, favoring the thick-barked, fire-resistant oaks, which in many areas have become the most dominant trees. A monoculture, as we know from agriculture, is particularly susceptible to invasions by pests. And of all our forest trees, none seems to be more attractive to gypsy moths than the oak!

As the gypsy moth spread through the forests of eastern Massachusetts early in this century, foresters and entomologists supplemented their early methods of control with more sophisticated weapons, chiefly parasites. They imported insects, including certain wasps and tachinid flies, known to parasitize gypsy moths in their native habitats in Europe and Japan. These parasites deposit their own eggs in the eggs, caterpillars, or cocoons of gypsy moths; after hatching, the young parasites eventually kill their hosts.

For the first half of this century the gypsy moth remained a pest chiefly in Massachusetts. Occasionally, as in the 1920s, there were severe infestations in various parts of the state where the insects surged to peak numbers and then collapsed from starvation, disease, parasites, and predators. Through the 1930s and 1940s the gypsy moth population seemed to have stabilized itself, fitting less disruptively into the forest community. Although the insect invaded Connecticut, New Jersey, and other nearby states, it seldom caused serious problems.

Then, after World War II, DDT was released for civilian use. Here was the miracle insecticide, a panacea for all of our pest problems. The U.S. Department of Agriculture, obsessed with this latest manifestation of man's technological ingenuity, decided to use DDT to blow the gypsy moth off the face of the Earth, or at least that portion of it within its own jurisdiction.

And so, wherever the gypsy moth was detected, the spray planes appeared and laid down their chemical barrage. DDT seemed to work fantastically well, killing gypsy moths far more efficiently than had any of man's other devices, before or since. But always, the following year, there was another outbreak of gypsy moths. Funds were appropriated, and the spray planes roared in once more over the treetops. Fish died, hawks and other birds declined in the woodlands, and public health authorities warned that excessive quantities of DDT had been detected in milk supplies.

And, ironically, it was during the heyday of DDT that the gypsy moth threw off its natural shackles to begin the massive extension of its range that we see continuing today.

Was this simply a coincidence? In October 1971 the Gypsy Moth Advisory Council, composed chiefly of foresters, entomologists, and industry people involved in the control program against this insect, met at the Department of Agriculture in Washington, D.C. During the meeting, Reitz I. Sailer, who has been active in gypsy moth studies with USDA's Agricultural Research Service for many years, spoke of that insect's "suddenly violent fluctuations" during the 1950s.

"I can't help but feel that we were seeing evidence of human interference with the natural balance that had stabilized the gypsy moth's population in the 1930s," Sailer said. "If you spray over a large area you annihilate all the parasites. We went from a policy of coexistence to one of annihilation, and we have not been successful. That's why we're here today."

At an earlier council meeting, William M. Cranston of New Jersey's Bureau of Plant Industry documented the procession of events for a specific area. He said the gypsy moth had been found occasionally in New Jersey from 1914 on, and at one time it had been eradicated there. It reappeared, however, and by

1955 (after nearby states had used DDT for several years) the insect was widespread in the northern part of the state.

"DDT was applied by aircraft at the rate of one pound per acre," he remarked. "Adjacent areas in Pennsylvania and New York were also treated. Approximately one hundred and fifty-five thousand acres were treated in New Jersey. Large acreages were treated from 1956 to 1963 with DDT, but it became evident in our 1963 egg mass winter survey that the gypsy moth was permanently established in New Jersey."

Robert Callaham, Director of Forest Insect and Disease Research for the U.S. Forest Service, pointed out the final irony. "The research and management effort languished during the DDT era," Callaham said. "Now we do not have adequate management techniques for the present resurgence."

The public outcry against DDT's side effects, led by Rachel Carson in *Silent Spring*, finally forced USDA and its cooperating state forestry departments to abandon the use of that discredited chemical for gypsy moth control. Yet USDA's approach to a complex environmental problem remained simplistic. The pest control people merely switched to another insecticide, Sevin, which breaks down more quickly than DDT and thus is not recycled through food chains.

The fatal flaw in this single-minded chemical approach remained. Like DDT, Sevin tends to perpetuate the problem, so that spraying must be continued year after year with only short-term relief. Enough insects survive each chemical treatment to produce the eggs that insure a bumper crop of gypsy moths the next summer. But vertebrate and invertebrate predators, which might have helped to restore the woodland's natural balance, recover much more slowly than their prey from a massive spraying program and thus lose control. So do parasites, since the alternate hosts they may depend upon for part of the year are wiped out by the insecticide and they too decline. The pest species almost inevitably resurges to peak numbers.

Moreover, the same biological laws that govern the gypsy moth and its predators apply to other predator-prey relationships. With their predators diminished, a variety of defoliators and other potential troublemakers enjoy a population explosion of their own. In the woodlands, as in the vegetable fields, an exclusive reliance on chemical insecticides creates new pests while failing to eliminate the old ones.

Sevin, like all of its chemical relatives, was introduced with unguarded optimism. Only with time have we learned about some of Sevin's nastier side effects, such as its potency in wiping out bees and other pollinating insects. Though Sevin apparently is not extremely toxic to birds, its use often coincides with the birds' nesting season, thus killing off the variety of insects that birds require to feed and raise their young.

Finally, the 1969 *Report of the Secretary's Commission on Pesticides and Their Relationship to Human Health* by the Department of Health, Education and Welfare disclosed evidence that Sevin causes birth defects in animals and thus must be considered suspect in its effects on human beings.

The authorities' single-minded reliance on chemical pesticides stems from a confusion of aims. There are three kinds of wooded areas where gypsy moths thrive:

1. Commercial woodlots, orchards, campsites, and nurseries.
2. Large multipurpose forest communities.
3. Private lawns and gardens.

The first is a place where the owner has a considerable investment in the quality of his trees. Defoliation by insect pests will slow plant growth and may kill some of the trees, and the owner has the right to protect his investment in any way that will not damage his neighbor's interests.

In the absence of more acceptable tools, he may be obliged to use chemicals; DDT, because of its mobility and persistence, obviously cannot be confined to its target area, nor can less-persistent pesticides such as Sevin when they are applied to tall trees from the air. The careful application in spot treatments of short-lived chemicals from the ground is often the least of evils at the present stage of pest management.

Turning to the second category, the use of chemical insecticides for the control of the gypsy moth over wide areas of our Eastern woodlands cannot be justified by *any* yardstick. Most trees are able to survive several successive defoliations (hemlock is an exception). Usually after two or three years of infestation the insects build to peak numbers and then "crash," falling victim to starvation, disease, or weather.

Foresters have learned that even when the loss of trees is high, most of the dead trees were old or unhealthy, so that the result is merely the compression of several years' mortality into one. Further, since the majority of trees attacked by gypsy moths usually are oaks, this process of "thinning" may have a beneficial effect on the forest. Maples and other trees, which may be suppressed in Eastern woodlands by oaks, are then able to gain a foothold, increasing the forest's diversity and strengthening it against future infestation.

A classic example of an agency's refusal to be stampeded in a crisis occurred recently at the Jockey Hollow Area of New Jersey's Morristown National Historical Park. In the late 1960s gypsy moths infested this area. Proposals were made to spray with Sevin. Since an experimental program with parasites had already been started there, however, the National Park Service declined to spray. Proponents of chemical control criticized this decision in 1969 as the gypsy moth defoliated large areas of the park for the third year in a row.

"Quite suddenly and dramatically in the summer of 1970 the gypsy moth infestation in Jockey Hollow completely and utterly collapsed," Park Superintendent Melvin J. Weig has reported. "Apparently, as the numbers of the pest insect increased, exceeding the habitat's carrying capacity, the polyhedral virus wilt disease began to take a heavy toll, and the parasites and other natural predators finished the job. Today [1971] it is practically impossible to find any significant number of egg masses in Jockey Hollow, and the natural collapse there has also spread to outlying, peripheral areas."

More than ten thousand oak trees died because of the prolonged severe infestation, and nearly as many were found to be in poor condition. Yet 75 percent of all the trees at Jockey Hollow survived the infestation in excellent health. The result was that the gypsy moth simply thinned out the forest and may have somewhat altered its composition of trees, to the forest's ultimate benefit.

Even so, loud and influential voices are raised in opposition when man lets nature run its own course.

"Think of all the board feet of valuable timber we'll lose," these voices cry, forgetting that almost none of the woodland in those Eastern states where the gypsy moth currently has a foothold is managed for commercial logging.

"Tourists will shun the area," other voices warn, ignoring the fact that most of the defoliation occurs for a short time each summer in the interior of the forests where few tourists venture. Most of the trees quickly refoliate when the caterpillars pupate. Areas heavily used by tourists, especially around campsites, usually are sprayed anyway.

"The insects will kill all the trees and deplete our watersheds," still other voices warn. But gypsy moths do *not* destroy entire forests (though extensive spraying, which might trigger serious outbreaks by other pests in successive years, could very well destroy a forest).

The ace up the sleeve for those who advocate chemical control is the claim, designed to unsettle conservationists and "bird-lovers," that "wildlife can't live in defoliated forests." In a joint study of woodlands being prepared by Roland C. Clement of the National Audubon Society and Ian C. T. Nisbet of the Massachusetts Audubon Society, this claim is denied. "In fact, the diversity of wildlife depends on the diversity and patchiness of the forest, especially in the shrub and herb layers," Clement and Nisbet write. "Hence, occasional defoliations benefit wild-life . . . Birds, in fact, nest successfully after much more severe disruptions caused by fire."

The only contention of the prochemical groups that makes sense is that a defoliated forest, with its dead trees, poses a fire hazard. Surprisingly, there are no studies to confirm this claim. Meanwhile, thousands of forest trees die as a matter of course for a great variety of reasons, including disease and old age.

Private lawns and gardens are the third kind of wooded area subject to invasion by the gypsy moth. In its quality and magnitude, this category brings a new element into the controversy. Now, more than ever before, people are fleeing the cities to invade and carve up the woodlands of suburbia. Many of them, in their ignorance of natural forces, are creating a woodland that is uniquely susceptible to ecological catastrophe.

"Greenery" is one of the big lures that bring people out of the city. The new suburbanite is proud of his trees and shrubs. However, though they inspire him with visions of the forest primeval, his trees probably are suffering from an overdose of modern civilization. Poisoned by the leaded fumes of passing autos, parched by drainage patterns that have been altered by drains and sewers, encased in concrete and strangled by a maze of underground pipes and wires, the suburban tree may hardly be in condition to withstand the attack of thousands of leaf-chewing caterpillars.

Nor can the homeowner expect relief from the caterpillars' natural predators and parasites, even if he knows about them. Suburbanites, many of them city-bred and disgusted by bugs and creepy-crawlies of any kind, generally use proportionately more chemicals about their property than any cost-conscious farmer. Most of the gypsy moth's insect enemies thus have been obliterated long before an infestation begins.

Even certain mice (white-footed mice are voracious predators on gypsy moths) and birds (which eat great quantities of the caterpillars) do not thrive in the average suburb. They quickly fall victim to a number of hazards, chiefly cats and dogs.

"Detailed studies of a few species have shown that they raise very few young in suburban situations," Massachusetts Audubon Society's Ian Nisbet says of songbirds. "It appears that suburban bird populations, especially in the inner suburbs, are maintained only by immigration from outside."

But shade trees are valued highly, both for their obvious practical and aesthetic virtues and as real property; court cases have affirmed that a magnificent old shade tree may be worth anywhere from $3000 to $6000. Several severe defoliations may kill such a tree, especially one weakened by suburbia's special ills. So Clement and Nisbet offer this advice to homeowners who wish to protect valuable individual trees:

"There are several short-lived chemical pesticides that can be applied as foliage sprays . . . For those who prefer not to use chemicals, the bacterial preparation *Bacillus thuringiensis* is effective when applied from the ground . . . The most important considerations are that treatments should be based on professional diagnosis of the pest problem so that trees are not treated unnecessarily, and that they should not affect the interests or the property of neighbors. This means, for example, that sprays should be applied by conscientious applicators, and should not be used under conditions liable to lead to drift."

In the Northeast, people and forests have lived with the gypsy moth for a long time. When DDT failed and had to be abandoned, the U.S. Department of Agriculture and its subsidiary Forest Service supplied no fresh ideas to deal with the problem. "You can't imagine the terrific day-to-day pressure on us here," a USDA scientist told me. "Every letter that comes in from a Congressman has to be dealt with right away — even those that could wait. There's a crisis atmosphere all the time, so there's usually no chance for long-range problem-solving. USDA in effect can't move until outside pressure becomes unbearable."

But now there are new pressures on USDA. To the gypsy moth's natural means of spreading its range (airlifted as a tiny caterpillar on its gossamer threads) man has added his own vehicles. Chief among these are trailers, campers, and motor homes, which are peculiarly adapted to the transport of gypsy moths because they stand for varying amounts of time in woodland or suburban habitats and then are driven to other parts of the country.

Vacationers, for instance, flood the Northeast with their trailers and campers just about the time when gypsy moths reproduce. Parked in woodlands and campgrounds, their vehicles provide attractive niches in which insects deposit their eggs. Despite a quarantine (involving frequent vehicle inspections) that USDA maintains in infested areas, these vehicles often slip through to carry the egg masses to southern and western states. Whenever gypsy moths are detected for the first time in other parts of the country, the location invariably is a campground, a mobile home park, or along an interstate highway.

In many cases the incipient infestation is quickly snuffed out. But gypsy moths appear with alarming frequency around the country today, posing a threat in states dependent on wood products for their economic health. It is this development that may tip the balance toward a comprehensive and successful gypsy moth control program.

The Gypsy Moth Advisory Council got its impetus from a few state and federal foresters who had been working on the problem for some time. They were frustrated by a lack of vital information about infestations and a lack of money to mount an integrated control program. The council, established several years ago to coordinate all of the individual efforts in the gypsy moth campaign, began as primarily a lobbying group.

The foresters and entomologists were fortunate in enlisting the aid of William H. Gillespie of West Virginia's Department of Agriculture as council chairman. West Virginia is one of the states whose commercial forests might be injured by an infestation of gypsy moth. Gillespie, skilled in political maneuvering, was able to interest a number of Congressmen in the control campaign, and Senator Robert C. Byrd of West Virginia managed to get funds from Congress for a "five-year plan."

Not long ago I attended a council meeting in Washington to hear about the plan's progress. From time to time a querulous voice was raised, asking why we didn't go back to the good old days of DDT. But in general the council members proved to be serious men, aware of the many complexities involved and anxious to get on with the job of finding sophisticated techniques to deal with those complexities. It was encouraging to learn that there is no more talk of "eradication"; the aim is to control the gypsy moth so that it takes its place in a balanced and healthy forest community.

"The biggest lack has been an evaluation of control," said the Forest Service's Robert Campbell. "We really don't even know how well the various techniques controlled gypsy moths, whether we're talking about parasites or DDT or burlap bags."

Campbell told of his efforts, using a computer, to predict the severity of gypsy moth outbreaks and the effects of successive defoliations on various species of trees. Entomologists spoke of their work with parasites and predators. USDA's Reitz Sailer, for instance, said that entomologists formerly had concentrated their search for Old World parasites in areas of heavy gypsy moth infestation; if the search can be shifted toward parasites that operate successfully in low density or stable areas, these new parasites might better control American gypsy moths at acceptable levels.

"I do not think that chemical control and biological control are compatible on a large area," Sailer said. "Spot treatments, all right. But over large areas you will kill all your egg parasites, and the gypsy moths will snap back." Several of the conference participants agreed that Sevin's side effects were undesirable, and told of continuing experimental work with new pesticides such as Zectran. For a long time, chemicals will be needed on a spot basis to supplement natural controls.

Participants also mentioned their increasing success with various applications of *Bacillus thuringiensis,* whose toxicity is confined to lepidoptera but whose long-term control of pests seems to be no more effective than that of more conventional insecticides: pest populations are temporarily reduced, but in the absence of a variety of other controls such as parasites and predators, the insects bounce back another year.

Probably the most encouraging reports dealt with the synthesis of the female moth's sex attractant into a new product called Disparlure. Scientists already have had considerable success with Disparlure, confusing males or luring them to traps where they can be sterilized or destroyed. Sterilized males, turned loose, mate with females and thus produce only infertile eggs.

At the moment, most of the techniques described at the

conference are at least several years away from large-scale use in the field. Enthusiasm must be checked. "Don't oversimplify or oversell this program to the public; don't get hopes too high," one of the participants warned.

And it was gratifying, after years of hearing conservationists described as "hysterical" when they warned against the hazards of massive spraying programs, to learn that today the shoe is on the other foot.

"Talk about hysterical people!" said a Massachusetts official. "We've got some of them, and they're literally screaming for us to spray. You can't blame them completely when you see thousands of caterpillars climbing over their trees. We're not having much mortality, but we've got aesthetic problems, and so we'll do some spraying in inhabited areas, instead of back in the woods as we used to."

Yet in parts of northern New Jersey, which once was badly infested, the gypsy moth populations are collapsing, leaving weak, stunted survivors that deposit small egg masses. And in Pennsylvania, the authorities are telling it like it is. "The gypsy moth is here to stay," a recent state press release admitted to the public. "We must learn to live with it since there is no hope of eradicating it or even preventing its spread."

The U.S. Forest Service's Robert Campbell takes a fresh view. "Part of our job now is to educate the public," he told me. "We've got to dampen the hysteria. The first step is to stop thinking of these caterpillars as something disgusting — nobody thinks of a *woolly bear* as disgusting. I dislike the tree mortality, of course, but to tell you the truth I enjoy being in the middle of a good defoliation. It's very exciting."

Bob Campbell has some exciting moments ahead.

A heron, dead from oil saturation on a coastal beach

MARVIN ZELDIN

From Your Crankcase
to the Sea

Friday, November 13, 1970, was not a good day for Berks
Associates, Inc., a company that rerefines used oil, such as the
oil drained from your car's crankcase when you pull into your
neighborhood filling station for an oil change.

Berks, a small company in a dwindling industry, has a plant
at Douglassville, Pennsylvania, about 40 miles north of Philadel-
phia. Berks had about 20 million gallons of oily sludge, the residue
of used oil after reprocessing, in five lagoons on company property. Rain-weakened walls of two lagoons broke and 3 million
gallons of sludge spilled into the Schuylkill River. Attempts to
contain the sludge failed and it oozed down the Schuylkill and
into the Delaware River. Fifty miles of the Schuylkill and 15
miles of the Delaware were contaminated. The sludge entered
the water supply intakes of several towns, and water supplies
were promptly shut off. Containment and clean-up operations
got under way immediately, under the National Contingency
Plan for oil and hazardous materials pollution.

Meanwhile, back at the plant, there was a threat of more
trouble. The rain-soaked walls of the lagoons were in danger
of collapsing and releasing the remaining 17 million gallons of
sludge into the Schuylkill. This posed an "imminent and substantial threat to the public health or welfare" from an "actual or

threatened discharge of oil" under the Water Quality Improvement Act which was signed into law on April 3, 1970. For the first time, that provision of the act was invoked by then Secretary of the Interior Walter Hickel. (Water pollution control has since been transferred from Interior to the new Environmental Protection Agency.)

The government went to court to abate the threat. The company agreed to shore up the walls of the lagoons, to build an emergency lagoon, to purchase and install an incinerator to burn the sludge, to remove the sludge from the lagoons, and then to landfill the empty lagoons, all under federal supervision.

Berks's Black Friday was the first test of the 1970 law which gave the government new legal tools to prevent and control oil pollution. The tools worked well. There was no doubt about the "imminent and substantial threat." The National Contingency Plan, a system to coordinate federal agencies' spill control and clean-up activities, also worked well. The Federal Water Quality Administration (now the Water Programs division of the EPA) provided the on-scene command and other personnel. The Coast Guard headed the clean-up operation. (The company is liable for the costs.) Other federal agencies also participated.

But there is more to the Berks story. The state of Pennsylvania had been aware for some time of the danger of oil pollution from the Berks plant. It had cited the company for violations 8 times in some 11 years prior to the spill — and fined the company a total of $300. Earlier in 1970, the Pennsylvania Department of Health had named Berks the fifth worst water polluter in the state. Beyond that, however, nothing had been done to *prevent* a Black Friday. Once again, a spill was required to dramatize the inadequacy of state and federal efforts to *prevent* pollution.

A recent investigation by the *New York Times* exposed one of the basic causes of this deplorable nation-wide situation. As the *Times*'s national environmental correspondent, Gladwin Hill, put it: "Most of the state boards primarily responsible for cleaning up the nation's air and water are markedly weighted with representatives of the principal sources of pollution." The *Times* probe revealed that "the membership of air and water pollution boards in 35 states is dotted with industrial, agricultural, municipal, and county representatives whose own organizations or spheres of activity are in many cases in the forefront of pollution." In California, for example, Hill wrote, "For years a board member dealing with pollution of Los Angeles harbor has been an executive of an oil company that was a major harbor polluter."

The *Times*'s discovery prompted Environmental Protection Agency Administrator William D. Ruckelshaus to write the governors of the 50 states and remind them that "it is imperative that the men and women who sit on these boards — and who are empowered to set and implement reasonable standards of pollution abatement — be influenced only by the general public interest and not by any vested interests." Ruckelshaus added: "The credibility of our efforts at every level to restore environmental conditions rests on our ability to pursue a rigorously independent course."

David D. Dominick, then EPA's Acting Commissioner for Water Quality, cited the Berks spill in a letter to the heads of state water pollution control agencies early in 1971. "One need only fly across our nation to know that many of the elements present in the Schuylkill River event are repeated at hundreds of points," he wrote. "All types of materials, from industrial and mining wastes to raw chemicals, are stored in lagoons often directly adjacent to rivers, streams, and lakes. This practice may have been acceptable and tolerable in the past. Times have changed, however, and I believe that we must take whatever measures we can to guard our waters against these potential damages."

Dominick urged the states "to determine the extent to which

your water may be threatened and to seek the cooperation of your municipal and industrial leaders in adopting remedial measures which will prevent environmental damage from this source."

The Berks spill also drew attention to another problem. Immediately after the spill, with the plant shut down, the collection of used oil from filling stations and industrial plants stopped in parts of the area. Slicks of used oil began appearing in some rivers and streams in Pennsylvania and in Delaware Bay. Slicks coming directly out of storm sewers were observed from the air. After the Berks plant went back into operation in early December, the oil slicks largely disappeared. Some collectors, filling stations, and industries had simply dumped their waste oil into sewers and streams to be rid of it.

They were not alone, for getting rid of waste oil is a national and international problem of vast dimensions. According to the American Petroleum Institute, an estimated 450 million gallons of used oil are disposed of each year in the U.S. "without complete assurance that some pollution potential doesn't exist." That is, says an API report on used oil, it is either put in sewers or is dumped on the ground or falls in the "mysterious category" of "fate unknown."

Worldwide, it is estimated that a total of 957 million gallons (3.3 million tons) of oil used in motor vehicles and industries winds up in the rivers and oceans each year. Used oil thus represents about two-thirds of the 5 million tons of oil added to the world's waters annually.

In the United States, the capacity of rerefining plants that process used oil has dropped almost 50 percent. The number of reprocessing plants has declined from about 150 to fewer than 50. Capacity of the plants still operating is estimated at 100 million to 125 million gallons a year.

"The rerefining industry is simply disappearing," a government official told us, for three basic reasons. First, rerefined oil no longer enjoys the excise tax subsidy — and consequent price advantage — it used to have. Second, the Federal Trade Commission requires the oil to be labeled "rerefined." This has reduced buyer acceptance. Third, the "virgin" lubricating oils manufactured by oil companies now contain many chemical additives to enable them to stand up over 4000 to 6000 miles. The days of an oil change every 1000 miles are long gone. While this is a boon to the motorist, the additives and suspended solids in the used oil are a bane to the rerefiners. Many of the rerefining plants are old and cannot handle the additive-laden used oil.

As a result, some used oil collectors have gone out of business. More and more oil is being dumped into sewers and streams. In addition to its direct pollution effects, used oil also decreases the efficiency of sewage treatment plants and at times causes fires in the plants. Some disreputable collectors mix used oil with fuel oil and sell it for home heating. They don't get many repeat sales, however, for the mixture generally clogs the burners.

Research is currently under way on converting waste crankcase and industrial oil into usable products — for home heating, for fueling industrial and power-plant boilers, etc.

The reuse of waste oil would mean conserving a valuable natural resource and eliminating a major source of oil pollution of the waters of the world. "Waste oil is a tremendous resource for energy in an energy-short world," a pollution controller told us. "Something's got to be done to put it to use and keep it the hell out of the environment."

One of the most likely markets for recycled and purified waste oil would be large consumers of fuel oil, such as electric utilities. But sales of rerefined waste oil to utilities would reduce the major oil companies' sales of their own residual fuel oil to those customers. Thus the API report is more concerned with disposal than with reclamation of used oil. The report concludes:

"Based on the studies conducted by this committee, it seems that the task of assuring nonpolluting disposal should be handled on a high priority basis by individual companies rather than the industry as a whole. While the problem of used industrial oil disposal is generally handled by the users, and is not likely to bring immediate discredit to the petroleum industry, oil companies have a more direct responsibility for pollution problems caused by service stations bearing their name."

A variety of proposals have been made which go far beyond the oil industry's limited approach. It has been suggested that an excise tax be imposed on "virgin" lubricating oil to finance a system of collecting and reprocessing used oil into readily useful products. It has also been suggested that legislation might be necessary to require systematic, licensed collection and disposal of used oil. And it has been suggested that the oil industry, as the producer of a product that adds so greatly to water pollution, itself initiate a national used oil conservation program.

Companies manufacturing and using aluminum cans and glass bottles are recycling more and more of those discarded products. They are conserving natural resources, reducing the solid waste burden — and enjoying public relations dividends. One wonders why an industry as public-relations conscious as the oil industry does not go and do likewise.

Postscript: A first step toward constructive national action to cope with the problem of used oil was taken by Congress in 1972. An amendment to the Federal Water Pollution Control Act directed the Environmental Protection Agency to study the problem and to give Congress a preliminary report by April 1973 and a final report by April 1974. Aspects to be covered include the amount of waste oil generated in the nation; existing and alternative collection and disposal methods; long-term biological effects of present disposal practices; the potential market for reclaimed oil products; and recommendations to stimulate reclamation and recycling of this energy resource.

GARY SOUCIE

How You Gonna Keep It
Down on the Farm?

HARASSED URBANITES, beset by noise, air pollution, power plants, airports, highways, congestion, and decay, have put The Farm on a pedestal. The last bastion of the good, simple, decent, pristine life. Even a decade of intense fighting over DDT has not shaken our faith in the new agrarian idealism. But more than a furlong separates The Farm of our romantic notion from the farm of today's agribusiness reality.

Would you believe, for instance, that American agriculture each year generates nearly 10 times as much solid waste as all our cities, towns, suburbs, and communities combined? That some of the feedlots supplying us with steaks and hamburgers have sewage problems the equivalent of one million people living on 320 acres, a population density 26 times that of Calcutta? That disposal of logging debris by prescribed burning produces more particulate air pollution than all our motor vehicles, industries, power plants, space heating, and burning dumps combined?

Each year agricultural activities generate 2.5 billion tons of solid wastes, more than half of all solid wastes from all sources. Included are manure and other animal wastes, crop residues and timber slash, and food processing wastes.

Animal wastes constitute the biggest share and the biggest

problem: 1.1 billion tons of fecal waste, 435 million tons of
commingled liquid waste, and another 200 to 400 million tons
of used bedding, paunch manure from slaughtered cattle, and
carcasses. According to Dr. Cecil H. Wadleigh, former director
of the U.S. Department of Agriculture's Soil and Water Conservation Research Division, "Waste production by domestic animals in the United States is equivalent to that of a human
population of 1.9 billion." Calculating a few years ago that the
annual production of manure exceeded a billion cubic yards, Dr.
Chester E. Evans of the USDA's Agricultural Research Service
wrote: "If this manure were divided up equally, every family
would receive 25 cubic yards a year as their fair share. This
would be enough to fill the average 9 x 15 living room to a
depth of 5 feet, or about chin level on most adults."

The environmental problems of animal wastes do not stem
so much from sheer volume, startling as these figures are, but
from their concentration and the manner of handling. When
animals were raised on family farms, each farmer had only a
manageable amount of waste to handle and he generally used
it as fertilizer. Today, animal and crop production are largely
separate enterprises and beef cattle, dairy cows, hogs, and chickens are raised in high-density feedlots and poultry houses. The
USDA estimates that more than half of the 600 million domestic
animals are raised under concentrated conditions. A large poultry
operation may produce 5 tons of chicken droppings daily. A
feedlot with 10,000 head of beef cattle generates 260 tons of
manure each day. This approximates the sewage problem of
a city of 164,000 people.

Farmyard and feedlot runoff waters — which may be 10 to
100 times as high in biological oxygen demand (BOD) as untreated
municipal sewage, and are rich in the nitrogen and phosphorus
nutrients that cause algal blooms and eutrophication — are a

major cause of stream and lake pollution. A 1966 study of the Potomac River revealed that most of the pollution of its upper basin is from animal wastes.

The biochemistry of animal wastes is an ecologist's nightmare. Thousands of chemical compounds may be present, depending on the particular animal species involved, the feed ration, climatic conditions, and other factors. Very little is known about these compounds or their environmental significance. Washed into streams or rivers, or percolated into the water table beneath the farm or feedlot, they can unleash their consequences on an unsuspecting population miles away.

Recent studies show feedlot wastes to be a major source of nitrate contamination in nearby wells and groundwater supplies. This is a first-order health hazard because nitrates in drinking water can cause methemoglobinemia (blue babies) in infants. Moreover, virtually nothing is known about the movement of nitrates and other contaminants in groundwater away from feedlots.

In hog pens and other areas where the wastes are acid, secondary amines may be produced and combine with nitrite to form carcinogenic nitrosamines. A large but indeterminate number of diseases that may be transmissible from farm animals to people further complicate the environmental health question. Histoplasmosis is a human disease, most often affecting the lungs, caused by a fungus that thrives on poultry droppings; there is a relatively high incidence of the disease in Midwestern and Middle Atlantic states, areas of concentrated poultry production. Other diseases transmitted through animal wastes include liver necrosis (listeriosis), an infectious jaundice (leptospirosis), cholera, parrot fever (psittacosis), about 30 enteroviruses, including poliomyelitis and Coxsackie, infectious hepatitis, brucellosis, many fungal infections, including thrush and cryptococcus, salmonellosis, trichinosis, and many worm infections. An Iowa State University report on animal waste management observed: "It is surprising, however, to note the lack of information or documentation for many animal diseases where human illness has been possible but not confirmed."

Some pollutants from animal wastes are airborne. About 90 percent of the ammonia in urine and manure quickly volatilizes into the air, where it is easily trapped by plants and water surfaces. Agricultural scientists have calculated that a 35-foot-deep lake a mile from a feedlot with 80,000 head of cattle "absorbs enough ammonia each year to raise its entire volume to a eutrophic level." Feedlots and other concentrated animal-raising areas have become a major source of flies. Dust from feedlots and farmyards may affect people with allergies and may carry trace chemicals and drugs from animal feeds or any number of pollutants.

Odor is generally regarded as the toughest problem facing livestock and poultry producers. Some waste treatment processes intensify the odor problem. Agricultural scientists admit virtually no headway is being made in the face of a high degree of ignorance about the causes of odors. Apparently the chemistry of stench is not a very popular field. A USDA soil scientist, Frank G. Viets, Jr., in a report on "The Mounting Problem of Cattle Feedlot Pollution," concludes that "perhaps the odor problem cannot be solved."

Land disposal of one sort or another is the dominant method of handling animal wastes. In some areas — particularly the Corn Belt and northern Great Plains — a substantial portion of animal manure is still used as fertilizer. But elsewhere, ponding or lagooning or simply making mountains of manure predominates. Manure fertilizer is not very popular with today's farmer. It takes a ton of high-quality feedlot manure to supply as much nitrogen as 22 pounds of ammonium nitrate fertilizer. Handling costs are high, storage problems severe (fertilizer may not be spread during the growing season nor during the winter where the ground freezes), and the manure must be worked into the soil. As two USDA scientists wrote in *BioScience,* "Farmers can buy and apply chemical fertilizer cheaper than they can apply compost obtained without cost."

Composting, or dehydration, reduces both weight and volume of manure, however, making disposal or spreading easier. And recycling of the nutrient values in manure would appear to make the most sense. Some agriscientists prefer spreading it — wet, dried, or treated — as fertilizer; others prefer treating and pellet-izing it so that it can be used as animal food. Each method has its problems. Great care must be taken in the use of organic fertilizers because of the dangers of runoff pollution, soil contami-nation, crop damage, and the distribution of weed seeds, diseases, and the like. Some scientists and public health officials feel uneasy about manure-based animal feeds; at present the Food and Drug Administration prohibits the feeding of fecal wastes.

Energy recovery is a distinct possibility. The Bureau of Mines of the U.S. Department of the Interior has demonstrated that manure and other animal wastes can be converted into fossil fuels like oil and gas. Writing in *Environment,* Dr. Hinrich L. Bohn of the University of Arizona suggests the production of methane (natural) gas from anaerobic digestion of animal wastes. According to Dr. Bohn, the manure generated by a 100,000-head feedlot could produce enough natural gas to supply a city of 30,000 people, while the by-product sludge would have twice the nutrient content for fertilizer as raw manure. Presently, Combustion Power Company in California is working on a turbine generator that could use animal wastes as fuel.

Agricultural crop production produces another 550 million tons of solid waste annually. Much of it gets burned, contributing to air pollution. There are 5000 cotton gins in the 14 cotton-producing states, and the big gins must dispose of up to 3000 pounds of waste per hour. Half of it is vented as dust into the atmosphere from exhaust fans (carrying pesticides and plant diseases with it), and the other half gets burned. The continuing mechanization of cotton fields is intensifying the problem. A hand-picked bale produces 50 pounds of waste at the gin, compared to over 2000 pounds for a machine-stripped bale. But even if left in the field, the residue would still have to be disposed of.

Sugarcane is a waste-intensive crop. After the sugar is squeezed out, most of the plant remains as waste. In the past, much of this sugarcane waste (called bagasse) was used to make paper, but the bagasse mills have not been able to compete with the wood pulp mills. Valentine Paper Company in Louisiana is the only notable exception.

Despite the increasing use of wood chips in papermaking, each year the forest products industry leaves 25 million tons of timber slash in our nation's forests. If it is burned it creates severe air pollution problems — limiting visibility to the point where it becomes a significant cause of auto accidents. (Apple-growers in the Pacific Northwest a few years ago sued the Forest Service, claiming the smoke from prescribed burning was inhibiting the proper color development of their apples.) If the slash isn't burned it spreads tree diseases and increases the likelihood of forest fires. A U.S. Forest Service study showed that forest fires originating in logging wastes are, on the average, seven times larger than those originating in uncut areas or where the slash has been disposed of. Virtually the only alternative to burning is chipping, but it costs $12 a ton to chip the debris as opposed to $1 a ton to burn it.

Agricultural crops and products are among the first to suffer from agricultural waste. Contaminated waters make the watering of livestock or the irrigation of crops more difficult. Houseflies and stable flies bred in feedlot manure or in peanut litter, rotting straw or other crop residues, may worry livestock to the point where there are material losses in beef production and a 25 percent decline in milk production. Plant diseases may be magnified in crop residues and field stubble. The best-known example is late potato blight, which annually ruins 4 percent of the potato crop; the disease originates in piles of potato culls on farms, along railroad tracks, and outside storage houses. Other crop destroyers attributable to plant residues include wheat mosaic, the European corn borer, blind-seed disease in seed grasses, sugarcane borer, and beet yellow virus.

Some crop residues do get recycled, and the greatest use by far is for mulch. Stubble and plant residues also may be plowed under as a soil conditioner. But plant disease and insect problems plague these reuses. Some crop residues are used as bedding for livestock and poultry, but after one short-term use they become waste matter again, this time contaminated by animal wastes. So, until someone figures out how to control these diseases and pests chemically, biologically, or genetically, farmers will continue to burn much of the crop wastes.

According to a 1969 report to the President on "Control of Agriculture-Related Pollution": "Precise estimates of the magnitude of wastes from processing agricultural products are not available. But a recent summary of published data indicates that their pollution potential expressed in pounds of biochemical oxygen demand (BOD) is equivalent to that produced by a population of more than 168 million people." Other studies put the BOD population equivalent at 275 million people. These wastes are produced by canneries, dairies, slaughterhouses and meat-packing plants, tanneries, sugar refineries, potato processing plants, textile mills, breweries, distilleries, and — overshadowing all the rest — pulp and paper mills.

Because processing wastes are usually water-borne (dumped

into municipal sewers or directly into rivers, lakes, bays, and oceans with or without treatment) and diluted to varying degrees with water used in processing, their pollution potential is usually evaluated in terms of pounds of BOD required rather than in terms of concentration of BOD in parts per million. Prior to dilution, some processing wastes have incredible concentrations of BOD: peavine ensilage juices may contain 75,000 parts per million (or 200 to 750 times that of raw municipal sewage). And that 1969 report says, "The acid whey produced annually from cottage-cheese processing amounts to a BOD equal to a population equivalent of 83 million people."

Fortunately, a great many by-products are produced from the culls, peelings, pits, trimmings, screenings, sludge, and other residuals, but not necessarily without environmental impact. In Florida a $30 million industry has been developed to make citrus molasses and other animal feeds from citrus peels, rags, and seeds, but the emissions from the drying plants have become a major source of air pollution in some communities. In the food processing industry, about 80 percent of all processing residuals are turned into by-products like animal feeds, charcoal, alcohol, oil, vinegar, and fertilizer. The remaining 20 percent is trouble enough, for canning and other food processing industries resist installation of expensive effluent treatment equipment because its use would be limited principally to those few months of the harvesting season. Some effluent is utilized as irrigation water, but the use of chemicals in certain processes limits this beneficial disposal process. For example, sweet potatoes often are peeled in a process that uses sodium hydroxide, a deflocculant that breaks soil down into smaller particles, limiting its ability to pass water.

¤   ¤   ¤

This report has been long on stating problems and short on solutions. Unfortunately, that's an accurate picture of today's agricultural waste management scene.

Recent trends in agriculture that emphasize concentrated production and higher yields per acre, and the absolute supremacy of concern for minimum cost over product quality, land enhancement, environmental protection, or any other principle — in other words, the transformation of agriculture into agribusiness — have compounded nearly all these problems. Consumer trends have further intensified the problems. Between 1940 and 1970, per capita consumption of beef in the United States more than doubled, half that increase coming between 1960 and 1966. The phenomenal growth in frozen, canned, and packaged foods has further aggravated the solid waste situation. Rinds, husks, peels, and other organic waste products that once made up a large part of our municipal refuse have been replaced by jars, bottles, cans, boxes, and other paper and plastic packaging. Meanwhile, the organic waste is accumulating out of sight and out of mind back on the farm.

The federal government, whose policies have done so much to fuel agricultural waste problems, is providing virtually no leadership in solving them. Farmers, ranchers, producers, and processors are left to fend for themselves. Thus the states have assumed principal responsibility for regulating agricultural waste, producing a crazy-quilt pattern of laws and rules inadequate to the situation. Buck-passing among the U.S. Department of Agriculture, the Environmental Protection Agency, and, to a much lesser degree, the Bureau of Mines is the order of the day in Washington. Jurisdiction is fragmented, and the emphasis is on research and navel contemplation rather than action.

In 1969 the Department of Agriculture and the Office of Science and Technology recommended a five-year program to combat the various pollution problems caused by agriculture. That program has gone virtually nowhere. In animal waste management alone, the 1969 report to the President recommended USDA expenditures in 1972 of $3.76 million for research and development, $178.43 million on action programs, and $550 million in federal loans to livestock producers and processors. According to Joseph T. McDavid, USDA director of press information, 1972 expenditures on animal waste management were $3.03 million for research and $8.02 million for action; he was unable to supply loan figures. In 1971, participants in a National Symposium on Animal Waste Management complained that of the nearly $80 million authorized for agricultural waste projects the previous year by the Solid Waste Disposal Act, Congress appropriated $64 million but the Nixon Administration had spent only $2.25 million.

The Department of Agriculture's zeal in the solid waste field might be gleaned from two remarks made to the writer. When asked what was actually being done today in terms of waste handling and disposal, Ray Schleeter of the press service in the Secretary's office said: "I can't conceive of any office in the department keeping tabs on what's being done with solid wastes. That's their problem," referring to farmers, producers, and processors. Carl W. Carlson, acting assistant administrator of the Agricultural Research Service: "Why are you interested in crop residues? It's just not much of a problem." Five hundred fifty million tons is not much of a problem?

Ultimately, all these organic wastes should be recycled. Land disposal, for fertilizer or as waste, and refeeding offer the most potential. Even energy production must not dominate agricultural waste disposal. As the Iowa State University study stated: "There is no such thing as waste organic material in the natural world. We call animal excreta waste and consider it offensive because it is not orderly in our sense of values. In the scheme of life, almost all of the compounds that make up living bodies and compounds that come from their metabolism must be returned to a condition in which they may again be used to build, repair, or provide energy for other protoplasm. Without a system of reducing organic matter to a form in which the elements composing it may be used again, almost all life would shortly cease on this Earth."

Waste is often defined as resources in the wrong place, and this is definitely the case for the agricultural wastes polluting streams and lakes, fouling the air from burning, and accumulating in mounds, ponds, and ditches.

Students of the agricultural waste problem have identified education as the foremost challenge in the immediate future. Educating agricultural producers about the techniques of proper animal waste management and the dire environmental consequences of improper waste management; educating policymakers at all levels of government; and educating the general public about the dimensions of the problem so they will demand action and be willing to pay the costs in higher prices and higher taxes.

Conservationists must be among the first to accept the challenge. As Dr. Cecil Wadleigh puts it: "There must be enlightened leadership. Those graced with the good fortune to stand on mountains and discern the bright horizons of a pristine environment have the right — even the duty — to help turn unawareness and indifference into understanding, concern, and action. Nothing gets done without someone being motivated."

An army of motorcyclists roars out across California's Mohave Desert on a cross-country race. Trail bikes of all sizes number 2½ million — the most numerous of all off-road vehicles

JACK HOPE

The Invasion
of the Awful ORVs

THE BOY RODE EXPERTLY. He gunned the small motorcycle across the sagebrush flat, throttled down as he came to a hill, and shifted his weight to provide more traction as he urged his machine up the slope. At the top he briefly disappeared from view, then came into sight beyond the dry creek bed, the throttle open again, a red cloud of dust fanning out behind. He vaulted a mound standing up, landing the snarling motorcycle on its rear wheel, buckling his knees at the right instant to absorb the shock. Then he reclimbed the hill, circling, sliding, sending up red flashes of dirt as a mourning dove flushed from the ground and retreated low over the sagebrush.

Eventually the boy tired of his sport and headed back toward the campground, where I stood watching. He rode up to me, stopped, and removed his crash helmet. He was a cute-looking kid, with a tanned face and a bright smile.

"Hi. Did you see me go over that ramp?"

I nodded toward the motorcycle. "What do you call that thing?"

"It's a Trail Seventy. A Honda."

"It looks dangerous. And it's noisy."

"It makes a helluva noise," he said enthusiastically.

"You put up a dove out there. How do you know it didn't have a nest? You could've crushed it."

"There's plenty of doves. Besides, I'm careful."

"Isn't it illegal to ride that machine around here?"

The boy shook his head. "This is national forest. You can ride them anywhere you want."

"Even off the trails?" I asked, knowing he was stretching the truth.

The boy turned uneasily on his motorcycle seat and glanced back toward the place where his family was camped. "My father says you can. He says if they didn't want us to ride, they'd put up a sign."

Out in the sagebrush another engine roared. A crash-helmeted man, about forty years old, steered a large motorcycle in our direction. He wore a white T-shirt, blue-and-white striped pants, cowboy boots, and large sunglasses.

"That's my father."

The man smiled as he stopped, and gestured toward his son.

"Rides pretty well for a nine-year-old, doesn't he?"

Nine! I pictured future generations being born with wheels instead of feet, with four-cycle engines filling the space within the cranium, a drive chain running down the spinal column, exhaust pipes protruding from the ears.

"I was going to wait another year, but all his friends have 'em. So I figured he'd better have one too."

"Well," I began awkwardly, "I was about to tell your boy he'd be a lot better off walking instead of riding a machine."

The man was visibly annoyed. "C'mon Billy," he said. "We got to go.

"This's a free country," he yelled to me as he revved up his engine. "Some people like to walk, and some like to ride. *We* like to ride."

At that he and Billy gunned their father-and-son machines and sped off, side by side.

Frustrated, I stood thinking of the various sorts of purgatory to which certain people could be subjected: 100-mile motorcycle rides with a prickly-pear cactus fastened to the seat; filling in eroded trail bike ruts with a teaspoon. But I couldn't decide who — in addition to Billy's father — would be made to suffer the punishment. The president of the Honda company? The Madison Avenue people who write the trail bike ads? The bureaucrats of the U.S. Forest Service? The inventor of the wheel? Who indeed?

The off-road recreational vehicle has taken America by storm. Little more than a decade ago, the machines collectively referred to as ORVs were nonexistent, or at least were not manufactured for recreational use. Today there are more than 4 million of their kind: 2.5 million trail bikes (small or lightweight motorcycles designed for use in rough terrain); 1.4 million snowmobiles; 200,000 dune buggies (dune buggy = an old Volkswagen chassis + a new fiber glass body + variations thereof); and 50,000 all-terrain vehicles (ATVs) that are either bathtub-shaped or flat, supported by either balloon tires or by a cushion of air that carries the vehicle over land or water.

And within five years, according to a government estimate, we can expect about 6 million more off-road vehicles to be in use in this country.

The definition of an off-road vehicle is somewhat arbitrary — and is generally determined by controversy. The four types mentioned have provoked the most debate. These machines are characterized by recent and rapidly growing popularity, by their capacity to travel over unpaved landscape, and by a price tag that is within the grasp of most Americans, ranging from $250 for the least expensive trail bike, to $1000 for a snowmobile or dune buggy, to $1500 for a balloon-tired all-terrain vehicle or the cheapest air-cushion "hovercraft." Most expensive of all vehicles capable of off-road travel are four-wheel-drive jeeps, and pickup trucks costing upward of $3000. All ORVs, of course, are powered by internal-combustion engines.

The rapidity with which the industry is developing indicates that within two or three years new or crossbred machinery will be added to the ORV category. Kits for converting snowmobiles with summer wheels are already available. And the companies have worked feverishly to produce miniature versions of some of their vehicles. Like the "Kitty Cat" snowmobile, a tiny machine designed for tiny children. (A recent advertisement pictures a five-year-old boy seated at the wheel of one of these motorized "toys.")

The most positive characteristic of off-road vehicles is that they are truly fun to operate. They are capable of speeds ranging from 15 to 80 miles per hour, and they provide the user with feelings of power, excitement, and control — sensations that, as the ad writers know only too well, appeal to most of us. And since the first of these vehicles hit the commercial market in the late 1950s, they have been embraced by a diverse segment of the American public, ranging from beachcombers in Southern California to conservative pillars of the church in Salt Lake City; from 4-H leaders in upstate New York to night-cruising deer poachers in northern Michigan.

But against the fun provided by those 4 million ORVs must be weighed a frightening list of grievances. For, by eliminating the need for physical effort in cross-country travel, by dramatically increasing the distance a man may cover in pursuit of his recreation (or in pursuit of anything else), these machines have created an ominous set of social and environmental problems.

Although half of the states have passed legislation regulating the use of some form of off-road vehicle, most of the laws are directed solely toward the snowmobile. Oregon and North

Dakota are the only states requiring a driver's license or permit to operate an ORV, and this restriction is limited to snowmobiles. In most places, an eight-year-old may legally operate an off-road vehicle. And as some parents have learned, too late, an eight-year-old can also be killed by the machine. Nearly 90 people die each year in snowmobile accidents alone. Data gathered by a Maine official indicates that snowmobiling causes 60 times more accidents than hunting (roughly 300 accidents per 20,000 snowmobilers versus 50 accidents per 200,000 hunters). In addition, many thousands of serious spinal injuries are attributable to the jarring ride of this machine.

The lack of legal attention to ORVs — and the lack of comprehensive statistical information on the extent of their use and misuse — is testimony to the fact that lawmakers and law enforcement agencies are inadequately prepared to cope with the off-road vehicle. As in the case of the automobile, our technological inventiveness has outstripped our ability or willingness to deal with these machines in a rational manner.

The ORV laws that have been enacted are superficial. In general, they require a small state registration fee (usually $5 or less), put an age minimum on operators (sometimes sixteen years, sometimes fourteen, sometimes ten, sometimes none at all), and are directed largely toward protecting the ORV user from himself. There are seldom provisions to safeguard the environment or to buffer that 98 percent of the public that does not own ORVs from the 2 percent that does. Often, the legal and administrative burden of coping with off-road machines falls upon such understaffed state agencies as departments of natural resources or park and forest commissions.

Unlike the automobile, whose use is confined largely to roadways, the snowmobile, all-terrain vehicle, or trail bike can travel almost everywhere — and does — making its use and impact impossible to monitor and control by normal means. Law enforcement officers can attend to only a small fraction of the offenses committed by ORV owners. Consequently, individuals whose summer cabins have been vandalized by winter snowmobilers, whose cattle have been stampeded by trail-bikers, or whose privacy has been invaded by operators of any of the off-road vehicles have resorted to somewhat misanthropic tactics to protect themselves from their tormentors. In New England the ORV has given new life to the "No Trespassing" poster business, and signs printed in recent years contain special bold-letter warnings to snowmobilers. In several Western states back-country hikers have piled logs into "motorcycle traps" (really blockades) along footpaths used by silence-shattering trail bikes. In New York, growers whose Christmas trees have been stolen by snowmobilers are patrolling their plantations with loaded firearms and delivering thieves to local authorities at gunpoint.

Many state and federal land-managing agencies initially welcomed the new recreational vehicles, permitting them to range unrestricted over vast portions of the public domain, printing leaflets advertising the opportunities for motorized tourists to "cruise to their hearts' content." Now they find themselves in the embarrassing and politically awkward position of having to restrict and police vehicle usage in order to reduce vandalism and environmental damage. ORV users have committed a bizarre array of illegal and irresponsible acts on public lands, ranging from the theft of outhouses in Southern California to the destruction of ancient Indian petroglyphs in several Southwestern states, from the "rustling" of moose calves in Wyoming to the stealing of the brass bar rail from the well-known ghost town of Garnet, Montana. (The rail was installed in 1867 and stolen in the winter of 1969–70.)

In the spring of 1971, two men were found guilty of chasing

and running over coyotes with snowmobiles in Grand Teton National Park in Wyoming. It was the fifth such incident at that park in a year. The U.S. Forest Service no longer permits snowmobilers to enter areas in the national forests where game animals winter. Rangers often have found the carcasses of winter-weakened deer and elk that apparently had been shot or run to death in the deep snow by snowmobilers.

As any trail-biker or snowmobiler will point out, the majority of the acts of vandalism are committed by a minority of ORV users. But this is irrelevant. A lone man on any of the ORVs can do a great deal of damage in a very short time. And given the shortage of enforcement personnel, the growing number of ORVs, and the lack of restrictions upon their use, the chances of arresting or preventing this damage are almost nil.

But far more serious is the fact that use of ORVs by large numbers of people can create environmental havoc. In Humboldt National Forest in Nevada officials had to post "No Vehicles" signs within a hilly region where hunters using jeeps and all-terrain vehicles had caused an estimated $50,000 worth of damage to soil and vegetation. The hunters tore down the signs and drove into the area anyway. At 80-acre Pierz Lake in Minnesota, where summer canoeists were once rewarded for their six-hour paddle with a catch of two-pound trout, a troop of 120 snowmobilers virtually cleaned out the lake in a single winter's day, packing out 556 pounds of fish. And in repeated hill-climbing expeditions in California's Panoche Hills, a 1200-acre area administered by the Bureau of Land Management, trail-bikers stripped away 60 percent of the vegetation.

In an attempt to control the use of off-road vehicles, some land-managing agencies ironically have invested tax dollars in ORVs of their own. New York State's Department of Environmental Conservation purchased a fleet of 43 snowmobiles for use in the Adirondack Forest Preserve. The machines are used both for routine work and to patrol the activities of snowmobilers. Some of the "routine" work could more properly be traced to the advent of the snowmobile. In an article in the department's magazine, *The Conservationist,* Conservation Officer Louis Fendrick writes of the pleasures of shooting foxes from a snowmobile as part of the state's predator control program.

Moreover, the U.S. Forest Service, the Bureau of Land Management, and state agencies have spent time and money in the development and maintenance of thousands of miles of ORV trails. Costs of trail construction vary greatly, but one federal land manager cited a typical expense of about $2000 per mile in preparing a pathway for trail bikes. Snowmobile trails are less costly to build since the surface need not be especially smooth, but they must be frequently groomed in winter to smooth out ruts and "moguls" at an estimated cost of $200 per mile per year.

And the wants of ORV users do not stop at the facilities already provided. Snowmobilers' associations demand more, better maintained, and more accommodating trails, with eight-foot-wide bridges across waterways, with snowbanks at road crossings cut back "at least 500 feet in both directions," with grades and slopes of no more than 25 percent, with one-way traffic only, with trail widths no less than ten feet, with "warm-up and test areas" near the beginning of trails, with parking lots for the autos and trailers that bring the snowmobiles, with spur trails into "interesting areas," with "occasional open areas for frolic and rest," with nearby lodges and restaurants, with warming shelters and camping facilities, and with access routes to first aid, fuel supplies, telephones, and repair shops. One snowmobilers' group complained that the trail situation on public land is "totally unrealistic unless trail opportunities are greatly expanded." Yet an upstate New York snowmobiler blithely testified before a legislative committee that "The cost to the state's taxpayers in welcoming this new wholesome outdoor sport is practically nothing, because no special facilities are needed."

Trails for off-road vehicles have been built in a well-meaning attempt to confine the machines to relatively small and patrollable areas. And well-meaning vehicle users usually stay on these trails. But in California's Sequoia National Forest, there were so many motorcyclists using established trails that heavy erosion resulted; the loose mountain soil, powdered by ORV tires, washed downhill into nearby waterways, damaging the spawning grounds of golden trout. The area was closed to further ORV use.

All-terrain and four-wheel-drive vehicles have similar erosional effects, except in areas where rainfall is light. There, their tracks persist as unaesthetic reminders for years. In the Southwest the ruts caused by four-wheel-drive military vehicles in 1942 during World War II maneuvers are still visible. All-terrain vehicles also damage aquatic vegetation. Dune buggies cause little ecological disturbance on flat, sandy beaches. But when driven a few yards inland, they disrupt the stability of seashore dunes by destroying their vegetative cover.

Snowmobile treads snip the terminal buds off snow-buried evergreens, disfiguring the trees and retarding growth. Damage to public and private timberlands has occurred from Maine to Oregon. But no one has projected the impact of thousands of errant snowmobilers on lumber or pulp production.

Snowmobiles exert more subtle pressures upon the environment. Resource managers report that the snow compacted by these machines forms icy blocks, reducing the soil's capacity to absorb moisture during the spring thaw, causing rapid runoff and erosion. Dr. Phillip Corbet, a Canadian wildlife specialist, reports that compaction also destroys the snow's capacity to insulate against the cold and to accommodate the burrows of small rodents that live beneath the snow's surface. Not many people would notice the disappearance of a million mice. But eagles, hawks, owls, coyotes, bobcats, and foxes would.

Noise is the most commonly cited ORV offense. A snowmobile emits about 82 decibels of racket at 50 feet — equivalent to that of a jackhammer or chain saw — and can be heard two miles away. Manufacturers could easily muffle the noise, but they fear it would hurt sales. For noise gives a feeling of power. Federal officials are urging that levels be reduced to 73 decibels at 50 feet, and a few states have passed such legislation — but laws of this sort are difficult to enforce.

More critical is the fact that snowmobiles and trail bikes operate in areas where noise is an abnormality. It is doubtful that anyone would pay attention to the sound of a snowmobile at the corner of 42nd Street and Broadway in New York City. But in a state park in New Hampshire the effect is shattering — to human ears, and to animals' nervous systems as well.

In winter most browsing and grazing animals are in poor physical condition; they live largely on the body fat stored during summer months and cannot tolerate extreme exertion. Most females are pregnant. Based upon a new study of snowmobilers' harassment of elk and deer in southeastern Idaho, wildlife biologists estimate that an *hour's* exposure to a snowmobile drains these animals of as much energy as a *week's* normal winter existence. Once harassed by the machines, they will break into a "panicked run" while the snowmobile is still three-quarters of a mile distant and out of sight; noise alone can do the damage.

The off-road vehicle has spread the problems of litter and pollution to areas that five years ago knew neither. The amounts of paper, bottles, tin cans, and exhaust fumes distributed by ORVs and ORV users have not been quantified. The Bureau of Land

Management, a federal agency that administers 453 million acres of public domain, notes simply that vehicle users make a "significant contribution" to the 50 million pounds of litter that the agency annually removes from its lands, and cites both exhaust and dust pollution caused by ORVs as "significant but undetermined."

ORV owners are often portrayed as a breed unto themselves, as a cutthroat band of barbarians divorced from the mainstream of society. But they are really only *Homo sapiens* with wheels, no more or less inclined to litter, poach, or vandalize than any other group. In fact, some vehicle clubs have taken commendable steps to patrol the activities and clean up the litter of their members. Unfortunately, self-patrol cannot make a dent in the tremendous number of problems caused by ORVs. Only dedicated and well-organized clubs can effect any sort of useful patrol. At this point, only a small percentage of all ORV operators belong to clubs, and even in those areas where clubs do patrol, land managers report that vehicle-caused problems are increasing.

More important, most damage done by ORVs is not intentional but simply a result of normal, legal vehicle operation. Most ORV owners do not deliberately pollute or litter or damage trails and stream banks. They do not purposely disturb wintering wildlife, or intentionally reduce the suitable living space for such wilderness species as cougars, wolves, and grizzly bears. They do not choose to intrude upon the nonmotorized recreation of hikers, campers, canoeists, or snowshoers. But they do. Such problems cannot be patrolled against.

Likewise, many of the social costs attributable to the ORV cannot be quantified. A woman living near Schenectady, New York, writes: "It is impossible to enjoy a quiet afternoon in the country when all one hears is the roar of snowmobiles. Needless to say, I am hoping for a snowless winter." What does it "cost" to know that there is no way of escaping a sight or sound that you detest? What does it cost a hiker who has climbed miles into the wilderness to suddenly hear the steady roar of a trail bike? What does it cost any of us to know that, since the 1968 snowmobile expedition to the North Pole (the first land expedition to reach the top of Earth since 1909), there is virtually nowhere one can go without encountering an internal-combustion engine?

Perhaps the most frightening aspect of the off-road vehicle is its capacity to influence thought. In many ways the impact of the ORVs parallels that of the automobile. Both contribute to the notion of the inseparability of man and machine. And both raise the question of whether we are really capable of controlling our vehicles, or whether the vehicles assume power of their own.

For most Americans the off-road vehicle did not become a personal reality until about 1968. Yet ORV owners and their clubs intimate that motorcycles and snowmobiles are as essential to the American way of life as public education or freedom of the press. They refer to their machines with such affectionate (and nonmotorized) nicknames as "buggy" or "sled" or "bike." And snowmobilers remark that before the machine their lives in winter were drab and dismal. One president of a snowmobile club in Eagle River, Wisconsin, musing on his fate if he were deprived of his machine, posed the question: "What would we be able to do around here except sit in front of the television?"

Some ORV owners go so far as to contend that their machines are necessary for cultivating an appreciation of nature. A strange thought, insofar as the ORV is designed to isolate its user from one of the primary realities of nature — the need for physical effort. And while there are few people who would deny a mechanical assist to anyone who is truly incapable of locomotion, it is worth remembering that 50 percent of our population is under the age of twenty-eight, and most Americans can manage self-propulsion. In any case, 210 million people mounted on snowmobiles would probably have a hard time finding any nature to appreciate.

Indeed, riding an ORV is one of the least independent, least rugged of all outdoor activities. Yet many advertisements for these machines imply the opposite. Consider this slogan: "Ready to make molehills out of mountains? Here's a bike from the Yamaha Enduro series that's blazing new trails through wilderness and back country across the land." Or: "Fun is there for whoever is alive enough to go after it. The new way to find it in the wintertime is with an Evinrude Skeeter." And for the man who wants to get back to nature the easy way: "The Honda Mini Trail 70. All the fun of backpacking without sore feet."

Some of the ads are strangely contradictory, urging one to "run away from civilization" or to "get away from it all" on a motorcycle or snowmobile, showing photos of neatly attired young couples who "ride rough" through woods, streams, and fields without so much as getting dusty.

Accommodation of the private recreational vehicle on public land places the Forest Service supervisor or state park commissioner in a curiously contradictory position. Although entrusted with protecting public resources, he condones a sport that creates unsolvable aesthetic and ecological problems. By constructing trails and publishing booklets that encourage motorized recreation, he actively promotes a pastime that is the ultimate in environmental frivolity. As with automobiles, trucks, and other vehicles, the ORV consumes nonrenewable resources in both its manufacture and use; but unlike most vehicles, the ORV can hardly be described as a necessary means of transportation.

The federal agencies that have had the fewest problems with

ORVs are those that have imposed the strictest controls upon
their use. The National Park Service has adopted the general
position that while the ORV is an acceptable means of transportation *into* a park, it is not an appropriate instrument for an
off-road environmental encounter. Within natural areas of the
National Park System, ORVs are usually restricted to paved auto
roads (or to paved, snow-covered auto roads in winter) and are
not permitted on hiking trails or in the back country. The ORV
is regarded by the National Park Service as no more or less sacred
than the automobile.

Questions of the right to recreational use of public lands have
been brought into sharper focus by the advent of the off-road
vehicle. The legal rule of thumb says that all of us have an
equal right to use the country's commonly owned land, providing
we do not infringe upon the rights or activities of other users,
or do not diminish the value of the recreational resources.

But the ORV operator is many times more capable of infringing
or diminishing than the man who walks, snowshoes, paddles,
or skis cross-country. He can cover 20 times more land — or
water — in a day than the man on foot or in a canoe, and thus
will interfere 20 times more with the recreational opportunities
of other land-users — by getting first pick of campsites and fishing
spots, by frightening away wildlife others might have seen, by
reaching more places more quickly. He interferes with those
seeking solitude by leaving highly visible and persistent reminders
of his passing. Since he can carry at least twice as much gear,
he leaves twice as much litter. And because of the weight and
horsepower of his machine, and the volume and constancy of
its sound, land managers have estimated that the motorized
outdoorsman can cause 200 times more physical damage to the
landscape and can create 100 times more noise than the walker.

Translating these factors into a policy decision, a land manager might decide to either limit ORV use to a given number of acres, or to completely prohibit their use. What factual information is available clearly favors the latter course. For there are no solutions to the problems created by the ORV; we can tolerate the machines only if we are prepared to accept a steady, rapid decline in both the quality and the effective size of our recreational environment.

ORV associations argue that opposition to their sport is partially based upon backpackers' selfish wishes to "have the outdoors all to themselves." They're right. Unfortunately, all of us — hiker and machine operator alike — seem to develop possessive attitudes toward things that are impossible to possess.

But while this is an interesting commentary on human nature, it has no meaning in terms of resource management. With a growing population and a declining pool of open space, each new use of land must be carefully justified. And the burden of proof rests upon the shoulders of the off-road vehicle enthusiasts and the ORV industry.

As more people want to do more things on the same acre of land, the man mounted on a machine inevitably becomes less of an asset. And by comparison, the man on foot becomes infinitely more valuable.

The Contributors

Index

The Contributors

HAL BORLAND is distinguished both as a naturalist and as a novelist. For more than three decades his perceptive nature essays have brightened the Sunday editorial pages of the *New York Times*. Among his many books are *Hill Country Harvest*, which earned the John Burroughs Medal, and a modern classic, *When the Legends Die*, which has recently been made into a major motion picture.

JO BREWER has written and lectured extensively on butterflies. Her book *Wings in the Meadow* has been reprinted in several editions, and she has contributed the text to *The Butterfly*, a new volume of color photographs of butterfly wings. She is assistant director of the Xerces Society, a new organization dedicated to the preservation of butterfly habitat.

PAUL BROOKS has explored many of the world's wildest places, from East Africa to the Arctic to Mexico — often by canoe. His books include *Roadless Area*, which received the John Burroughs Medal; *The Pursuit of Wilderness;* and *The House of Life*, which draws a personal portrait of Rachel Carson from her writings, her letters, and the author's close work with Miss Carson while he was editor-in-chief at Houghton Mifflin Company.

ARCHIE CARR, professor of zoology at the University of Florida and the world's foremost authority on sea turtles, is one of those rare scientists who possess great literary gifts — as acknowledged by his winning of the John Burroughs Medal and an O. Henry Award. His books include

The Windward Road, Ulendo, and *So Excellent a Fishe,* the last the story of the great oceanic reptiles he has studied for two decades.

AIMÉ GAUVIN, a native of Maine, returned home four years ago after nearly a quarter-century as a radio newsman in New York City. He writes regularly for *Maine Times,* a crusading, environmentally aware weekly newspaper, and the *Eastern Maine Sunday Reporter.*

C. E. GILLHAM, a conservation old-timer who died in 1970, "had been around" in his seventy-two years. He was a hired bounty hunter who tracked down Arizona's only white wolf; a Mississippi Flyway waterfowl biologist who discovered the nesting grounds of Ross' goose; the territorial biologist for Alaska before statehood. He wrote several books on the Far North and was a regular contributor to out-of-doors magazines.

FRANK GRAHAM, JR., an *Audubon* field editor, is author of the best-selling *Since Silent Spring,* which chronicled the worldwide battle for a sane use of pesticides following publication of Rachel Carson's history-changing book. He has written two other important environmental books — *Man's Dominion,* tracing the story of the conservation movement in America; and *Disaster by Default,* on politics and water pollution.

JACK HOPE is the author of forthcoming books on the crisis in America's national parks and on the Hudson River. A former senior editor of *Natural History,* he has contributed articles to many national magazines, including *Harper's Magazine* and *Smithsonian.*

ALVIN M. JOSEPHY, JR., is an eminent authority on American Indian affairs and Western American history. His numerous books include *Red Power,* on the Indians' fight for freedom; *The Indian Heritage of America;* and *The Patriot Chiefs.* A vice-president at American Heritage, he authored a special report for President Nixon on government Indian policy and was a consultant to the Public Land Law Review Commission.

JOSEPH WOOD KRUTCH followed many distinguished careers — as drama critic, teacher, philosopher, man of letters, and for the last twenty years of his life, an articulate commentator on the mysteries of nature. From an adobe brick home in his adopted Arizona, he wrote such books as *The Desert Year, Grand Canyon, The Voice of the Desert,* and *The Great Chain of Life.* His honors included the Emerson-Thoreau Medal of the American Academy of Sciences. Dr. Krutch died in 1970 at the age of seventy-six.

GEORGE LAYCOCK is a highly respected environmental writer, an *Audubon* field editor, and the author of several important conservation books: *Alaska: The Embattled Frontier,* which was the first volume in The Audubon Library; *The Diligent Destroyers,* a critical look at the industries and agencies that are defacing the American landscape; *The Alien Animals,* on the dangers of importing exotic wildlife; and *The Sign of the Flying Goose,* the story of our national wildlife refuges.

JOHN MADSON is a professional conservationist who has written a widely acclaimed series of life history booklets on American gamebirds and mammals and a guide to careers in wildlife management. Assistant director of conservation for Winchester-Western, he has been honored with the Jade of Chiefs, highest award of the Outdoor Writers Association of America, and the Conservation Education Award of the Wildlife Society.

WESLEY MARX, a California environmental writer and lecturer, is best known for his first book, *The Frail Ocean,* which sold several hundred thousand copies. His articles have appeared in *Atlantic, American Heritage, The Reporter,* and *National Wildlife.* He wrote a recent Sierra Club "Battlebook," *Oilspill,* and the text for *The Meeting Place,* a forthcoming pictorial book on the Pacific shore.

FAITH McNULTY, a member of *The New Yorker* staff, writes often on America's threatened wildlife. She has two important books to her credit: *The Whooping Crane,* which details the long and difficult fight to save this great bird from extinction; and *Must They Die?,* which exposes the campaign by federal and state agencies and stockmen to exterminate the prairie dog with poisons, and the resulting threat to the rare black-footed ferret.

SIGURD F. OLSON, northern Minnesota's famed voyageur-natural-ist-author, has written a long series of classic books on the canoe-country wilderness astride the boundary of the United States and Canada. Among them are *The Singing Wilderness, Listening Point, The Lonely Land,* and the autobiographical *Open Horizons.* He has led the ongoing fight to protect that wilderness from a host of destructive invasions — airplanes, mining, logging, dams, motorboats.

SKIP ROZIN is a young free-lance writer who lives in New York City and who concentrates on human ecology, on people who live close to nature. He has traveled widely in Europe, North Africa, and South America, and has written a yet-unpublished novel set in a small, isolated fishing village in Labrador.

GARY SOUCIE is an *Audubon* field editor who specializes in the technical aspects of conservation issues. He is president of the Environmental Policy Center in Washington, D.C., and formerly was executive director of Friends of the Earth and eastern representative for the Sierra Club. He was chairman of the conservation coalition against the supersonic jetliner.

EDWIN WAY TEALE has written more than two dozen books on natural history, including the four volumes on the American Seasons which earned him a Pulitzer Prize. His most recent book was *Springtime in Britain,* the account of 11,000 miles of travel from Land's End to the very tip of Scotland. He is presently writing the story of Trail Wood, his own sanctuary in northern Connecticut.

MARVIN ZELDIN is a Washington-based writer and consultant who specializes in environmental issues. Formerly director of information services for the Conservation Foundation, he represented *Audubon* at the United Nations Conference on the Human Environment in Stockholm.

Index

DATE DUE
